AMUSEMENT PARKS
of New Jersey

AMUSEMENT PARKS
of New Jersey

JIM FUTRELL

STACKPOLE
BOOKS

Copyright © 2004 by Stackpole Books

Published by
STACKPOLE BOOKS
5067 Ritter Road
Mechanicsburg, PA 17055
www.stackpolebooks.com

Printed in the United States of America

10 9 8 7 6 5 4 3 2 1

FIRST EDITION

Cover design by Wendy Reynolds

Photographs by the author and other illustrations from the author's collection, unless otherwise noted.

Library of Congress Cataloging-in-Publication Data

Futrell, Jim.
    Amusement parks of New Jersey / Jim Futrell.–1st ed.
      p.   cm.
    ISBN 0-8117-2973-7 (pbk.)
    1. Amusement parks–New Jersey–History. 2. Amusement
parks–New Jersey–Guidebooks. 3. New Jersey–Guidebooks. I. Title.

GV1853.3.N52 F88   2004
791.'06'809749

                                                      2003023082

CONTENTS

Foreword vii
Acknowledgments ix
Introduction xi

A History of the Amusement Park Industry 1
A History of the Amusement Park in New Jersey 23

Steel Pier 47
Keansburg Amusement Park and Runaway Rapids 62
Clementon Amusement Park and Splash World 75
Jenkinson's Boardwalk 87
Casino Pier and Water Works 96
Playland's Castaway Cove 112
Bowcraft Amusement Park 118
Land of Make Believe 124
Storybook Land 133
Funtown Pier 141
Wild West City 149
Gillian's Wonderland Pier 153
Morey's Piers 162
Six Flags Great Adventure 182
Fantasy Island 200
Blackbeard's Cave 207

Other Amusement Facilities 211

Index of Major Rides in Operation in New Jersey 213
Bibliography 217
Index 219
About the Author 227

FOREWORD

REMEMBER THAT GREAT SONG, "UNDER THE BOARDWALK," BY THE DRIFTERS from the summer of 1964? That's the song that comes to my mind when I think of New Jersey amusement parks. Being a landlocked midwestern boy, the image of a carousel along a boardwalk near an ocean was a wonderful fantasy.

Of course, there's much more than just pier and boardwalk parks in the state. New Jersey has one of the most diverse collections of amusement parks in the country. Sixteen of those parks are featured in this book. Among them are many nostalgic shore parks, funky and fun 1950s-era roadside attraction parks, a genuine trolley park, and a huge corporate theme park that gets more than 3 million visitors a year. How lucky to be able to have all those fun parks within a few hours or less of each other!

This book is an amazing read. From the oldest park in the state, Atlantic City's Steel Pier, to the most recent, Blackbeard's Cave in Bayville, you'll learn of the dreams, ambitions, and challenges of those whose main jobs are to put smiles on people's faces. Except for Six Flags Great Adventure, Jackson, the parks are all family owned and operated. That means you'll probably find the owners at the park every day. They'll be out selling tickets, running a ride, or sweeping up. That's what owner-operators do, and that's what makes their parks so special.

When long-time friend and colleague Jim Futrell asked me to write the foreword to this book, I didn't hesitate for one second, because I knew it would be a quality product. As he proved in his book on Pennsylvania parks, he is thorough, accurate, and insightful, and his stuff is fun to read. He knows his parks and he knows New Jersey, and if you're investing the time and money in a book, you certainly want a man of his credentials to write it. Sit back and enjoy, and as you read the stories and look at the pictures, you may just be lucky enough to hear the sound of that carousel!

Tim O'Brien
Parks and Attractions Senior Editor
Amusement Business

ACKNOWLEDGMENTS

NO BOOK IS POSSIBLE WITHOUT THE SUPPORT OF NUMEROUS INDIVIDUALS. This one is no different. From the amusement parks themselves to their employees to the support and encouragement provided by friends, family, and coworkers, this book was the result of more than my efforts. Were it not for the generosity of the following people, this book would not have been possible.

Thanks would have to start with Kyle Weaver of Stackpole Books, who came up with the idea of a series of books profiling America's amusement parks. Thanks also have to go to his assistant, Amy Cooper, for all her hard work.

The owners and staff of New Jersey's amusement parks were very cooperative, and I am certainly grateful for all of their assistance: Anthony Catanoso of Steel Pier; Robert Conti of Steel Pier Helicopters; Bill and Hank Gelhaus of Keansburg Amusement Park; Larry Baker and Sarah Crea of Clementon Amusement Park and Splash World; Pat Storino, Marilou Halvorsen, and Toby Gerlach of Jenkinson's Boardwalk; Bob Bennett, Bill Erwin, and Floyd Moreland of Casino Pier and Water Works; David and Scott Simpson of Playland's Castaway Cove; Steve Marke of Bowcraft Amusement Park; Chris Maier of Land of Make Believe; John, Esther, John Jr., and JoAnne Fricano of Storybook Land; Bill Majors and Carmen Ricci of Funtown Pier; Michael Stabile of Wild West City; Roy and Jay Gillian and John Kavchok of Gillian's Wonderland Pier; Jack, Will, and Dolores Morey, Joanne Duffy, and Joanne Galloway at Morey's Piers; Kristen Siebeneicher and Karen Yuchinski at Six Flags Great Adventure; Ed Florimont and Diane Georgy of Fantasy Island; and Ned Bevelheimer of Blackbeard's Cave. I would also like to thank Isabel Miller for sharing her memories of Bowcraft Amusement Park.

Denise Putlock of the New Jersey Amusement Association deserves special recognition for her enthusiastic support of this project.

Also of great assistance were three historians, each with their own special expertise. Thank you to Charles Jacques, for sharing his knowledge of amusement park history; Douglas Foulks, who gave information on Keansburg Amusement Park; and Jerry Woolley, for his assistance with Jenkinson's Boardwalk.

Thanks also are due my friends and family for all their support during the two-year process of making this book a reality. In particular, I would like to recognize my sister Mary for her editing expertise, and Dave, Terry, and Davey Hahner for their help in choosing the pictures.

But four people more than any others deserve my special gratitude for making this book a reality: my wife and best friend, Marlowe, and our sons Jimmy, Christopher, and Matthew. They share and appreciate my passion for amusement parks, and I hope they will always remember the good times we had exploring the delightful variety in New Jersey.

INTRODUCTION

FEW STATES IN THE COUNTRY CAN MATCH THE QUANTITY OF AMUSEMENT parks found in New Jersey. In addition, New Jersey probably has the greatest *variety* of amusement parks found in any state. By visiting the state's amusement parks, you can almost trace the evolution of the industry, from Clementon Amusement Park, one of the last surviving trolley parks; to 1950s roadside attractions such as Storybook Land, and Wild West City; to Land of Make Believe, a pioneering theme park; to Six Flags Great Adventure, one of the largest theme parks in the country. Almost any type of amusement park can be found in New Jersey. But what really sets the state's amusement industry apart is the largest collection of waterfront amusement parks in the world, including Keansburg Amusement Park, one of the oldest; Morey's Piers, one of the largest; and the revived Steel Pier, along the famous Atlantic City boardwalk.

What also sets the New Jersey amusement industry apart is the dominance of family-owned facilities. While the huge corporate-owned theme parks dominate the industry as a whole, the family-owned park is alive and well in New Jersey. Of the seventeen parks profiled in this book, only one is not owned by a family. The others are not just businesses, they are cherished family heirlooms, which gives each one its own special personality.

Each of New Jersey's amusement parks, large and small, family- or corporate-owned, has a special story behind it, representing the dreams and hard work of generations of individuals. I have tried to convey those stories so that you can truly appreciate each park's special personality when you visit.

Before you venture out, here are a few general tips to make your day more enjoyable:

- *Dress comfortably.* Make sure you wear comfortable shoes that are broken in. Wear cool, loose-fitting clothes, but not too loose, as they might get caught on something. Take along a jacket and a rain poncho, just in case.

- *Pack lightly.* You're going to be walking around all day, so don't weigh yourself down with a lot of stuff. Many parks have lockers where you can store things you might need during the day.

- *Eat a good breakfast.* Arriving at the park hungry means that you might waste time that could otherwise be spent riding. Don't stuff yourself with greasy food, however, which doesn't mix well with rides.

- *Arrive early.* Typically the best time of day at an amusement park is the first hour it's open, before the bulk of the people show up. This is often the best time to ride some of the big rides.

- *Hit the big rides first.* While most visitors tend to rush to the big rides first, the lines will only increase as the day wears on, although they usually grow shorter in the evening, when the roller coasters tend to be running faster. Try to avoid the big rides between noon and 5 P.M.

- *Follow the rules.* All parks have certain rules and regulations and set height limits for certain rides and attractions. A great deal of thought has gone into developing these limits, and they are there to protect you. Please respect them. Also note that in the state of New Jersey, a rider responsibility act requires customers to follow posted rules and regulations.

One of the great things about amusement parks is that they are constantly evolving and changing. While every effort had been made to ensure the accuracy of this book, some changes may have occurred. Please call ahead to confirm admission policies and operating hours.

A History of the Amusement Park Industry

HUMAN BEINGS ARE, BY NATURE, SOCIAL CREATURES. SINCE THE BEGINning of time, people have sought ways to come together and escape the pressures of everyday life. As humankind started to settle in villages, festivals and celebrations became a popular way for the community to relax. As villages grew into cities, parcels of land were set aside as sort of a permanent festival. In medieval Europe, these places were known as pleasure gardens.

In the 1500s and 1600s, pleasure gardens sprang up on the outskirts of major cities. At a time when Europe's cities were crowded, dirty, disease-ridden places, these pleasure gardens provided a welcome respite. In many ways, they were similar to today's amusement parks, offering landscaped gardens, live entertainment, fireworks, dancing, games, and even primitive amusement rides, including the forerunners of today's merry-go-rounds, Ferris wheels, and roller coasters.

Pleasure gardens remained extremely popular until the late 1700s, when political unrest and urban sprawl caused a decline that lasted until the mid-1800s. While most of the pleasure gardens are now faded memories, two still exist. Dyrehavs Bakken, which opened in 1583 outside Copenhagen, Denmark, is the world's oldest operating amusement park, and the Prater in Vienna, which got its start in 1766 when the emperor turned a portion of his private hunting preserve over to public amusement, is now a beloved Viennese tradition.

1

Coming to America

As the pleasure garden was dying out in Europe, a new nation, the United States, was growing into a world power. Immigrants flocking to cities such as New York, Philadelphia, and Boston clamored for recreation. Entrepreneurs responded by developing picnic groves and beer gardens throughout America.

Jones Woods, widely accepted as America's first large amusement resort, opened along the East River in New York in the early 1800s. Its attractions included bowling, billiards, gymnasium equipment, a shooting gallery, donkey rides, music, dancing, and a beer garden. Jones Woods' popularity was short-lived, however, as the rapid growth of Manhattan soon overtook the resort.

The continuing demand for amusement in New York was soon answered on a peninsula in Brooklyn known as Coney Island, named for the coneys, or wild rabbits, that inhabited the area. The seaside location provided a cool getaway in the hot summer months, and in 1829, a hotel catering to visitors appeared on the sands. By the early 1850s, pavilions offering bathing, dining, and dancing were being constructed at Coney Island. Around 1875, a railroad to the resort was completed, and the destination's popularity quickly increased. Entrepreneurs responded by opening cabarets, vaudeville theaters, fortune-telling booths, games, and rides such as small carousels. Here, in 1867, a creative restaurateur named

Coney Island was the center of the amusement industry in the early twentieth century.

Rocky Point, Narragansett Bay, R. I.   *Visited aug. 6, 1908*

Rhode Island's Rocky Point was one of America's earliest amusement parks, opening in 1847.

Charles Feltman invented the hot dog. The resort's first major amusement device opened in 1877, when the Iron Tower was installed. This 300-foot-tall observation tower was relocated from the 1876 Philadelphia Centennial Exposition, where it was known as the Sawyer Observatory. Just seven years later, in 1884, the modern roller coaster was invented when LaMarcus Thompson built the Switchback Railway along the seashore. Throughout its history, however, Coney Island was never an amusement park, but a neighborhood in Brooklyn that featured a collection of amusements, including several independent amusement parks.

Early amusement resort growth was not confined to New York. In 1846, large crowds gathered at a family farm in Bristol, Connecticut, to view a failed science experiment. The size of the crowd convinced the farm's owner, Gad Norton, that there was a big need for a recreational gathering place in central Connecticut. Norton converted his farm into an amusement resort called Lake Compounce, where people could enjoy picnicking, boating in the lake, listening to band concerts, and dancing. Today Lake Compounce continues as the oldest operating amusement park in the United States. Another early amusement resort, called Rocky Point Park, opened nearby in Warwick, Rhode Island, in 1847. This seaside resort continued to operate until 1995.

In the years following the Civil War, the personality of the country changed as America's cities became increasingly congested and industrialized. Farmers flocked to the cities to find jobs in the new factories. The growing congestion encouraged many to seek out recreation away from the cities. Many amusement resorts opened along the ocean shore or by a lake, where people could find a cool getaway in the hot summer. But the primary engine for the development of the amusement park in America was the trolley company.

In the wake of the opening of the first practical electric-powered street rail line in Richmond, Virginia, in 1888, hundreds of trolley lines popped up around the country almost overnight. At that time, utility companies charged the trolley companies a flat fee for the use of their electricity. The transportation companies looked for a way to stimulate weekend ridership to make the most of their investment. Opening amusement resorts provided the ideal solution. Typically built at the end of the trolley lines, these resorts initially were simple operations consisting of picnic facilities, dance halls, restaurants, games, and a few amusement rides. These parks were immediately successful and soon opened across America.

Becoming an American Institution

The amusement park became an institution in the wake of the 1893 World's Columbian Exposition in Chicago. This world's fair introduced the Ferris wheel and the amusement midway to the world. The midway, essentially a wide walkway lined with an array of rides and concessions, was a huge success and set the precedent for amusement park design for the next sixty years.

The following year, Capt. Paul Boynton borrowed the midway concept and opened the world's first modern amusement park, Paul Boyton's Water Chutes, on Chicago's South Side. Boyton was a colorful figure who served in the Union navy during the Civil War and fought in the Franco-Prussian War. In 1874, he stowed away on an ocean liner with the intent of jumping overboard 200 miles out to sea to test an "unsinkable" rubber lifesaving suit. He was apprehended but was eventually permitted by the captain to jump overboard 30 miles off the coast of Ireland. Boyton safely made it to land, achieving international fame. He followed that accomplishment by becoming the first person to swim the English Channel. In 1888, he settled in Chicago, where he started an aquatic circus and raised sea lions in Lake Michigan. Soon he came across a Shoot the Chutes water ride in Rock Island, Illinois, where it had been invented in 1889. Boyton was intrigued by the simple ride, in which a boat traveled down an inclined plane into a body of water. This was the first major water-based amusement ride and the forerunner of today's log flumes and splash-down rides. Boyton purchased the rights to the Shoot the

Chutes and tested it in London in 1893 before setting it up in Chicago as the centerpiece of his new park.

Unlike the primitive trolley parks, which were just starting to come into their own, Boyton's Water Chutes was the first amusement park to charge admission and use rides as its main draw, rather than picnic facilities or a natural feature such as a beach or a lake. Patrons from all over Chicago flocked to Captain Boyton's operation to ride the 60-foot-tall Water Chutes. More than five hundred thousand people showed up in that first season alone. Boyton's park relocated to a larger site in 1896, but it closed in 1908, eclipsed by larger and more modern facilities. However, the success of his Chicago park inspired him to open a similar facility, Sea Lion Park, at the fledgling Coney Island resort in New York in 1895. The park featured not only a water chute ride, but also the Flip Flap, one of the first looping roller coasters, and a sea lion show that foreshadowed those at today's theme parks.

Sea Lion Park was Coney Island's first true amusement park—a collection of rides and shows in a fenced area to which patrons paid admission. With the opening of Sea Lion Park, Coney Island became the center of the amusement universe. Entrepreneurs from all over flocked to develop new rides and attractions for the masses. George Tilyou, a successful Coney Island restaurant operator, opened Steeplechase Park in 1897. The park, with its well-manicured gardens, took amusement to a whole new level. Soon the park became internationally renowned for its signature Steeplechase ride, which allowed patrons to experience the thrills of a horse race by riding wooden horses along eight parallel, undulating tracks.

The success of Steeplechase Park hurt business at Sea Lion Park, and in 1902, Boyton sold the struggling operation to businessmen Frederick Thompson and Elmer Dundy. The two men found fame at the Pan American Exposition in Buffalo, New York, in 1901, when they introduced their successful Trip to the Moon, one of the first simulator attractions. After moving it to Steeplechase Park, where they operated it for the 1902 season, they wanted to set out on their own. The result of this ambition was Luna Park, reportedly named after Dundy's sister. Described in advertisements as "an electric Eden unlike anything that had ever been built before," it was characterized by its fanciful "Arabian Nights" style of architecture outlined by 250,000 electric lights. At a time when electrical lighting was rare in most houses, Luna Park created a sensation, attracting over forty thousand patrons at its opening in May 1903.

Luna Park represented a new genre of amusement park known as the exposition park, which looked to the Chicago World's Fair for inspiration. These parks featured elaborate buildings with fanciful designs out-

Birds Eye View of Luna Park, Coney Island, N. Y.

Coney Island's Luna Park was the first exposition park.

lined with thousands of electric lights. There were attractions that were considered very complex for their time, such as re-creations of famous disasters, scaled-down replicas of distant lands, and displays of prematurely born infants being cared for with technology so advanced that even hospitals had yet to install it. Unlike the more pastoral trolley parks, exposition parks tended to be raucous, packed with attractions, and located close to urban centers. Among the more famous exposition parks were White City in Chicago (opened in 1905); Luna Park in Pittsburgh (1905); Luna Park in Cleveland (1905); and Wonderland near Boston (1906). While most larger cities featured an exposition park, the phenomenon was largely short-lived because of high overhead and the high cost of the new attractions they added. However, one remains in operation: Lakeside Park in Denver, which opened as White City in 1908, and still features its elaborate Tower of Jewels.

Perhaps the grandest exposition park of them all was Dreamland, which opened across the street from Coney Island's Luna Park in 1904. Dreamland tried to top Luna Park in every respect. At the center of the park was a 375-foot-tall tower, the buildings were outlined with a million electric lights, and the entire place was adorned with elaborate facades, fountains, pools, and floral displays. Among the attractions were Lilliputia, a complete city populated by three hundred little people, and the huge Fighting the Flames show, which claimed to have a cast of four thousand. With the opening of Dreamland, Coney Island was at its zenith, with three immense amusement parks and dozens of individual concessions catering to the millions that flocked there. Steeplechase's Tilyou was quoted as stating, "If Paris is France, then Coney Island between May and September is the world."

Even a fire at Steeplechase Park in 1907 that burnt the park to the ground failed to put a damper on things. After charging customers 10 cents a head to view the "burning ruins," owner George Tilyou immediately rebuilt the park bigger and better than ever. The Steeplechase ride remained and encircled the Pavilion of Fun, a 5-acre building featuring rides and fun house devices.

Unfortunately, fire became a constant nemesis of Coney Island, with twenty major conflagrations striking the resort area through its history. The largest completely destroyed Dreamland as it was preparing for the 1911 season. Never as successful as Luna Park or Steeplechase, it was not rebuilt, although other amusement attractions soon moved in on the ruins to take Dreamland's place. The destruction of Dreamland signified the beginning of Coney Island's slow decline, however. The following year, Luna Park went bankrupt, but it managed to hold on until 1944, when it too was done in by fire. Steeplechase closed in 1964 and sat abandoned for two years before being demolished. Into the 1980s, many of Coney Island's remaining landmarks succumbed—the once great restaurants and bathhouses, and three of its greatest roller coasters, the Bobsled in 1974, the Tornado in 1977, and the Thunderbolt in 1982.

Dreamland at Coney Island was the largest and most spectacular exposition park.

Although only a fraction of its original size, Coney Island has hung on, and it is enjoying a renewed appreciation with its surviving vintage attractions, such as the 1920 Wonder Wheel and the 1927 vintage Cyclone roller coaster, both now listed as national landmarks.

The success of Coney Island during the early part of the twentieth century helped spread the amusement park industry throughout the country. Trolley companies, breweries, and entrepreneurs opened parks by the hundreds. The number of operating parks grew from approximately 250 in 1899 to nearly 700 in 1905. By 1919, more than 1,500 amusement parks were in operation in the United States. In 1913, *World's Work* magazine described the growth as "a hysteria of parks followed by a panic." *Billboard* magazine sounded a cautionary message in 1909: "The great profits made by some of the park men produce a mania for park building, which can well be compared to some of the booms in mining camps. Men from almost all professions of life flocked to this endeavor, and without knowledge or particular ability in this line endeavored to build parks." Soon every major city had at least one major park.

Amusement parks during this time had a much different personality than they do today. A review of the industry by *Billboard* magazine in 1905 summed up the keys to a successful attraction as "plenty of shade, attractive landscaping, sufficient transportation, first class attractions (live entertainment) and a variety of good up to date privileges," as rides and concessions were then known. Rides were almost an afterthought in the article and only mentioned after an in-depth discussion of the importance of a summer theater, presenting summer stock, vaudeville, and concerts, which it considered to be the heart of the park. But that personality would soon change.

The Golden Age

With amusement parks opening at such a rapid pace in the early twentieth century, patrons were looking for more thrilling attractions, and soon a whole new industry sprang up to fulfill this need. The William F. Mangels Company was founded at Coney Island in 1890 and in 1914 introduced the whip, one of the first mass-produced rides. The Eli Bridge Company started operations in 1900 and to this day continues to manufacture the Ferris wheels that are a midway staple. Other companies founded during this period include the Philadelphia Toboggan Company, one of the largest manufacturers of roller coasters and carousels, which started making rides in 1904. In 1912, the Dayton Fun House Company was formed. This company was the forerunner to National Amusement Devices and, later, International Amusement Devices, one of the largest and most prolific builders of amusement rides before folding in the mid-1980s. The Dodgem Corporation opened in 1919 in Salisbury Beach, Massachusetts, introducing bumper cars to amusement parks.

In the competition to sell the most rides, innovation was the watchword of the era. Riverview Park in Chicago built a roller coaster called the Potsdam Railway in 1908, in which the cars were suspended beneath the track rather than riding above it. In 1912, John Miller, the most prolific ride builder of this era, patented a system of holding a roller coaster to the track that remains in use to this day. This new system, called underfriction, made it impossible for roller coasters to leave the tracks, forever changing the nature of roller coasters from mild-mannered scenic railways to true thrillers.

New technology such as the wide-scale rollout of underfriction roller coasters converged with the booming economy and the newfound popularity of the automobile in the 1920s to drive the amusement park industry into its Golden Age. As most trolley companies had long since divested their amusement park operations, a whole new generation of entrepreneurs flocked to the industry, building amusement parks that catered to the automobile trade. The automobile led to the closing of dozens of smaller amusement parks throughout the country that were unable to provide large parking lots, but the surviving parks boomed, and thrill rides were the primary draw. America was in a mood to play, and there was an insatiable demand for thrills and entertainment at America's amusement parks.

Business continued booming through the 1920s, and amusement parks were constantly looking for new ways to thrill patrons. Roller coasters became larger and more thrilling, and every year a new ride was introduced to the masses. The Tumble Bug, a large ride featuring cars traveling along a circular undulating track, immediately became a favorite upon its invention in 1925. In 1926, Leon Cassidy constructed the first rail-guided dark ride at Tumbling Run Park in Bridgewater, New Jersey, leading to the formation of the Pretzel Amusement Company, a major manufacturer of dark rides. The Tilt-A-Whirl was also introduced to the midway that year. In 1929, inspired by the Winter Olympic bobsled tracks, Norman Bartlett introduced the Flying Turns, a roller coaster whose trains traveled down a trough rather than on tracks, at Lakeside Park in Dayton, Ohio.

Enterprising businessmen were not the only ones getting involved in the industry. In 1928, Westchester County, New York, recognizing the value of having a recreational community gathering place, acquired a collection of ramshackle amusements along the shores of Long Island Sound and replaced them with Playland. Unlike most amusement parks of the era,

The original layout from 1928 of Playland in Rye, New York, was so successful that it has changed little since.

which had gradually evolved over several decades, Westchester County carefully laid out Playland to provide the optimal mix of rides and attractions. This precise planning was a predecessor to the design of the large corporate theme parks that would open three decades later. The main attractions were arranged around a lushly landscaped mall, and the kiddie attractions were located in a separate smaller amusement park. In addition to the park's main roller coaster, the Aeroplane, a milder ride, the Dragon Coaster, was located just across the midway. Recreation attractions such as an ice rink, swimming pool, beach, and nature preserve complemented the amusements, and a large parking lot accommodated the growing number of automobiles. Towering above it all was the music tower, which broadcast peaceful music throughout the park. People flocked to the facility, with attendance the first season reaching 2.8 million. The basic design of Playland has changed little to this day, although many of the rides and attractions have been updated to appeal to new generations.

Hard Times

As Playland was setting new design standards for the amusement park industry, the stock market crash of 1929 drove America into the Great Depression. With unemployment peaking at 33 percent, consumers had little money to spend on entertainment, let alone a day at an amusement park. The Depression took a horrible toll on the industry, and hundreds of parks closed across the country. By 1935, only four hundred amusement parks remained open. With capital virtually nonexistent, parks did whatever it took to hang on. Popular strategies to attract crowds included food giveaways and live entertainment, or "flesh shows," as they were known. Not all was bleak, as this became the golden age of big bands, which toured amusement parks from coast to coast. The crowds that big bands attracted to many amusement parks were credited with saving dozens of amusement parks during the 1930s.

Fortunately, things did improve, and amusement parks slowly started to get back on track by the late 1930s. Long-deferred maintenance was done, and new attractions were added. But dark clouds were looming on the horizon once again. In late 1941, America entered World War II, and soon the resources of the nation were focused on the war effort.

The war was a mixed blessing for the amusement park industry. On one hand, with the economy booming in support of the war effort, patrons flocked to amusement parks located near industrial centers and military installations, providing a much-needed cash infusion for the parks. At the same time, gasoline rationing severely hindered operation at parks not easily reached by public transportation. In fact, many parks closed for the duration of the war and in some cases never reopened. Also, with the nation's industrial output fully focused on wartime production, amusement parks could not add new rides, and material shortages made maintenance of existing rides difficult.

When World War II finally ended, America and the amusement park industry enjoyed a period of postwar prosperity. Attendance and revenues grew to record levels, and new parks opened across America. But the world was a rapidly changing place. Veterans sought to capture their portion of the American dream and start families. Many flocked to the suburbs. Entrepreneurs reacted by developing a new concept that soon became as much of a fixture in suburbia as the tract home—the kiddieland, a special amusement park featuring rides just for kids. The concept had actually been developed in 1925, when C. C. Macdonald opened the Kiddie Park in San Antonio, Texas, which remains in operation. Kiddielands grew from fewer than two dozen in 1950 to more than 150 operating throughout the country by 1960. They were located primarily in large cities such as New York, Chicago, and Los Angeles. Even the primary monument to suburbia, the shopping center, got into the act as several constructed their own kiddielands, with the first opening at Northgate Mall in Seattle in 1950. The kiddieland boom was short-lived. Rising property values and an aging target market shut most of them down by the late 1960s. Though some grew into full-fledged amusement parks, fewer than a dozen kiddielands from this era remain in operation today, including Pixie Playland, Concord, California; Funland, Idaho Falls, Idaho; Hoffman's Playland, Latham, New York; and Memphis Kiddie Park, outside Cleveland.

As America was flocking to the suburbs, the core of the industry, the large urban amusement park, was being left behind in the face of aging infrastructure, television, urban decay, and desegregation. Coming off the capital constraints of the Depression and World War II, many parks were struggling to update and stay competitive. It seemed that these parks were becoming increasingly irrelevant as the public turned elsewhere for entertainment. What was needed was a new concept to reignite the industry, and that new concept was Disneyland.

The Theme Park Era

By the 1950s, Walt Disney was an internationally renowned filmmaker. He often spent Sunday afternoons with his kids at a local amusement park, lamenting the fact that there was nothing that the family could enjoy together. Disney initially considered building a small entertainment facility at his movie studio, featuring a train, boat and stagecoach rides, a Wild West Town, and a circus. But as his dream grew, so did the size of the project.

When Disneyland first opened in 1955 on a former orange grove in Anaheim, California, many people were skeptical that an amusement park without any of the traditional attractions would succeed. There were no roller coasters, no swimming pool or beach, and no midway games. Instead of a midway, Disneyland offered five distinct themed areas—Main Street, Adventureland, Frontierland, Fantasyland, and Tomorrowland—

providing guests with the fantasy of travel to different lands and times. Disneyland was an immediate success, attracting nearly 4 million people in its first year of operation. The theme park era was born.

Robert Ott, former chairman of Dorney Park in Allentown, Pennsylvania, credits Disney with changing many things—"the way parks are organized, cleanliness, the use of lights and colors." Says Ott: "He catered to the customers, made them happy. His magic flowed into amusement parks. We all benefited from it." Carl Hughes, chairman of Kennywood, one of America's best remaining traditional parks, con-

Opened in 1955, Disneyland, in Anaheim, California, set off the theme park era.

curs: "The standards changed. You couldn't get away with dirty midways and surly employees." It was a whole new era of the amusement park industry.

While Disneyland is often given credit for being the first theme park, the concept had actually been evolving for more than a decade before Disneyland, as several smaller attractions opened that embraced a single theme. Many of these attractions, which helped inspire Disney, are still in operation today. These include Knott's Berry Farm in Buena Park, California, which started building its Ghost Town in 1940; Holiday World (originally Santa Claus Land), which opened in 1946 in Santa Claus, Indiana; Santa's Workshop, North Pole, New York, which started in 1949; Paul Bunyan Center, which opened in Brainerd, Minnesota, in 1950; and Great Escape (formerly Storytown USA) in Lake George, New York, which first welcomed visitors in 1954.

As important as the opening of Disneyland was, Ott remembers another event that was also important in changing the face of the industry in the 1950s. In 1958, the industry trade association, then known as the National Association of Amusement Parks, Pools and Beaches, took a tour of Europe. Since the European industry was largely wiped out during World War II, it had been rebuilding with a level of sophistication not yet found in American parks—intricate flowerbeds, elaborate landscaping, and flashy new rides adorned with thousands of electric lights. "That trip changed the industry," Ott recalled. "We brought back new and more sophisticated ideas." While these new ideas created an even more complex industry in America, implementing them was quite expensive. For parks struggling to come back from the Depression and World War II, it was too much.

The excitement created by Disneyland and the ideas from Europe opened a new era for amusement parks, but the industry suffered some growing pains. A variety of parks attempted to cash in on Disney's concept, but many lacked the appeal of Disney or simply did not have the financial resources. In 1958, Magic Mountain opened west of Denver when it was only partially completed, and it closed almost immediately. It later reopened and now exists as a shopping village with a few rides. Pacific Ocean Park, widely credited with making the pay-one-price admission an industry standard, opened in Ocean Park, California, in 1958 with the backing of CBS, but it closed down in 1968 due to high maintenance bills. Pleasure Island debuted near Boston in 1959, but it could never get its main attraction, a giant robotic replica of Moby Dick that was supposed to rear out of a body of water, to work properly. It closed in 1969, never achieving its hoped-for popularity. But the most spectacular failure was Freedomland in the Bronx. Built in the shape of the United States, the park opened in 1960, incomplete and overbudget. From the beginning, it was plagued by accidents, poorly planned attractions, insufficient capacity, and a robbery. Furthermore, the park was constructed atop a former landfill on improperly graded land. The buildings shifted as they settled and required expensive repairs. It struggled on until 1964, when it collapsed under a mountain of debt.

It wasn't until 1961, when Six Flags Over Texas opened between Dallas and Fort Worth, that another major theme park was finally successful. Backed by the land development firm Great Southwest Corporation, the park was the first in what today is the largest theme park chain in the world. Six Flags adapted traditional amusement park rides to a theme park, introducing the log flume to the industry in 1963 and building the first Runaway Mine Train roller coaster in 1966.

Following on the success of Six Flags, which proved that the theme park was a viable concept apart from Disney, theme park development during this time took off. Between 1964 and early 1965, fifteen theme parks opened, and *Amusement Business* reported that twenty additional projects were in the works. While these tended to be smaller, short-lived roadside attractions, the success of Six Flags had caught the attention of major corporations, such as Clairol, Penn Central, ABC, Marriott, Taft Broadcasting, and Mattel, which were soon planning their own parks. Even Bob Hope considered opening a theme park in Los Angeles in the 1960s. Among the major parks opening during this time were the first Sea World theme park, which debuted in San Diego in 1964; Six Flags Over Georgia in Atlanta in 1967; Astroworld in Houston in 1968; Magic Mountain near Los Angeles, Six Flags Over Mid-America outside St. Louis, and the immense Walt Disney World in Florida, all in 1971; and Opryland in Nashville in 1972. What these parks had in common was a location close to interstate highways on the outskirts of town, high standards of design and operation, and disdain for traditional amusement park attractions such as wooden roller coasters and midway games.

That disdain, however, changed in 1972 when Taft Broadcasting opened Kings Island near Cincinnati. Kings Island was different from most theme parks. Its roots were found in a very successful traditional amusement park—Coney Island in Cincinnati—which had been regarded as one of the most successful and best-run amusement parks in the country. Walt Disney even visited Coney Island to observe their operations while planning for Disneyland. Its success was a double-edged sword, however, because it became increasingly difficult to accommodate growing crowds in its cramped location on the Ohio River. In addition, flooding was a constant nuisance. As a result, in 1969 it was decided to relocate the park to a larger site in the suburbs, where it would become

The Racer at Kings Island, outside Cincinnati, introduced the wooden roller coaster to the theme park.

a major theme park. Given Coney Island's success, its owners had no reservations about including traditional amusement park attractions, even persuading renowned roller coaster designer John Allen to come out of retirement and build two wooden roller coasters—the twin-track Racer and the smaller Scooby Doo (now the Beastie). The new park was called Kings Island.

People flocked to Kings Island and lined up for hours to ride the Racer. Kings Island proved that people were still longing for traditional thrills, and the industry responded by opening more theme parks. In 1973, Carowinds opened near Charlotte, followed by Great Adventure in New Jersey and Kings Dominion in Richmond in 1974; Busch Gardens Williamsburg in Virginia in 1975; and Minneapolis's Valleyfair and the two Great America parks in California and Illinois in 1976. While these parks continued to embrace many of the design standards of their earlier cousins, their resistance to more traditional amusement park rides was not as strong as had been the case with their predecessors.

Trying to Compete

While theme parks increasingly dominated the industry in the 1960s and 1970s, the old traditional parks were facing hard times. Several factors made it difficult for many parks to compete in this new climate. Aging rides and buildings were in need of expensive upgrades, and the increasing sophistication of attractions at the theme parks made new attractions increasingly expensive to both purchase and maintain. The congested urban location of many of the older parks made expansion difficult, and urban decay often caused the loss of family business. Finally, increasing land values prompted many park operators to sell their facilities to developers. As a result, the industry saw the sad closings of many large urban traditional parks—parks that used to be the cornerstones of the industry.

Not all was bleak, however. Many traditional amusement parks learned from theme parks and revitalized their operations. One of the most dramatic examples was Cedar Point, located halfway between Cleveland and Toledo, in Sandusky, Ohio. Once known as the "Queen of American Watering Places," by the late 1950s the park was a shell of what it had been earlier in the century. In 1957, investors purchased the attraction with the intention of redeveloping the park. A local outcry persuaded them to retain the amusement park and rebuild it, using flashy new theme-park-style rides and adding themed areas. By the 1970s, Cedar Point was widely recognized as one of the most successful amusement parks. Building on this success, the owners purchased a theme park in 1978, Minnesota's Valleyfair. Today the company owns five amusement and theme parks.

Cedar Point was not the only example of a traditional park successfully adapting to a theme park environment. Hersheypark in Pennsylvania revived its business by adding a series of themed areas. Other parks, such as Kennywood in West Mifflin, Pennsylvania; Geauga Lake (now Six

Riverview, in Chicago, was one of the greatest of the urban traditional parks to close in the 1960s.

Flags Worlds of Adventure) in Aurora, Ohio; Riverside (now Six Flags New England) in Agawam, Massachusetts; and Lagoon in Farmington, Utah, maintained their traditional atmosphere but incorporated ideas pioneered by theme parks, including uniformed employees, live entertainment, costumed characters, and theme-park-style rides such as log flumes, observation towers, and monorails.

Competition and New Concepts

Theme park development had slowed dramatically by the late 1970s, simply because most of the markets large enough to support such a facility now had a park. As a result, most theme park operators concentrated on expanding and improving existing facilities. Most attention was focused on topping one another with record-breaking roller coasters. Sparked by the interest generated by Kings Island's Racer, the seventies saw a roller coaster arms race. New record-breaking heights were achieved, and in 1975, Knott's Berry Farm and Arrow Development Corporation built a steel Corkscrew looping roller coaster. Soon looping roller coasters were must-have attractions for successful theme parks. The intense competition sparked innovations in ride technology, which reached a level of complexity never before experienced. Most rides were now computer controlled and made by new high-tech manufacturing processes.

This was all extremely expensive, and rapidly increasing manufacturing costs coupled with a downturn in the industrial economy, which provided the picnic business that so many traditional parks relied upon, brought about another wave of park closures in the late 1970s. By the end of the decade, nearly one hundred amusement parks had closed forever.

As the industry entered the 1980s, opportunities for new theme parks were limited, and the demand for large thrill rides was waning due to an aging population and increasing costs. The popularity of water attractions skyrocketed during the decade, however, as they could be enjoyed by the entire family and provided a fun way to cool off on a hot summer day. New concepts included the river rapids (introduced in 1980), the splashwater (1984), and the "dry" water slide (1986). It was an era of tremendous growth for water parks, which eschewed traditional rides for water slides. The first water park, Wet 'n Wild, opened in Orlando in 1977, but the concept truly took off in the 1980s. By 1983, water parks were so popular that Geauga Lake in Aurora, Ohio, became the first amusement park to add a full-scale water park to its lineup of traditional amusement park attractions.

The ride simulator was another attraction that many amusement parks thought would be the wave of the future during the 1980s. Small versions such as the Astroliner had been available since 1978, but the opening of Star Tours at Disneyland took the experience to an entirely new level. Industry observers predicted that simulators would supplant traditional thrill rides, because they could easily be reprogrammed into a new ride experience every few years. Most major theme parks added a simulator, but the lines at the roller coasters did not grow any shorter.

Many American theme park operators also turned their attention overseas. Disney became the first major American operator to expand overseas, opening Tokyo Disneyland in Japan in 1983. It soon became the world's most popular amusement park and set off a wave of theme park construction in Asia, turning it into the second-largest amusement park market in the world.

The Industry Today

By the late 1980s, amusement park operators realized something very surprising: As the "baby boom" generation got older, they were not retiring from enjoying thrill rides like previous generations had done. The roller coaster innovations in the late 1970s failed to satiate their appetite for thrills, and in 1988 the arms race began anew with the construction of the 170-foot-tall Shock Wave at Six Flags Great America in Gurnee, Illinois (now dismantled). It held the record for only a year, however. The following season, Cedar Point in Sandusky, Ohio, constructed Magnum XL 200, the first roller coaster to surpass 200 feet in height. The arms race continues unabated to this day, peaking in the year 2000, when about a hundred roller coasters opened around the world. In fact, that year the world's record for the largest and fastest roller coaster changed hands three times—from Goliath at Six Flags Magic Mountain (255 feet tall and 85 miles per hour) in February, to Millennium Force (310 feet tall and 92 miles per hour) in May, to Steel Dragon at Nagashima Spaland in Japan (318 feet tall and 95 miles per hour) in August. That record stood until 2003, when Cedar Point opened Top Thrill Dragster, which stands 420 feet tall and has a top speed of 120 miles per hour.

The year 1988 was also significant in that the development of new theme parks in the United States resumed, some being built in cities that had been considered too small for such an attraction in the 1970s. These included Sea World Texas in San Antonio (1991); Visionland, near Birmingham, Alabama (1998); Legoland, near San Diego, California (1999); and Jazzland (now Six Flags New Orleans), New Orleans, Louisiana (2000).

In the 1990s, the amusement park industry enjoyed a level of prosperity not seen since the 1920s. Theme parks were opening around the world and attracting record numbers of people. Although some parks did close, the traditional parks that survived the hard times have learned to compete and have become beloved local institutions.

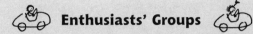

Enthusiasts' Groups

There are dozens of organizations for people interested in amusement parks or specific rides. The largest of these are listed here:

American Carousel Society

3845 Telegraph Rd.
Elkton, MD 21921-2442

www.carousel.org/acs/

Membership includes three newsletters, a convention summary newsletter, a biennial census of operating wooden carousels, a membership directory, and convention materials.

American Coaster Enthusiasts (ACE)

7700 Shawnee Mission Pkwy.
Suite 201
Overland Park, KS 66202

www.aceonline.org

Publications include *Roller Coaster!*, a quarterly magazine, and *ACE News*, a bimonthly newsletter. Normally hosts five events a year in North America.

Dark Ride and Fun House Enthusiasts

P.O. Box 484
Vienna, Ohio 44473-0484

www.dafe.org

Publishes *Barrel of Fun*, a quarterly newsletter, and hosts at least one event a year.

The Dark Ride and Fun House Historical Society

22 Cozzens Ave.
Highland Falls, NY 10928

www.laffinthedark.com

Features an on-line newsletter.

European Coaster Club

Six Green Lane
Hillingdon, Middlesex UB8 3EB
England

www.coasterclub.org

Publishes *First Drop*, a bimonthly magazine, and hosts six to eight events a year, most often in Europe.

(continued on page 20)

Enthusiasts' Groups
(continued from page 19)

National Amusement Park Historical Association (NAPHA)

P.O. Box 83
Mt. Prospect, IL 60056

www.napha.org

The only club following all aspects of the amusement and theme park industry. Publishes *NAPHA News*, a bimonthly magazine, and *NAPHA NewsFLASH!!!*, a monthly newsletter. Hosts two to four events annually, primarily in North America.

National Carousel Association

P.O. Box 4333
Evansville, IN 47724-0333

www.carousel.org/nca/

Membership benefits include the quarterly magazine *Merry-Go-Roundup*, a biennial census report of existing carousels, and a biennial membership listing. Hosts an annual convention and a technical conference.

Roller Coaster Club of Great Britain (RCCGB)

P.O. Box 235
Uxbridge, Middlesex UB10 0TF
England

www.rccgb.co.uk

Publishes *Airtime*, a bimonthly newsletter, and a yearbook. Hosts six to eight events a year, primarily in Europe.

There is also a wealth of clubs around the world targeting specific regions or interests. These include Coaster Enthusiasts of Canada, Coaster Riders of America, Coaster Zombies, Florida Coaster Club, Freundeskreis Freizeitparks (Germany), Great Ohio Coaster Club (GOCC), Kentucky Coaster Club, Mid Atlantic Coaster Club (MACC), Rollercoaster Friends (Belgium), Western New York Coaster Club (WNYCC), Wild Ones Coaster Club, and Wild West Coaster Club.

The distinction between theme and traditional parks has become blurred, with theme parks adding thrill rides that have little connection to their original themes and traditional parks adding themed areas. And the two have always shared a desire to entertain their customers and respond to an ever-changing society.

Consumers seemed to have less free time available for entertainment in the 1990s, so the industry responded with a new concept: the family entertainment center. Unlike larger parks, which required one or two days to fully enjoy, family entertainment centers emphasized activities that could be enjoyed in a short amount of time. Most cities now feature one or more of these facilities, which can range from a large game arcade to a miniature amusement park complete with go-carts and kiddie rides.

Although the industry is increasingly dominated by major corporations and large, high-tech thrill rides, there is a renewed sense of appreciation for the industry's heritage. Two amusement parks—Pittsburgh's Kennywood and Playland in New York—are now listed as national historic landmarks, as are numerous rides throughout the country, such as the Giant Dipper roller coaster at a revived Belmont Park in San Diego and Leap the Dips at Lakemont Park in Altoona, Pennsylvania, both saved due to grassroots preservation efforts. A few parks, most notably Arnold's Park in Iowa and Conneaut Lake Park in Pennsylvania, have found new life as nonprofit community assets. The few remaining family-owned parks have found ways to peacefully coexist with the large, corporate-owned competitors. Few regions of the country better reflect the industry today than New Jersey. Of the sixteen major parks, only one is owned by a major corporation. The remainder are family-owned.

As the amusement park industry enters the twenty-first century, it is enjoying unprecedented popularity. In all corners of the world, people flock to their local parks, and thanks to advances in technology, they are

Kennywood, near Pittsburgh, is one of the traditional amusement parks that has thrived in the theme park era.

thrilled in ways never before imagined—400-foot-tall roller coasters with speeds exceeding 100 miles per hour; linear induction motors launching rides at unheard-of acceleration rates; 300-foot-tall free falls; and dark rides in which riders become part of the action. More than 300 million people flock to American amusement parks annually, which is more than twice the number in 1970, despite the fact that the number of parks has remained consistent at around six hundred. The industry seems to have entered a new golden age.

A History of the Amusement Park in New Jersey

THROUGHOUT THE COUNTRY, THE AMUSEMENT INDUSTRY CAN CREDIT different influences in their development. In Pennsylvania and Ohio, the numerous industrial cities attracted amusement parks. In New York City, the entrepreneurial energy driven by waves of immigrants turned Coney Island into the center of the amusement park universe. More recently, Florida's position as a tourist mecca earned it the title of "theme park capital of the world." But in New Jersey, the energy that drove the development of the amusement park industry came from the pounding surf of the Atlantic Ocean.

Today the Jersey shore is one of the country's favorite vacation destinations, attracting millions of visitors annually, and as a result, it is home to nine of the state's sixteen amusement parks. While the Atlantic Ocean was the most influential factor in the growth of the amusement park industry and remains its focus today, that was not always the case. For much of the early 1800s, a lack of transportation options limited the use of the shore primarily to fishing villages and the occasional summer visitor.

The earliest amusement resorts in the state tended to thrive in the densely populated areas in the northern part of the state, near New York City. One of the earliest examples was Elysian Fields in Hoboken. Col. John Stevens, the founder of Hoboken and one of the inventors of the steamboat, started the park. Beginning in 1784, Stevens developed Hoboken as a resort to generate traffic for the ferryboats he operated in the Hudson River. A wooded six-mile path along the river was one of the original attractions. This was later joined by a mineral water spa, a tavern, a hotel, and by the 1830s, a few primitive rides, including a 100-foot-tall

Observation Tower and the Pleasure Railway, a contraption consisting of three-wheeled cycles propelled by riders around a circular track. In 1846, Elysian Fields achieved renown as the location of the first regular organized baseball game, but by then Hoboken was developing into a major city, and Elysian Fields was soon developed for other purposes.

By the Sea

By the 1850s, improvements in transportation and perceptions about the medicinal benefits of the sea air started attracting people to the ocean. Following the end of the Civil War, a variety of interests created seaside communities in rapid succession to accommodate the growing crowds. This led to a need for entertainment and accommodations that businesspeople were all too happy to fill.

One of the first resorts was Long Branch, located in the central part of the state, which gained popularity with Southerners following the Civil War as a place to escape the summer heat and malaria of the South. It also achieved prominence when President Ulysses S. Grant started spending summers there in 1869. A racetrack opened in 1870, a steamboat pier in 1878, and waterfront pavilions soon thereafter. An amusement pier opened in 1902, and a boardwalk followed in 1912.

Religious organizations were responsible for the founding of a number of seaside communities, which they initially established as summer religious camps. These included Belmar (1872), Ocean City (1879), and Ocean Grove (1869). Most other communities, including Point Pleasant Beach (1877), Keansburg (1904), Seaside Park (1909), and Seaside Heights (1913), were started by real estate speculators who saw the opportunity to sell lots to residents of Philadelphia and New York City for summer bungalows.

Almost invariably a boardwalk was constructed in these communities, where entrepreneurs ran concessions to cater to the crowds. These included bathhouses, restaurants, and almost always a large pavilion anchored by a carousel. By the early twentieth century, almost every town along the Jersey shore had its own carousel.

While most resorts and their associated amusements were modest in scope, a few really stood out. One of the largest resorts was Asbury Park, founded by James Bradley in 1871. In 1887, it received its first major amusement facility when Ernest Schnitzler built a 10,000-square-foot building to house a carousel. The carousel was soon joined by a Crystal Maze, and in 1892, one of the first Ferris wheels ever constructed was added. A larger, more elaborate Ferris wheel topped by an 85-foot observation platform that riders could access by disembarking at the top of the wheel opened in 1895. Other amusements and a boardwalk soon fol-

Asbury Park was one of New Jersey's first seaside resorts and was anchored by Palace Amusements since 1887. This photo shows the Palace's 1895 Ferris wheel with the observation deck on top.

lowed. By the early 1900s, Asbury Park was one of the largest amusement areas in the state.

Meanwhile, at the southern end of New Jersey, real estate speculators began selling lots in what is now known as Wildwood during the 1880s to Philadelphians looking for a summer retreat. In 1888, the first ocean-side pavilion was constructed. A carousel opened in 1892, and other oceanfront entertainment facilities soon followed, including the community's first pier in 1890. Today Wildwood is the largest amusement area on the Atlantic coast.

Playground of the World

As successful as these resorts were, there was one place against which all other resorts would be measured: Atlantic City, the heart of New Jersey's amusement industry in the latter half of the nineteenth century. In 1850, Atlantic City was just a small settlement, but once the town was linked to Camden by the railroad in 1854, growth took off. Hoteliers flocked to the town, with the first hotel opening in 1853. Ironically, the oceanfront property was considered worthless until 1870, when hotel owner Jake Heim implored the city council to do something about the mess that the tourists created by tracking sand into his business. The result was the world's first Boardwalk. It was a simple affair, just a mile long and 8 feet wide, and it was taken down and stored each winter. After being replaced by a larger portable boardwalk in 1880, a permanent one was erected in 1884, followed by the current 5-mile-long, 60-foot-wide version in 1896.

The Boardwalk shifted the focus of the town to the waterfront, where the hotels tended to gravitate. With millions of people now flocking to the Atlantic City Boardwalk, it also became a center of amusement industry innovation, as entrepreneurs tried to find ever more creative ways to entertain the masses. The first recorded amusement facility in Atlantic City, the Sea View Excursion House, opened in 1869. The Excursion House was built to accommodate vacationers and included a railroad terminal, a hotel, and a number of concessionaires catering to travelers, among them a carousel and a rotary swing, a 15-foot-tall device resembling a Ferris wheel.

In fact, Atlantic City can claim to be the birthplace of the midway favorite, as several Ferris-wheel-type rides predated the opening of what is considered the first Ferris wheel in Chicago in 1893. A ride called the Encyclopedial Wheel was built in 1872 and consisted of four 30-foot-tall wheels, each accommodating sixteen people. As the wheels turned, they also revolved on a turntable.

Another early ride, which closely resembled the Ferris wheels of today, was the Observation Roundabout, opened by William Somers in 1891 along the Boardwalk. Although the wooden ride burned down the next year, it was immediately rebuilt as two 40-foot-tall wheels operating side by side.

But amusement ride innovation did not stop with the Ferris wheel. Atlantic City's first roller coaster opened in 1885, when LaMarcus Thompson, the inventor of the roller coaster, opened a Switchback Railway in Atlantic City. Based on the ride he opened at Coney Island the year before, the ride consisted of two parallel tracks. A car traveled down one track to the other end, where it was hauled to the top of a second tower and released down the other track for the return trip.

While the Switchback Railway was popular, Thompson's greatest contribution to the emerging amusement industry in Atlantic City was the opening of the Scenic Railway in 1887. Unlike the Switchback Railway, the Scenic was similar to modern roller coasters, with a lift hill and a complete loop of track, but it had a building at one end of the ride through which the trains traveled, filled with elaborate scenes of faraway lands that were illuminated as trains passed by. The Scenic Railway caused an international sensation, and soon similar versions were being erected around the world, including two additional ones in Atlantic City.

Another popular amusement invented in Atlantic City was the Haunted Swing, one of the first illusion rides, in 1893. Riders sat on a bench while the room revolved around them, giving them the feeling that they were being flipped upside down. It too was a popular attraction at amusement parks through the early part of the twentieth century, and a number of contemporary versions are in operation today.

As important as amusement rides were at Atlantic City in the late 1800s, by the beginning of the next century they were taking a backseat to live entertainment. The emerging dominance of live entertainment was driven by what is perhaps Atlantic City's greatest contribution to New Jersey's amusement industry: the popularization of piers as entertainment facilities. Before Howard's Pier opened in 1882 in Atlantic City, piers were primarily thought of as docking facilities for ships. But in Atlantic City, the chance to stroll high above the crashing waves of the ocean and be entertained by dance halls, theaters, picnic areas, sunbathing pavilions, and other amusements led to a wave of pier development that lasted until World War I.

Howard's Pier collapsed in a storm within a few months of its opening, but it was immediately replaced by a new 750-foot-long pier. This one lasted until 1890, when it was demolished for an expansion of the Boardwalk. In 1884, Howard's Pier was joined along the Boardwalk by Applegate's Pier, which stood 625 feet long and featured an ice water fountain as one of its main attractions. Applegate's Pier became one of the leading amusement facilities in 1891, when Capt. John Young, one of

Young's Pier featured one of the first looping roller coasters.

STEEPLECHASE PIER, ATLANTIC CITY, N. J.

Steeplechase Pier was the first pier in Atlantic City to emphasize rides over live entertainment.

the city's greatest promoters, acquired it. Young had grown up in the area and started speculating in Atlantic City real estate in the 1880s. He soon acquired a carousel along the Boardwalk. When he purchased Applegate's Pier, he changed the name to Young's Pier, tripled the length to nearly 2,000 feet, and brought in attractions such as a tram to shuttle people around the pier, a carousel, and in 1902, one of the first looping roller coasters ever built. A fire destroyed Young's Pier in 1912.

A third pier, Iron Pier, opened in 1886 and was sold in 1898 to food magnate H. J. Heinz as a showcase for his products. It was destroyed by a storm in 1944. The great Steel Pier, which for years was the heart of the resort, debuted in 1898 and gained a neighbor in 1899 when Auditorium Pier opened.

Auditorium Pier's opening was fought by neighboring pier owners, who used a clause in the city code to prohibit it from being linked to the Boardwalk. This meant that customers had to climb up a set of stairs from the beach to get to the pier. In addition, a restraining order was obtained against the opening day headliner, so she had to be smuggled in in a steamer trunk. Though it was soon connected to the Boardwalk, the pier was never successful, and in 1902 the great Coney Island park owner George Tilyou purchased it. In 1904, he converted it into Steeplechase Pier, adding a large fun house and rides, creating Atlantic City's first pier to emphasize amusement rides over live entertainment.

Captain Young was also responsible for the last great pier to be constructed in Atlantic City. Called Million Dollar Pier due to its construction cost, the pier featured the world's largest ballroom, a theater, an exhibit hall, and an aquarium when it opened in 1906. Young built an elaborate home at the end of the pier that he modestly called One Atlantic Ocean, and he enthralled visitors with his daily net hauls in which a net was lowered into the ocean to bring up a variety of sea life. Some fish were displayed in the aquarium, others served in the restaurant, and some even sold to customers.

The last of the Atlantic City piers was Garden Pier, which was built as a vaudeville house in 1913 and has survived to the present day as Atlantic City's Arts Center.

By the early twentieth century, Atlantic City was at its zenith. It boldly proclaimed itself to be Playground of the World, and millions flocked to its hotels and piers. Publicity stunts such as eating contests, flagpole sitters, and the Miss America competition were common occurrences. But by now, amusement rides had taken a backseat to live entertainment and were tough to find outside Steeplechase Pier.

Looking Inland

As important as the growth of the seaside resorts were to the emergence of the amusement industry in New Jersey, inland development also had a major impact in the late nineteenth and early twentieth centuries. As

Hillside Park near Newark was one of New Jersey's early trolley parks.

Palisades Park's Cyclone was one of the top roller coasters of its era.

in other states, trolley companies near the major cities in New Jersey opened amusement parks to generate ridership on the evenings and weekends. Most of the development was concentrated around the two major urban areas: Newark in the north and Camden in the south.

Among the parks opening in the north were Electric Park, Newark (1903); Hillside Pleasure Park, Belleville (1904); Olympic Park, Maplewood (1904); and Fairyland, Passaic (1905). In the Camden area were Tumbling Dam Park, Bridgeboro (1893); Washington Park on the Delaware, Woodbury (1895); Woodlynne Park, Camden (1901); Bellewood Park, Pattenburg (1902); and Clementon Lake Park, Clementon (1907). Other parks that opened elsewhere in the state included Lenape Park, Mays Landing (1908); and White City, Trenton (1908). By 1910, some thirty amusement parks were in operation in the state.

Of all the parks that opened during this period, by far the most famous was Palisades Park. Sitting on a bluff overlooking Manhattan, 200 feet above the Hudson River, Palisades Park was started in 1898 by the Bergen County Traction Company. The park initially attracted patrons with its peaceful picnic groves, horse ride, miniature train, and carousel. That changed in 1909, when a major expansion was launched. One of the largest features was the world's largest electric sign. Spelling out the name of the park, the 400-foot-long sign featured 18-foot-tall letters and had ten thousand electric lights. It reportedly could be seen 50 miles away.

When the Schenck Brothers acquired the operation in 1910, expansion kicked into high gear with the addition of three roller coasters and rides in genuine automobiles, a real novelty at the time. The Schencks continued to operate the park into the 1930s, when they sold the operation to focus on their motion picture businesses.

A Maturing Industry

Through the early 1920s, the industry in the state held its own. Some parks opened, such as Belvidere Beach in Keansburg (1912) and Columbia Park in Union Hill (1919). Others, such as Newark's Electric Park (1912), Woodlynne Park (1912), Washington Park on the Delaware (1913), and Bellewood Park (1916), closed in the face of increasing competition and the inability to accommodate the increasingly important automobile trade.

As it did in the country as a whole, New Jersey's amusement industry boomed in 1920s, with the number of parks operating in the state increasing to nearly forty. With transportation improvements, several seaside towns saw increased traffic and responded by offering new amusement facilities to the masses.

In 1921, Atlantic City saw Central Pier open on the site of the burned remains of Young's Pier, while Rendezvous Park, an elaborate amusement park with the latest amusement rides, including a large roller

Columbia Park in Union Hill featured this Noah's Ark fun house when it opened in 1919.

coaster, opened nearby. Central Pier is still in existence as a go-cart facility, but Rendezvous had a much shorter life, being purchased by the city in 1924 for the site of the current Convention Hall.

But the greatest impact of the industry's expansion was felt farther south, in the quieter resorts of Ocean City and Wildwood. Ocean City saw its first amusement parks open, with the debut of Stainton's Playland (1929) and Gillian's Fun Deck (1930). Meanwhile, Wildwood, which had featured limited amusement facilities, saw its first large-scale amusement park development in 1919 with the opening of Playland, which featured a carousel, an Old Mill dark boat ride, and the Jack Rabbit, a large wooden roller coaster. Following in quick succession were Sportland Pier in 1928 and Marine Pier in 1931. The inland areas also saw new parks opening, including the short-lived Dreamland in Elizabeth (1922) and Bertrand Island, which opened on Lake Hopatcong in 1925.

But as the 1920s ended, the industry entered a quiet period as the Depression and World War II diverted attention elsewhere. While some parks opened, such as Casino Pier in Seaside Heights (1932), Casino Amusements in Asbury Park (1932), and Playland in Ocean City (1939), overall development was quiet. Although the number of parks in the state fell from around thirty-five to about twenty-five, the dropoff paled into comparison to that in many other states.

Prosperity

As America entered a new age of prosperity in the late 1940s, the industry in the state entered its greatest era, as New Jersey benefited from some of the major trends that dominated the period: the development of interstate highways and the growth of suburbia.

The growth in the state during the 1950s caught the attention of amusement park developers, and New Jersey rode a new wave of development. In response to the postwar baby boom, kiddielands became popular diversions in suburban areas throughout the country. New Jersey joined areas such as Long Island, Los Angeles, and Chicago as a hotbed of kiddieland development, with more than a dozen opening, primarily in the northern part of the state. Included were kiddielands in Bayonne, Pennsauken, River Edge, and Saddle River Township. Even shopping malls got into the act, with Bergen Mall in Paramus opening a small outdoor kiddieland in 1957. In 1962, Kiddieland opened inside Cherry Hill Mall in Cherry Hill. While it lasted only a few years, it was regarded as the first indoor kiddieland, a new concept that enjoyed renewed popularity in the 1990s. By the late 1960s, however, rising property values closed most of the kiddielands. New Jersey's last true

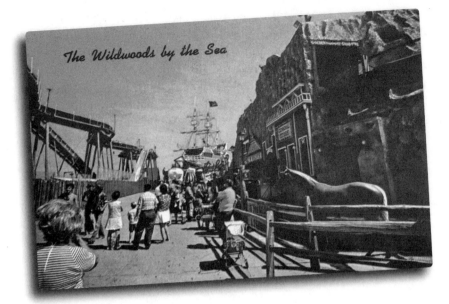

Hunt's Pier in Wildwood was known for its unique attractions.

kiddieland, Kiddie Karnival in Pine Brook, closed in 1987 when it was taken over by the state for a road project.

Themed roadside attractions also became popular features in New Jersey during the 1950s. Like kiddielands, they catered to the automobile culture, but instead of rides, they emphasized a themed environment. The two most popular themes were nursery rhymes and the Wild West. At least five storybook parks and three Wild West parks opened throughout the state. While some, such as Storyland Village in Neptune City (1956 to 1962), Adventure Village in Egg Harbor Township (1959 to 1969), and Cowboy City in Farmingdale (late 1950s to 1966), were shuttered after only a few years due to increasing property values, New Jersey still has the heaviest concentration of these facilities in the country, including Storybook Land in Cardiff (1955) and Wild West City in Netcong (1957).

But these new types of attractions were not the only ones to benefit from the spread of interstate highways in the 1950s. The state's seaside resorts, in particular Wildwood, also benefited from improved accessibility and underwent tremendous growth. The amusement industry in Wildwood had stagnated since Ocean Pier was destroyed by fire in 1943. But with vacationers flocking to the resort to stay in the flashy new motels being built throughout the town, a new generation of parks debuted, including two in 1957 alone.

At the southern end of the Boardwalk, Joe Barnes purchased a dilapidated thirty-year-old pier that housed the city's convention center and converted it into an amusement pier, Fun Pier. Throughout the 1960s, Fun Pier stood out as a showplace of rides built by Universal Design, a manufacturer started in the early 1960s in Wildwood to develop low-cost versions of theme park rides for smaller parks. Among their products displayed at Fun Pier were a Sky Ride, monorail, and sky tower.

Farther north, William Hunt built an all new pier atop the charred remains of Ocean Pier. Called Hunt's Pier, it soon became one of the most popular amusement parks in the state, with its high-quality custom-built attractions that were comparable to many of the rides being built at the new corporate theme parks that were just starting to spring up throughout the country. These attractions included Jungleland in 1959, the Gold Nugget Mine Ride in 1960, and the Pirate Ship Skua, one of the last old-style fun houses in 1962.

A Swinging Place

No other amusement park in the state, or in the country for that matter, saw the level of prosperity in the 1950s that Palisades Park experienced. The roots of this success dated back to 1934, when Jack and Irving Rosenthal purchased the park. The Rosenthals were drawn to the amusement industry at a young age to support their impoverished family. Starting with a pail and shovel concession at Coney Island in 1906, the brothers moved on to the other amusement areas and had become so successful that in 1913, the now teenage brothers took over operation of the rundown Golden City Park in Canarsie, New York, which they later sold.

At the time of the purchase, Palisades Park was losing $80,000 annually. But the Rosenthals' business acumen and flair for publicity allowed them to quickly turn the operation around and make it one of the most popular amusement parks in the country. Even fires in 1935 and 1944 that destroyed major portions of the park failed to stop them. In fact, the park was considered so important to public morale that it was given a special waiver after the 1944 fire to obtain building materials rationed due to World War II to assist in the rebuilding.

But it was when the Rosenthals teamed up with Sol Abrams and Morgan Hughes that Palisades Park reached its zenith. In 1949, Abrams joined the staff as publicity director. Soon the park was attracting thousands of patrons with stunts such as merchandise giveaways, talent contests, free live entertainment, and almost every kind of beauty contest imaginable. The park achieved national publicity when it sponsored an elephant that water-skied down the Hudson River. Eddie Fisher and Deb-

Unique and Historic Attractions

Alice in Wonderland, Storybook Land
One of the most creative walk-throughs in the country, this attraction begins with a trip down the rabbit hole through the famous children's story and ends by finding your way out through a maze of giant playing cards.

Carousel, Gillian's Wonderland Pier
Carved by the Philadelphia Toboggan Company in 1926, the ride represents one of the company's finest works with 48 hand-carved horses.

Carousel, Six Flags Great Adventure
One of the few antique carousels in the country that was manufactured in England. It is also one of the oldest, dating back to 1881, and features twenty-four horses and twelve roosters.

Den of Lost Thieves, Wildwood Boardwalk
This independently operated dark ride on the action-packed Wildwood Boardwalk allows riders to participate by shooting at targets and amassing points throughout the ride.

Floyd Moreland Carousel, Casino Pier and Water Works
Assembled in 1910, this ride represents one of the finest examples of the carousel art, with fifty-eight animals including horses, camels, a lion, a tiger, and a donkey. This ride is the last carousel in New Jersey to still operate in its oceanfront pavilion, once common in every resort community.

Fun House, Jenkinson's Boardwalk
Built in 1998, this is a contemporary reincarnation of what was once an amusement park staple.

Helicopter, Steel Pier
This is a ride in a real helicopter over the Atlantic coast. Reaching speeds of 110 miles per hour during the four-minute trip, riders travel as high as 500 feet above the ocean.

Houdini's Great Escape, Six Flags Great Adventure
An updated version of the Haunted Swing illusion rides of the late 1800s, this heavily themed ride gives the impression that you are being flipped completely upside down.

Sky Ride, Morey's Piers–Spencer Avenue
No ordinary sky ride, this one reaches heights of 100 feet as it travels over and through the massive Great White roller coaster structure.

(continued on page 36)

Unique and Historic Attractions
(continued from page 35)

Spook House, Keansburg Amusement Park and Runaway Rapids
Dating back to 1931, the Spook House is the oldest operating non-water-based dark ride in the country.

Wipe Out, Morey's Piers–25th Avenue
This twelve-line fiberglass giant slide represents one of the last examples of what was a common attraction in the 1960s and 1970s. This ride is the attraction that started the Morey's Piers complex, the country's largest waterfront amusement complex.

bie Reynolds announced their engagement at the park. Palisades posters were seen in the movie *West Side Story,* and the park was the topic of a hit song by Freddie "Boom Boom" Cannon in 1962.

Abrams also followed the lead of Disney and reached deals with comic book publishers. Superman became the park's spokesman, with advertisements for Palisades Park appearing in every Superman comic book. In addition, rides were themed to Harvey Comics characters such as Casper the Friendly Ghost.

Morgan Hughes came to Palisades Park in 1950 as a ride concessionaire. On behalf of an associate, he agreed to set up the first Rotor ride in America at Palisades Park. Upon seeing the popularity of the ride, he realized that there was an unmet demand for the exciting new rides being developed in Europe, and he formed an importing business. Hughes set up relationships with twelve different European ride manufacturers, and through the 1950s and 1960s, each new season saw several of the newest and most exciting European rides introduced to North America at Palisades Park. Rides included the Bayern Kurve, Calypso, Cortina Bob, Matterhorn, Zugspitz, Reisenrad Ferris wheel, and the Jet Star and Wildcat roller coasters.

Changing Times

But while the industry boomed in the 1950s, things started to decline in the 1960s. By now more than fifty amusement parks were operating throughout the state, but the continuing spread of interstate highways and the increased popularity of air travel forever changed travel patterns. While some seaside resorts such as Wildwood and Ocean City continued to thrive, others, particularly Atlantic City, Asbury Park, and

Keansburg, started to lose the summer trade, sending their amusement parks into a slow downward spiral.

While the decline in the older seaside towns was slow, the large urban traditional amusement parks were all but wiped out during the 1960s. The first one to go was Olympic Park, straddling the towns of Maplewood and Irvington. The park originally opened in 1904 on the site of a picnic grove that had been popular with the area's German community since 1887. In 1921, under the leadership of Henry Guenther, Olympic Park became one of the largest amusement parks in the state. The park built the Dip-lo-do-cus in 1924. It was the first roller coaster with spinning cars, a concept reintroduced to the country in New Jersey in the 1990s. The park thrived through the 1950s, but time caught up with it, and by 1965 Olympic Park closed in the face of security problems, increasing taxes and labor costs, and skyrocketing property values.

At the opposite end of the state, Riverview Beach in Pennsville was the next large urban park to go. Although the site along the Delaware River was used for recreation purposes as early as 1845, in 1891 it became a full-fledged amusement park. From the 1920s into the 1960s, the park was known for its two large wooden roller coasters, the Wildcat and the Hummingbird. During this period, the most popular way to reach the park was via excursion boats that connected the park to Philadelphia and Wilm-

Roller Coaster, Riverview Beach, Pennsville, N. J.

Riverview Beach in Pennsville was one of the great amusement parks in New Jersey to close in the 1960s. LAKE COUNTY MUSEUM, CURT TEICH COLLECTION

ington. But when boat service was discontinued in 1961, the park went into a decline. The Wildcat coaster burned down in 1964 and was not rebuilt. In the end, the park became quite rundown, and in 1968, it quietly closed. The 63-acre site was subsequently converted into a public park.

But the most devastating loss was the closing of Palisades Park in 1971. Unlike Olympic Park and Riverview Beach, Palisades Park succumbed to its own success. By the late 1960s, the combination of the Rosenthals' high management standards, Morgan Hughes's flashy rides, and Sol Abrams's publicity was drawing an estimated 7 to 10 million people to the park annually. Since its earliest days, Palisades Park had a tense relationship with the densely populated residential communities surrounding the facility. By the late 1960s, this had reached a head with traffic congestion choking neighborhood roads and a rough element starting to hang out at the park. In the end, one of the surrounding communities attempted to block access to Palisades' overflow parking lots, and the property was rezoned to apartment use, which greatly increased the park's real estate taxes. Irving Rosenthal, who had outlived his brother, was now seventy-five and had no heirs. As a result, he sold the 38-acre site for apartment development, and Palisades closed following the 1971 season.

The announcement of the closing caused a great uproar, and several schoolchildren even wrote to President Nixon, imploring him to keep the park open. Initially Hughes attempted to lease the park for an additional season while plans were advanced to relocate Palisades Park to a new site in nearby Mount Olive. But the proposed lease fell through, ending Palisades' seventy-three-year history.

However, plans progressed for the new park, which would occupy 150 acres, feature seventy rides, and incorporate many of the best elements of the new theme parks springing up around the country. But the proposal faced opposition from the local community, and when it was rejected in a nonbinding referendum in November 1973, plans for a successor to Palisades Park fell by the wayside. The defeat seemed to suck the life out of Rosenthal, who died a little more than a month later at age seventy-seven.

The proposed Mount Olive amusement park was one of a number of new amusement parks proposed for New Jersey in the 1970s, as investors sought to cash in on the theme park boom that was taking America by storm. While most never made it past the proposal stage, including a proposal to develop a $600 million World's Fair theme park at Liberty State Park in Jersey City and a plan to convert an abandoned 942,000-square-foot automobile plant in Edgewater into an indoor theme park, a couple did open. Warner Brothers Jungle Habitat, a 1,000-

acre drive-through safari and theme park, managed to open in 1972, only to close just a few years later, in 1976. In the end, the only successful theme park to see the light of day in the 1970s was Six Flags Great Adventure, which opened in 1974.

Splish Splash

One new trend to emerge in the late 1970s was the invention of the water slide, and a number of parks in New Jersey were among the first in the country to embrace the concept. Since there were almost no water slide manufacturers, in 1977 two amusement parks, Sportland Pier in Wildwood and Gillian's Wonderland Pier in Ocean City, hired the great roller coaster designer John Allen to design water slides for them, introducing the attraction to the state. Within the next two years, nearly every park along the shore joined in, adding their own versions.

Water slides also played a key role in the development of one of the most unique amusement parks to open in the state—Action Park in Vernon. With a focus on participatory rides rather than traditional amusement park attractions, Action Park first opened in 1977 at the Vernon Valley ski resort. Its first attraction was an alpine slide, in which riders piloted small sleds through a trough constructed on a ski slope. The slide was a huge success, and the park started adding other participatory attractions such as water slides, go-carts, bumper boats, kayaks, speedboats, and a skateboard park. In its heyday, the park attracted nearly 1 million visitors annually to some of the most creative rides around, including the only 360-degree vertical loop water slide ever constructed. But Action Park fell on hard times and went bankrupt in 1996. A new owner acquired the facility, removed all of the non-water-based attractions, and reopened the park as Mountain Creek Waterpark in 1998.

The 1970s were a decade when many longtime traditions in New Jersey died. From its earliest days, the amusement industry in the state had been closely associated with the antique carousels that had operated in many areas since the late nineteenth century. But starting in the mid-1970s, increasing prices paid by collectors for the hand-carved animals, combined with growing capital needs by many of the parks, resulted in the sale of many of these priceless artifacts. In 1975, eighteen carousels were in operation in the state, but one by one they were sold, including the ones at Playland, Wildwood (1976); Lenape Park, Mays Landing (1977); Playland, Ocean City (1979); Casino Amusements, Asbury Park (1984); Keansburg Amusement Park, Keansburg (1984); Jenkinson's South, Point Pleasant Beach (1985); Gillian's Fun Deck, Ocean City (1987); Palace Amusements, Asbury Park (1989); and Clementon Amusement Park, Clementon (1990). Today just three antique carousels operate in the state.

But the most dramatic transformation that occurred in New Jersey's amusement industry in the 1970s was the continued decline of the industry in Atlantic City. Ever since the 1960s, decreasing business plagued the grand hotels along the Boardwalk, and many closed and were subsequently demolished, resulting in a loss of one-third of the city's hotel rooms by the mid-1970s.

Local leaders thought that the surest path to revitalization was to permit casino gambling. After several failed attempts, a voter referendum approved the proposal in 1976, and plans were made to erect sparkling new casinos along the faded Boardwalk. Pier owners initially celebrated the arrival of casinos, thinking the increased traffic would benefit their businesses. But once the first casino opened in 1978, they discovered that the crowds drawn to the casinos were not interested in enjoying the amusement piers.

Steel Pier, once the anchor of the Boardwalk, was the first to go when Resorts International purchased the struggling operation in 1978 and shut it down. Million Dollar Pier closed in 1980 and was converted into a shopping mall, and Central Pier removed its amusements in 1983. Finally, Steeplechase Pier, which was acquired by Resorts International in 1982, was shuttered in 1986 and subsequently demolished. For the first time since 1869, there were no operating amusement rides in the onetime capital of the New Jersey amusement industry.

The Turbulent 1980s

Unfortunately, the turmoil that impacted the amusement industry in Atlantic City was commonplace throughout the state during the 1980s. The most tragic event of the decade occurred at Six Flags Great Adventure, when a fire was started in the park's Haunted Castle by a patron trying to find his way through the darkened corridors with a lighter. In the end, eight people died, and government regulators worked to implement increased safety standards. That resulted in most of the state's dark rides and walk-through attractions being shuttered, as it was not feasible to implement the new standards. In fact, about ten such attractions in the state were shut down, and just one vintage dark ride, the Spook House at Keansburg Amusement Park, remains in operation. While the loss of these rides was sad, in the end, the incident resulted in much higher safety standards throughout the state.

The state also saw a number of disheartening park closures during the decade. In 1983, Bertrand Island, one of the state's last major traditional inland amusement parks, was shut down for a proposed real estate development. Dating back to 1925, the lakeshore facility was well known for its Wildcat roller coaster and Mill Chute rides. But the park

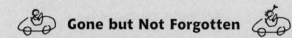

Gone but Not Forgotten

While New Jersey is still blessed with a wealth of amusement parks, all too many are now memories. Approximately 250 different amusement parks have operated in the state. Here is a list of some of the better-known ones that no longer exist.

Action Park, McAfee, 1977 to 1996.
Adventure Village, Egg Harbor Township, 1959 to 1969.
Alcyon Park, Pitman, 1892 to 1945.
Bayonne Kiddieland, Bayonne, early 1950s to late 1960s.
Bayonne Pleasure Park, Bayonne, 1909 to mid-1930s.
Bellwood Park, Pattenburg, 1902 to 1916.
Belmar Playland, Belmar, 1966 to 2000.
Belvidere Beach, Keansburg, 1912 to 1933.
Bergen Point Park/Uncle Milty's, Bayonne, early 1900s to early 1970s.
Bertrand Island, Lake Hopatcong, 1925 to 1983.
Brigantine Castle & Amusement Pier, Brigantine, 1976 to 1984.
Burlington Island Park, Burlington, 1910s to 1934.
Captain Good Times, Turnersville, 1989 to 1994.
Casino Amusements, Asbury Park, 1932 to 1990.
Casino Arcade, Wildwood, 1916 to 1980.
Central Pier, Atlantic City, 1921 to 1993.
Children's Storybook Farm, Parsippany, mid-1950s to late 1960s.
Colombia Park, Union Hill, 1919 to 1930s.
Cowboy City, Farmingdale, 1950s to 1966.
Days of Fun, Florence, 1950s to 1970.
Dinosaur Beach Adventure Park, Wildwood, 1996 to 1998.
Dreamland Park, Elizabeth, 1922 to 1939.
Ed Brown's Playground, Allaire, 1991 to 1999.
Electric Park, Newark, 1903 to 1912.
Exhilarama, Voorhees, 1992 to 1996.
Extension Kiddieland, Trenton, early 1950s to late 1960s.
Fairyland, Springfield, early 1960s to 1982.
Fairy Tale Forest, Oak Ridge, 1957 to 2003.
Fun City, Sea Isle City, 1971 to 2000.
Fun Fair, Point Pleasant Beach, 1965 to 1987.
Fun Pier, Wildwood, 1957 to 1987.
Gillian's Fun Deck, Ocean City, 1930 to 1987.
Gingerbread Castle, Hamburg, mid-1950s to late 1960s.
Hartman's Park, Beach Haven, 1960 to 1984.
Herman's Amusements/Schiffel's, Point Pleasant Beach, 1949 to 1987.

(continued on page 42)

Gone but Not Forgotten
(continued from page 41)

Hillside Pleasure Park/Riviera Park, Belleville, 1904 to 1927.
Hunt's Pier, Wildwood, 1957 to 1991.
Kiddie Karnival, Pine Brook, 1950s to 1987.
Kiddieland, Pennsauken, mid-1950s to mid-1960s.
Kiddieland, Saddle River Township, early 1950s to late 1960s.
Kids World, Long Branch, 1985 to 1987.
Lincoln Park, Paulsboro, 1890 to 1906.
Long Branch Pier, Long Branch, 1902 to 1987.
Marine Pier, Wildwood, 1931 to 1976.
Million Dollar Pier, Atlantic City, 1906 to 1981.
Nolan's Point, Lake Hopatcong, 1920s to 1933.
Ocean Pier, Wildwood, 1905 to 1943.
Olympic Park, Maplewood, 1904 to 1965.
Palace Amusements, Asbury Park, 1887 to 1988.
Palisades Park, Cliffside Park, 1898 to 1971.
Playland/Marine West/Nickels Midway Pier, Wildwood, 1919 to 1998.
Rendezvous Park, Atlantic City, 1921 to 1924.
Riverview Beach, Pennsville, 1891 to 1968.
Scheutzen Park, Jersey City, 1875 to 1964.
Sportland Pier, Wildwood, 1928 to 1982.
Stainton's Playland, Ocean City, 1929 to 1955.
Steeplechase Pier, Atlantic City, 1899 to 1986.
Storyland Village, Neptune City, 1956 to 1962.
Tivoli Pier, Atlantic City, 1988 to 1995.
Tumbling Dam Park, Bridgeboro, 1893 to 1946.
TW Sports, Egg Harbor Township, 1994 to 2001.
Warner Bros. Jungle Habitat, West Milford, 1972 to 1976.
Washington Park on the Delaware, Woodbury, 1895 to 1913.
White City, Trenton, 1908 to late 1910s.
Woodlyne Park, Camden, 1901 to 1912.
Wuest Casino, Point Pleasant Beach, early 1930s to 1975.

fell into disrepair in the 1960s, and after a last attempt to revitalize the operation, Bertrand Island closed in the face of increasing land values and maintenance bills.

The state's oldest amusement resort, Long Branch, also saw the loss of its amusements during the decade when a spectacular fire destroyed Long Branch Pier in 1987. The pier had been in the midst of a revitalization that began in 1978 when it was acquired by a new owner. Anchor-

Bertrand Island was a once popular park that succumbed in the 1980s.

ing the improvements was a huge haunted house, and in 1985 the pier added Kids World, a child-oriented theme park that generated positive publicity throughout the region. But on June 9, 1987, faulty electrical wiring ignited a gas line, and in three hours, the 425-foot-long pier was a total loss. Although the owners reopened an undamaged portion of the pier within five days, the loss was insurmountable, and the amusement park era of Long Branch ended.

Perhaps the greatest loss during the 1980s was the amusements in Asbury Park. Although the town had been plagued by urban decay through out the 1960s and 1970s, the amusement area, clustered along the Boardwalk and the nearby shore of Wesley Lake, managed to hold its own. The area along the Boardwalk was anchored by Oceanic Amusements with a small steel roller coaster, the Galaxy. Nearby was the Casino, with its antique carousel, Mad-O-Rama dark ride, and fun house, along with the larger Palace, with its 1895 Ferris wheel, carousel, Orient Express and Haunted Castle dark rides, fun house, and other rides.

But with the overall decline of the town, local leaders saw their salvation in a massive $750 million redevelopment of the waterfront. A developer group, with the assistance of the city, started acquiring property and demolishing buildings. The aging amusements were not part of the developer's plans. In 1987, Oceanic Amusements was shuttered. The following year, the Palace closed. The hand-carved carousel horses were sold off to collectors, while the carousel frame and the historic old Ferris wheel were sold to an amusement park in Mississippi. The Casino managed to hold on until 1990, but by then its antique carousel horses had been sold to collectors and replaced with fiberglass animals. After more than one hundred years, the amusement park era in Asbury Park had come to a sad end. What made its demise even sadder was that in 1992, the developer went bankrupt, leaving the half-completed skeleton of a condominium tower and the abandoned shells of the Palace and Casino as a testament to their failed vision.

Even Wildwood, the state's largest resort, went through a rough patch in the 1980s. The city boomed through the 1970s, when it became one of the country's most competitive amusement markets, featuring seven different amusement facilities. Leading the good times were Hunt's Pier and its one-of-a-kind attractions, and the Morey family, an aggressive upstart that opened their first pier in 1969 and in 1976, expanded by purchasing Marine Pier. But as the resort reached the 1980s, a number of facilities began declining in the face of aging owners, deteriorating facilities, and the growth of the Moreys' operations. In 1980, the Casino Arcade closed after sixty-four years of operation, followed by the fifty-four-year-old Sportland Pier in 1982. One of Wildwood's oldest amusements, the sixty-five-year-old Jack Rabbit roller coaster at Nickels Midway Pier (the former Playland), was demolished in 1984 in the face

Long Branch, the state's oldest amusement resort, saw its pier burn down in 1987.
OWEN KANSLER AERIAL PHOTOGRAPHY, LINDEN, NEW JERSEY

of high maintenance bills, while Fun Pier, which had been in decline since two fires in 1984, closed in 1987.

One year later, the Hunt family sold their pier to an investor group. They lacked the Hunts' creativity and started removing many of the rides that had made the pier famous, including the Flyer roller coaster, the Pirate Ship Skua, and the Jungleland ride. Attempts to turn around the pier were unsuccessful, and it closed in 1991.

Meanwhile, in Atlantic City, attempts were made to revive the moribund amusement park industry. As part of its $193 million expansion, the Tropicana Casino in Atlantic City reintroduced amusement rides to the Boardwalk with the 1988 opening of Tivoli Pier, a $19 million indoor theme park. Among its attractions were a roller coaster that gave riders a simulated view of the Atlantic City skyline; On the Boardwalk, a dark ride tracing the history of Atlantic City; and the Biggest Six Ferris Wheel, a 50-foot-tall Ferris wheel based on the casino's Big Six wheel game. The park's limited number of attractions failed to generate the necessary crowds, however, and Tivoli Pier closed in 1995.

On the Rebound

By the time Tivoli Pier closed, the number of parks in the state had dropped to around twenty, less than half the number in operation thirty years earlier. But there were definite signs throughout New Jersey that the hard times were ending.

In Atlantic City, Steel Pier, which had been destroyed by a fire in 1982, was completely rebuilt and reopened in 1993 as an amusement pier, signaling a rebirth of the industry in the town. In the northern part of the state, Keansburg was in the midst of a comeback anchored by a revitalized Keansburg Amusement Park, which was rescued from an almost sure demise. In 1995, the descendants of the person that opened the park in 1904 repurchased the struggling facility and launched a major expansion and renovation. Even the state's largest park, Six Flags Great Adventure, got into the act, launching the largest one-year expansion ever seen at a theme park, with the addition of twenty-four rides in 1999.

The most dramatic example of the comeback of the industry in the state occurred in Wildwood. By the early 1990s, four of the town's seven amusement facilities had closed. While one facility, Casino Arcade, was converted to other uses, the three piers quietly sat as underutilized assets. But starting in 1993, a revival was launched. The former Fun Pier, which was purchased by the Morey Organization shortly after it closed in 1987, was reopened as the Wild Wheels Raceway and Adventure Pier (now Morey's Pier–Spencer Avenue). Sportland Pier became a go-cart facility, and in 1996, the abandoned Hunt's Pier reopened as Dinosaur Beach

Adventure Park. Unfortunately, Dinosaur Beach closed after the 1998 season, the same year the town's oldest amusement park, Nickels Midway Pier, removed its rides to make room for a water park. But by now Wildwood was in the throes of a full-fledged rebound. The Morey Organization had taken control of four of the town's five amusement piers and was working to integrate its holdings in to a unified amusement facility tied in to the town and Wildwood's now-chic collection of 1950s Doo Wop–style motels.

While the abandoned remains of the Asbury Park's Palace and Casino Amusement buildings still stand as testaments to the challenges that the industry has faced, they are thankfully the exceptions. But even in Asbury Park, there is hope. In the late 1990s, a preservation group, Save Tillie, was formed to try to preserve the Palace and Casino buildings. While they have battled deterioration of the Palace and resistance from developers, they have succeeded in getting the Palace placed on the National Register of Historic Places. Even the Palace's old Ferris wheel and carousel returned to Asbury Park after the park in Mississippi to which they had been relocated closed in 1999. They are currently in storage, awaiting a time when they can again be placed in operation.

As the amusement park industry in New Jersey enters the twenty-first century, it has weathered numerous challenges but continues to thrive, still driven by the rhythmic pounding of the Atlantic surf.

Steel Pier

OPENED 1898

ATLANTIC CITY IS ONE OF AMERICA'S COMEBACK COMMUNITIES. FOR NEARLY a hundred years, until the 1960s, it was America's greatest seaside resort. After a three-decade period of decline, the storied resort is again becoming a popular destination, driven by the giant casinos that have replaced the grand hotels of an earlier generation. This comeback is not just limited to the hotels along the oceanfront, but also extends to what was the heart and soul of the Boardwalk, Steel Pier. What had once been given up for dead as the relic of the "old" Atlantic City has been born anew and is again the city's leading amusement facility.

Entertainment over the Sea

In 1897, a group of businessmen formed the Atlantic City Steel Pier Company to develop the largest and most modern pier in Atlantic City. Although there were other piers in operation at the resort, they tended to be smaller facilities whose poor construction made them susceptible to storm damage. The new pier would be different, however. Built at a cost of $350,000, it would be constructed of iron pilings extending 1,621 feet from the Boardwalk, driven deep into the ocean bed, and topped by steel girders on which the wooden pier deck was placed.

On top of the deck were a series of buildings larger and more elaborate than anything the city had previously seen. Fronting the Boardwalk was the Casino building. Designed in the Italian Renaissance style, the 150-by-120-foot, two-story building served as the pier's entrance and

Steel Pier
c/o Atlantic Pier Amusements
1050 Route 47 South
Rio Grande, NJ 08242-1506
609-345-4893
866-386-6659
www.steelpier.com

was distinguished by two graceful towers. The first level was promoted as "the great lounging place, where visitors can watch the throngs as they move to and thro on the walk." A cherry wood grand staircase linked visitors to the second floor, where they could enjoy smoking lounges, fully stocked reading rooms, and the Casino Theater, a large auditorium hosting the latest in band concerts.

From the back of the Casino, a two-story open-air promenade led to a 70-by-150-foot dance pavilion. Behind the dance hall was a 1,000-square-foot aquarium highlighted by a collection of sea lions. Beyond that was the 50-by-50-foot sun parlor, where visitors could enjoy the seaside weather. At the end was a fishing pier where "courteous attendants furnish bait and lines." The entire pier was decorated with five hundred potted plants and thirty-five hundred electric lights, with power provided by the pier's own plant.

On June 18, 1898, "the handsomest and most luxuriously appointed pier in the world" opened with a lavish ceremony highlighted by an appearance from Annie Oakley. Visitors flocked to the facility to enjoy the latest in concerts and live entertainment. One of the performers was a young W. C. Fields. In what was a revolutionary concept at the time, Steel Pier's 10-cent admission gave customers access to all of the shows and attractions, one of the first documented instances of what is now commonplace policy in the amusement industry.

The original Steel Pier, shown here in 1907, reflected the refined nature of the era.

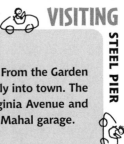

LOCATION

Steel Pier is located at the heart of the Atlantic City Boardwalk. From the Garden State Parkway, take Exit 37, the Atlantic City Expressway, directly into town. The pier is located directly across from the Trump Taj Mahal at Virginia Avenue and the Boardwalk. Parking is available for a nominal fee in the Taj Mahal garage.

OPERATING SCHEDULE

Steel Pier is open at noon on weekends from Palm Sunday weekend through early June, and at 1 P.M. on the week after Easter. Closing time varies from 6 P.M. to midnight. Between mid-June and Labor Day, Steel Pier is open weekdays from 3 P.M. to midnight and weekends from noon to 1 A.M. Steel Pier is also open weekends in September and October from noon to 6 P.M.

ADMISSION

Admission to Steel Pier is free, with rides and attractions available on a pay-as-you-go basis. Ride tickets cost about 75 cents each, and rides require from three to seven tickets. Discounted tickets books are also available. A pay-one-price wristband is available for around $30 on nonholiday weekdays. The Rocket and helicopter rides charge separately and do not accept ride tickets or pay-one-price wristbands.

FOOD

Steel Pier features about ten food outlets serving a wide variety of easy-to-eat foods. Most of the food stands are located in the International Food Court along the Boardwalk at the entrance to the pier.

FOR CHILDREN

Steel Pier has about eight kiddie rides and a three-level play structure, all located at the front of the pier. Favorite kiddie rides include the Little Leaper roller coaster, the Big Trucks, and the Mini Rocket. There are also a number of rides for the entire family, such as the Ferris wheel and double-deck merry-go-round.

SPECIAL FEATURES

Don't miss the Crazy Mouse, the first roller coaster in the United States with spinning cars.

TIME REQUIRED

Visitors can enjoy Steel Pier in about three hours.

TOURING TIPS

Take a helicopter tour. Few amusement rides can combine the height and speed of Steel Pier's helicopter, and the view of the Atlantic coastline is spectacular.

(continued on page 50)

VISITING (continued from page 49)

STEEL PIER

Try to visit during the week to take advantage of the pier's pay-one-price days. One price permits access to all rides in the amusement park with the exception of the Rocket and helicopter.

As one of the country's largest seaside resorts, Atlantic City offers a wide variety of other activities. In addition to more than a dozen casinos, you can stroll the world's original Boardwalk and take a ride in a rolling chair, a tradition since 1887. Attractions along the Boardwalk include Fralinger's, which has been selling saltwater taffy since 1885; the Ripley's Believe It or Not Museum; Garden Pier, home to the Atlantic City Art Center; and Central Pier, although a shadow of its former self, is the last of Atlantic City's amusement piers still in its original form, with a go-cart track and game concessions, along with its original elaborate entrance building. The nearby Ocean Life Center aquarium has Steel Pier's original Diving Bell on display. Park Place on the Boardwalk, scheduled to open in 2005, will be a Monopoly-themed shopping mall erected on the former Million Dollar Pier.

Steel Pier became a must-see attraction at the resort. The pier was lengthened to over 2,000 feet in 1908 with the addition of the Marine Ballroom, a 24,000-square-foot building that could hold up to seven thousand people. But soon the pier began to rest on its laurels and stagnated.

The Showplace of the Nation

In November 1924, a fire broke out across the Boardwalk from Steel Pier. Before it was over, two hotels had been destroyed and the pier's entrance damaged. This seemed to send a signal to the current owners that new blood was needed, and in June 1925, they sold the pier to Frank Gravatt.

Gravatt was a classic American success story. Starting with nothing, he worked his way up as a motorcycle salesman, automobile dealer, and real estate investor. He formed an investment group to acquire the pier for $2.1 million, but as the deal was being finalized, the other investors pulled out, leaving Gravatt solely responsible for the bank loan.

But it was Gravatt who realized the potential of Steel Pier and forged ahead to remake the facility. The pier that Gravatt took over had changed little in nearly two decades. Admission was still 10 cents, and the house band was the same one that had appeared at the pier since the beginning. Needless to say, the throngs that inundated the place in the early years had thinned considerably.

Gravatt immediately went to work to transform the pier for the 1926 season and over the next few seasons spent $1.75 million on improvements. He enlarged the Marine Ballroom and added a 5,000-seat arena at the end of the pier for water shows, expanding the pier to its ultimate length of 2,298 feet. The original dance hall was converted into two theaters—the 2,250-seat Music Hall and the 1,400-seat Ocean Hall. A 1,000-seat Children's Theater was constructed, while the original Casino Theater was expanded. In the Casino Building, a 20,000-square-foot exhibit hall was created that became the longtime home to a showcase of General Motors products.

One of Gravatt's first moves was to replace the house band by contracting with John Philip Sousa to bring his band to the pier every summer. Steel Pier became Sousa's summer home until his death in 1932. Sousa was just the first of dozens of big-name acts that would grace Steel Pier over the next several decades, establishing its reputation as the "Showplace of a Nation."

To help him fill all of the new space he created, Gravatt hired George Hamid to be the promoter. Hamid was one of America's great showmen. He got his start in 1907, when, as an eleven-year-old, he was worked as a tumbler with Buffalo Bill's Wild West Show. By 1913, he started booking circus and vaudeville acts. He acquired White City Amusement Park in Worcester, Massachusetts, purchased the New Jersey State Fair, started a circus, and eventually operated a chain of movie theaters. He came to Atlantic City in 1924 to operate Rendezvous Park, a short-lived amusement facility, where he caught Gravatt's attention.

Working together, the two men elevated Steel Pier to one of America's great attractions. Continuing the policy of one price for all attractions, Gravatt operated on a value premise. He kept prices low, filled the pier with attractions, and counted on a high volume of crowds. Although the first season was so plagued by poor weather that Sousa called himself the Rain God, by the end of the 1927 season, Steel Pier was solidly profitable.

Always on the lookout for unique attractions, the new owners added one of Steel Pier's most famous attractions in 1928, the Diving Horse. Part of the Water Circus, the Diving Horse act consisted of a rider guiding a horse to the top of a 45-foot platform, from which the horse and rider plunged into an 11-foot-deep tank.

The act actually dated back to 1874, when Dr. W. F. Carver was returning to his home in Nebraska on a stormy night. A bridge he was crossing collapsed plunging horse and rider 40 feet into the Platte River. While they both swam to safety, Carver wondered if he could train a horse to do that voluntarily. In 1878, he had perfected the act and started touring. By the time it came to Atlantic City, his daughter Lorena had taken over.

In 1929, another unique attraction debuted when the Steel Pier Grand Opera Company of Atlantic City was formed. Into the 1940s, the company performed operas in English, introducing thousands of people to opera who might not otherwise have had the chance.

The pier achieved national prominence in 1930, when Alvin "Shipwreck" Kelly set a world flagpole-sitting record, by occupying a flagpole on top of the Casino building for forty-nine days and one hour.

As the pier entered the 1930s, the combination of abundant activities and a single admission price, by now 50 cents, allowed the pier to thrive in troubled times. With dozens of activities, the pier was promoted as "a vacation unto itself." These included movies, dance orchestras, opera, a Hawaiian village, a Hollywood exhibit featuring movie props, ballet, diving horses, the water circus, a human cannonball, vaudeville acts, circus acts, a wild animal nursery, and corporate exhibits. Sometimes attractions tended to be a bit bizarre. In 1931, Tinytown, a village populated by little people, began a two-year run. There were also boxing cats and a 65-foot-long embalmed whale carcass.

Despite the depressed economy, Steel Pier added attractions throughout the 1930s. In 1932, Gravatt purchased John Rockefeller's 240-foot-long yacht, renamed it SS *Steel Pier,* and pressed it into service for sightseeing cruises. However, in September 1932, when the ship was headed to New York, it hit a storm and had to travel around the state to Camden to escape rough waters. The boat was sold soon afterward.

In the mid-1930s, the basement of the Casino building was converted into a complex of six fun houses with names such as the Haunted Castle, Laughland, Davy Jones Locker, and the Blue Grotto.

The Haunted Castle was one of six fun houses that operated on Steel Pier's lower level from the 1930s to the 1960s.

In 1935, Gravatt played a key role in reviving what has become one of the city's most high profile traditions—the Miss America Pageant. The pageant had been canceled in 1927, and after being revived in the early 1930s, it was held in other cities. Gravatt brought the pageant back to Atlantic City and held it at Steel Pier until 1939, when it moved to Boardwalk Hall, where it remains to this day.

Gravatt, who was now known as the "Salt Water Barnum," and Hamid had succeeded in building Steel Pier into one of the most prestigious entertainment venues in the country. An act was not considered to have made it until it appeared at the pier. Throughout the 1930s and 1940s, the country's biggest names in show business made appearances, including Frank Sinatra, Tommy Dorsey, Glenn Miller, Count Basie, Duke Ellington, Benny Goodman, Rudy Vallee, Gene Krupa, Bob Hope, Red Skelton, Abbott and Costello, and the Three Stooges. A 1934 appearance by Amos 'n' Andy set a new attendance record of thirty-nine thousand.

Many weekends, the pier was so busy that it would remain open from 8 A.M. Saturday to 2 A.M. Tuesday. It was not unusual to find people asleep for the night on the pier's sun deck. In fact, an article in *Colliers* magazine in the late 1930s detailed the abundance of activities at the pier and told the story of one customer who had to be taken to the hospital after collapsing from hunger after spending seventeen hours on the pier without eating. Among the activities he engaged in were two movies, an opera, a vaudeville show, a water circus including high-diving Hawaiians and horses, two Hawaiian and Filipino orchestras, the Girl in the Fish Bowl illusion, and the Laughland and Haunted Castle fun houses.

Changing Hands

By the late 1930s, the weak economy was catching up with Steel Pier. In 1939, the pier narrowly avoided being sold at public auction after mortgage holders launched foreclosure proceedings. While Gravatt continued to own the pier, Hamid left in 1940 to focus his efforts on the nearby Million Dollar Pier, which he had purchased in 1938. Operations were further hampered by World War II. In March 1942, the government imposed brownout conditions on the city, meaning that the pier had to extinguish its massive billboards. The exhibit hall was converted into a recruiting station, and manpower shortages made staffing the shows difficult. In fact, the Diving Horse show was canceled in 1944.

By now Gravatt was looking to sell, and Hamid stepped in. On May 7, 1945, Hamid completed a deal to acquire Steel Pier for $2.5 million. Hamid's showmanship combined with the booming postwar economy to quickly turn Steel Pier around.

Installed in 1947, the Diving Bell was one of Steel Pier's most fondly remembered attractions.

Another Steel Pier landmark made its debut in 1947 with the opening of the Diving Bell. Located near the ballroom over the ocean, the Diving Bell took fifteen riders on a journey below the surface of the ocean. For the next four decades, the Diving Bell was a Steel Pier icon, even though most riders recall seeing only muddy water from the Bell's windows.

Over the next two decades, Steel Pier thrived under the direction of Hamid and his son, George Jr. In 1948, the pier became one of the first places people could see television when one was installed in the Ocean Theater. The Tony Grant Stars of Tomorrow Show, featuring child performers, debuted in 1949. A Ripley's Believe It or Not attraction began a fifteen-year run in 1951, while the Diving Horse act was revived in 1954. One of the displays featured at the pier that year was a particularly poignant reminder of the larger concerns of the era—the Atomic Exhibit, which detailed the effects of an atomic blast.

In March 1962, a storm tore through the region and the swelling seas pushed a barge into the pier, destroying a 450-foot section and separating the Marine Ballroom at the far end from the rest of Steel Pier. Damage was estimated at $1.5 million, and with the summer season rapidly approaching, crews had to work around the clock to repair the pier. Amazingly, the rebuilding job was completed in 108 days, and Steel Pier was ready for the season as planned.

By the 1960s, most of Steel Pier's competitors in Atlantic City and elsewhere along the Jersey shore started to emphasize amusement rides. Although the Steel Pier added a few in 1963, including Swinging Gym cages and the Rocket, which simulated a trip through outer space, it resisted a wholesale investment in rides, maintaining its focus on live entertainment.

Hamid was not afraid to keep up with the times, booking the hottest rock-and-roll acts of the era, including the Rolling Stones, Beach Boys, Herman's Hermits, Frankie Avalon, Tiny Tim, Gary Lewis, the Banana

Splits, and Ricky Nelson, who set a new attendance record when 44,200 showed up to see him in 1958. As successful as Hamid was, he did occasionally make a mistake. He turned down an appearance by Elvis Presley in 1957, thinking no one would be interested in someone with such an unusual name.

Other changes were also made. In 1967, the pier acquired a 100-foot-tall Ferris wheel that originally operated as part of the U.S. Royal tire exhibit at the 1964 New York World's Fair. While the wheel was enclosed in a giant tire at the fair, it operated unadorned at Steel Pier. In addition, the basement fun houses were closed in the late 1960s, while General Motors moved out of the exhibit hall in 1968. Replacing GM was Animal World, an indoor zoo with seventy-five animals including Goliath, billed as the world's largest horse.

In December 1969, while Steel Pier slept for the winter, the wiring in one of the 70-foot-tall billboards perched on the roof of the Marine Ball-

Aerial view of Steel Pier from the 1960s shows the towering billboards that advertised coming attractions and sponsors. The Rocket Ship, a simulated trip into outer space, can be seen about halfway up the pier.

The Mystery Ride was a popular ride until it was destroyed by fire in 1969.

room shorted out. Soon the ocean end of the pier was in flames. For more than three hours, over two hundred firefighters worked to extinguish the blaze. Although the fire was fanned by 40-mile-per-hour winds, those same winds managed to save the pier, as they kept the flames from spreading to the remainder of the pier. When the fire was finally brought under control, a 56,000-square-foot area at the end of the pier was a total loss. The Marine Ballroom, Aqua Circus arena, one of the movie theaters, and the Mystery Ride, a dark ride that had been at the pier for over a decade, were all gone.

While it was a devastating loss, the Hamids took the fire as an opportunity to completely renovate the pier. The destroyed area was rebuilt, and a new six thousand-seat Aqua Circus arena anchored the end of the pier, one thousand seats bigger than its predecessor. In place of the Marine Ballroom was the Golden Dome ballroom, a 110-foot-diameter geodesic dome with walls that could be opened to the sea air.

The Hamids also purchased the Philadelphia Aquarama, a defunct aquarium, and relocated all of its equipment to Steel Pier. Located in the former Animal World, the new attraction was named Ocean World and included thirty tanks displaying a variety of marine life, along with a six hundred-seat stadium featuring a porpoise and seal show.

George Hamid passed away in 1971, but his son George Jr. pressed on. However, Steel Pier was finding it increasingly difficult to attract crowds in the face of an overall decline in Atlantic City. The advent of interstate highways and air travel in the 1960s made it easier for people to travel to more distant resorts, and many of Atlantic City's grand old resort hotels were closing and being demolished.

While it was increasingly difficult to attract customers in the face of the overall decline in Atlantic City, Hamid stood by the principles that made Steel Pier such a success. The movie theaters showed only G-rated movies, and in a reflection of the times, Hamid publicly stated that he would not book acid rock acts or permit marijuana to be smoked on the premises. But with business continuing to decline, Hamid sold the pier in 1973 to three local businessmen—Maxwell Goldberg, Al Gardner, and Milton Neustadter—while remaining on as manager.

The group was intent on turning around the fortunes of Steel Pier and launched a $2.5 million renovation program for the 1976 season. The combination of the decline in Atlantic City as a destination and additional live entertainment venues springing up throughout the country made it increasingly difficult to fill the theaters with big-name acts. As a result, the Midway and Music Hall theaters were demolished to make room for a major expansion of the amusement rides. The newly created section was dubbed the International Rides area and included several rides imported

from Europe. The main attraction was the City Jet, a 36-foot-high steel-track roller coaster designed by Anton Schwarzkopf that featured a compact, 1,362-foot-long layout. Other new rides included the Lost City dark ride, a two-level Venetian carousel, the Skooter bumper cars, two spinning rides, the Himalaya and Cyclotron, and a number of kiddie rides.

Elsewhere, the huge billboards on the Casino building that announced coming acts were removed as part of a restoration of the building, while

In 1967, Steel Pier added this 100-foot-tall Ferris wheel that originally operated at the 1964 New York World's Fair.

the Casino theater was renovated into the Music Hall, a modern two thousand-seat theater. The aquarium was converted into Ocean Discovery, featuring Flipper's Sea School, a dolphin show, while the world's largest miniature train layout, which was originally part of the Lionel Exhibit at the 1939 New York World's Fair, was also installed. A number of other favorite attractions remained, including the Diving Bell, the Water Circus, the Golden Dome dance hall, and Tony Grant Stars of Tomorrow Show. Everything was still available for a one-price admission, which was increased to $5.

The "New" Steel Pier, as it was called, opened to high expectations on May 29, 1976, with a season full of big-name acts, including Jimmy "J. J." Walker, the Bay City Rollers, Frankie Valli and the Four Seasons, Ella Fitzgerald, Tony Bennett, Jerry Lewis, and Isaac Hayes. But the crowds did not materialize, and in August the pier was hit by Hurricane Belle, resulting in $1 million in damage and the closure of the Diving Bell, Water Circus, and several other attractions.

In November 1976, voters approved a referendum legalizing gambling in the city, setting off a flurry of real estate speculation in the town. Steel Pier was placed on the market. As Lawrence Alper told *Amusement Business,* "Since casino gambling was approved, practically everything in the resort is for sale." Although the City Jet was moved to Massachusetts, not much else changed at the pier in 1977, as the owners waited to cash in.

After two deals to sell the pier were announced and subsequently fell through, the owners started making plans for the 1978 season, feeling it would be their last. The pay-one-price admission, which dated back to the beginning, was done away with in favor of a pay-as-you-go policy. The porpoise show was replaced by an exhibit featuring twenty-four live sharks and an 18-foot replica of a Great White shark, a Flight to Mars dark ride and a water slide were added, and the Golden Dome was converted into a disco. But with the town's attention focused on gambling, Steel Pier just could not attract crowds the way it once did. In fact, attendance at the Water Circus was so light that the performers asked for donations to help feed the diving horses.

In July, Resorts International, which opened Atlantic City's first casino that May, purchased the pier for $5.6 million. They had no interest in operating the pier in its current format, especially given the extensive repairs that were required. During 1979, a few concessions operated in just the front portion of the pier, and by 1980, it was completely closed and used for storage while alternate uses were evaluated. The end seemed to have come in December 1982, when an arson fire destroyed much of the remains.

Rebirth

The burnt remains sat on the beachfront for nearly three years, but in 1985, Resorts International commenced plans to develop a $10 million replacement pier. The initial proposal called for the pier to be an extension of a new hotel that they were developing across the Boardwalk. At 1,000 feet, it would be less than half the length of the original. Built out of reinforced concrete, it was designed to support a twenty-story hotel tower. Among the features the new pier was to include were an aquarium, aviary, 37,000-square-foot ballroom, meeting rooms, swimming pool, boat docks, and heliport.

Upon completion of the pier in 1986, however, construction on the remaining features never came to fruition, and the pier sat vacant. In 1988, Donald Trump purchased the entire unfinished hotel project, including the pier. He then proceeded to complete the hotel, which he named the Taj Mahal.

For the next few years, the new pier saw little use, with the exception of an occasional helicopter landing. But in 1992, the Trump Organization leased the pier to the American Cancer Society, which held a summer-long fund-raising carnival with attractions such as a merry-go-round, elephant rides, bungee jumping, go-carts, and miniature golf. Though the carnival was not successful, the operators of the go-cart track, the Catanoso family, thought that the pier offered potential as a family entertainment alternative to the casinos along the boardwalk.

Natives of Wildwood, New Jersey, brothers Anthony, Charles, William, and Joseph Catanoso were initially insurance brokers catering to the amusement industry. They soon started opening go-cart tracks throughout the state, which is how they became involved with the Steel Pier carnival.

The Catanosos teamed up with Taft Johnson and Edward Olwell and approached the Trump Organization with their proposal. They signed a one-year lease and just twenty-two days later opened sixteen rides on the reconstructed Steel Pier. The Catanosos knew that the pier as it was originally positioned with its abundance of live entertainment could not succeed in the face of competition from the casinos, and thus emphasized rides. Given the short time frame they had to prepare the operation that initial season, smaller rides such as a Scrambler, Tilt-A-Whirl, bumper cars, and kiddie roller coaster were featured.

They did, however, seek to honor the roots of Steel Pier by offering some limited entertainment. One act was a modern diving horse act featuring mules, dogs, and ponies diving into a pool from up to 30 feet in the air. Anthony Catanoso placed a priority in bringing back the act, based on the number of requests he had received from people. "Everyone had a diving horse story," he recalled.

But times had changed, and the revived show was greeted by protests by animal-rights groups. While the protestors succeeded in stopping the show at the end of the 1993 season, the revitalized pier received nation-wide publicity.

Based on the success of the initial season, the Catanosos signed a longer-term lease and made plans to upgrade the ride lineup for 1994. About a dozen new rides were added, including the Sky Flyer, which flipped riders upside down; a 100-foot-tall Ferris wheel; the Disco Star, a high-speed circular-track ride; and two roller coasters. The Little Leaper was a kiddie coaster, and the Wildcat was a steel-track ride standing 50 feet tall and 1,837 feet long. Steel Pier also debuted a new double-decker merry-go-round adorned with scenes portraying the Atlantic City of old.

Given the limited space available, the rides at Steel Pier continuously evolve as new rides replace existing ones. Among the major additions were spinning rides such as a Magic Carpet, in 1997, and a Wipeout and Chair Swing, both in 1998. In 1999, the Wildcat was replaced by the Crazy Mouse, a throwback to the Wild Mouse rides of the 1950s, in which 180-degree turns give the illusion of being about to plunge over the edge. But this 49-foot-high, 1,377-foot-long ride, manufactured by Reverchon of France, also features an unusual twist—the cars spin. Steel Pier's

Steel Pier's helicopter ride provides an excellent overview of the facility's attractions and of Atlantic City.

Crazy Mouse was the first roller coaster in the United States to feature spinning cars.

Steel Pier introduced another U.S. first the following season, with the installation of the Rocket. Using a system of steel cables and springs linked to two 144-foot-tall towers, the Rocket catapults a two-person capsule 220 feet in the air.

The appearance of Steel Pier changed in 2002 when the Giant wheel was removed. Taking its place was a landing pad from which visitors could embark on helicopter tours of Atlantic City. During the four-minute, seven-mile trip, riders reach speeds of up to 110 miles per hour while traveling as high as 500 feet above the ocean.

Also in 2002, after leasing log flumes as concessions for about five years, Steel Pier acquired its own log flume, the Big Splash, a 750-foot-long ride from Reverchon of France that included drops of 30 and 40 feet. After a one-year absence, a Ferris wheel returned to the pier in 2003 in the form of a 66-foot-tall model manufactured by Techno Park of Italy.

Given the popularity of the Crazy Mouse, Steel Pier decided to replace the go-cart track with another steel-track roller coaster in 2004.

Steel Pier Today

Although it offers different features than the Steel Pier of old, today's Steel Pier continues in the spirit of the original, providing family-oriented entertainment along the famed Atlantic City Boardwalk and featuring approximately twenty-seven rides. The entrance to Steel Pier can be found directly across the Boardwalk from the entrance to the Trump Taj Mahal casino.

Entering the pier through a tunnel lined with games, visitors will come across most of the pier's kiddie rides, along with the double-deck merry-go-round. Beyond this are found the Crazy Mouse roller coaster, Ferris wheel, and giant slide. The end of the pier features the Grand Prix go-carts, log flume, and helicopter flight.

Keansburg Amusement Park and Runaway Rapids

OPENED 1904

THIS IS A STORY AS MUCH ABOUT A TOWN AS IT IS ABOUT AN AMUSEMENT park. Along the south shore of Raritan Bay in northern New Jersey sits Keansburg. On clear days, New York City's Verazzano Narrows Bridge can be seen from the beach. Manhattan is a mere 18 miles away over the water.

A Real Estate Investment

In the early twentieth century, the area of Keansburg was nothing more than a nondescript piece of marshland. Its proximity to New York City, however, caught the eye of William Gelhaus a century ago. Born in 1871, Gelhaus was a baker and part-time real estate investor living in the nearby town of Atlantic Highlands. In 1904, he teamed up with five partners to purchase much of the marshy waterfront in Keansburg to create a summer resort. They planned to fill the marshland with sand dredged from the bay, and then sell 25-foot-wide lots for $100 each on which to build summer bungalows. At the time, Keansburg consisted of little more than a couple of waterfront pavilions and a camp operated by a Newark-based German gymnastics club. Among the first orders of business was to develop a boardwalk along the bay to serve as a recreation destination for the expected throngs of vacationers. This was the beginning of Keansburg Amusement Park.

Gelhaus and his associates formed the New Point Comfort Beach Company in 1906 to develop the town. The business was based in an office resembling a log cabin, in which Gelhaus also lived. Initially formed to develop and sell lots, the

Keansburg Amusement Park and Runaway Rapids
P.O. Box 189
Keansburg, NJ 07734
732-495-1400
www.keansburgamusement
park.com

62

New Point Comfort Beach Company soon became a diversified holding company. A water company was established to service the bungalows and businesses; two banks, Keansburg National Bank and Keansburg Building and Loan Company, were chartered to provide loans to home buyers; and to ensure that the home buyers could get to the fledgling resort, the Keansburg Steamboat Company was established.

Founded in 1909, the steamboat company served as an important link to New York City during the early years, shuttling people from Battery Park at the southern tip of Manhattan to a 2,000-foot-long pier constructed along the mile-long Boardwalk. Steamship service started in 1910, offering round-trip service to New York for 50 cents. The company quickly grew from one used boat to half a dozen by the 1920s, linking the town with New York City. Locals called the fleet "Gelhaus's Navy."

As the town grew, Gelhaus sought to concentrate his interests and sold the real estate company, retaining the steamship service and the Boardwalk. With his efforts now focused on the waterfront, the Boardwalk underwent a tremendous period of growth. In 1910, the New Point Comfort Hotel and a dance hall were erected at the entrance to the pier. The park's first mechanical ride, a Ferris wheel, premiered in 1911. During the years he owned Keansburg Amusement Park, Gelhaus saw himself as more of a landlord, renting out space to individual concessionaires rather than owning the concessions himself.

In the early years, Keansburg's beach ran right up to the Boardwalk.

Amusement park improvements came in rapid succession during this decade. A Scenic Railway roller coaster opened in 1912, and in 1914, concessionaire Nick Droge erected a large pavilion to house an elaborate new carousel. The carousel ride dated back to 1884 and initially operated at Midland Beach Park in Staten Island, New York. It was returned to the William F. Mangels factory in Coney Island, New York, in 1913 to be modernized before being transported to Keansburg on a barge. The animals, carved by Charles Looff, included twenty-eight jumping horses, sixteen standing horses, three goats, two dogs, a lion, and a dragon. There were also three chariots and a spinning tub. To provide music, Droge acquired an immense 30-foot-long band organ from the Italian firm of Gavioli, said to be the largest band organ ever imported into the United States.

Other major changes also took place along the Boardwalk in 1914. With the company's growth, Gelhaus's log cabin was replaced by a substantial new stucco building with a drugstore on the first floor and offices upstairs. A restaurant has long since replaced the drugstore, but the building remains the home of the park's offices.

A trolley line was extended into Keansburg, but given the popularity of the steamboats, ridership lagged and service was discontinued in 1921.

As the growth of the amusement area increased, larger structures were built to accommodate the crowds. One of these, the Auditorium,

Keansburg Amusement Park's largest ride was the Jack Rabbit, a large wooden roller coaster that operated from 1919 until the 1930s. JOHN M. CARUTHERS COLLECTION

LOCATION

Keansburg Amusement Park and Runaway Rapids is located in northern New Jersey on the shores of Raritan Bay. Take Exit 117 off the Garden State Parkway, following the signs for NJ Route 36 East. Go straight for 4 miles on Route 36 East. Take the jughandle for Laurel Avenue, then turn left to cross over Route 36, and follow Laurel Avenue for 1 mile into Keansburg. Parking is available for a nominal fee.

OPERATING SCHEDULE

Keansburg Amusement Park and Runaway Rapids opens for the season the last weekend in March. Keansburg Amusement Park operates on a limited basis (not all rides and attractions open) daily from early April through mid-June, opening at noon on weekdays and 11 A.M. on weekends. From mid-June through Labor Day, Keansburg Amusement Park opens at 10 A.M. Closing time varies, depending on the time of year.

Runaway Rapids opens at 10 A.M. starting Memorial Day weekend and daily from mid-June through Labor Day. Closing time varies, depending on the time of year. Runaway Rapids sometimes closes early for private functions, so confirm with the park before visiting.

ADMISSION

Admission to Keansburg Amusement Park is free, with rides available on a pay-as-you-go basis. Ride tickets cost about 75 cents each, and rides require from one to six tickets. On selected days, a pay-one-price admission is available for under $25 that permits access to all rides in the amusement park except for the go-carts, for which there is an additional charge.

Admission to Runaway Rapids is a separate charge of less than $20 and is available as a two- or three-hour pass. A discounted admission is available after 5 P.M. A "dry" admission is available for under $10 for those who do not want to use the water slides.

Combination passes permitting access to both Keansburg Amusement Park and Runaway Rapids are available for around $30.

FOOD

Keansburg Amusement Park and Runaway Rapids features more than twenty food outlets, including two in Runaway Rapids, ranging from sit-down restaurants to portable carts providing a wide variety of dining options. There are no restrictions on bringing food and beverages into the park, but picnic facilities are not available.

FOR CHILDREN

Keansburg Amusement Park has long featured one of the country's largest collections of kiddie rides. Currently nearly two dozen are located in two kiddie

(continued on page 66)

VISITING (continued from page 65)

areas at either end of the park. Included are a large number of carefully restored vintage kiddie rides, along with newer ones such as the Sea Serpent roller coaster, Frog Hopper, Safari Jeeps, and flume.

SPECIAL FEATURES

Keansburg Amusement Park's Spook House is one of the oldest operating dark rides in the world. While simple by today's standards, it is true trip back in time and should not be missed.

Few amusement parks have a better collection of vintage kiddie rides than Keansburg. Among the classics are the whip, Jolly Caterpillar, cars, airplanes, merry-go-round, and miniature train.

TIME REQUIRED

A visit to Keansburg Amusement Park and Runaway Rapids can easily occupy an entire day. If time is limited, the major rides and attractions can be enjoyed in about four hours.

TOURING TIPS

Try to visit on one of the park's pay-one-price days. One price permits access to all rides in the amusement park with the exception of the go-carts.

Plan to be at the park at dusk, as the sunset over Raritan Bay is truly stunning.

was built on the site of the original dance hall in 1915. This large structure was located in the heart of the amusement area and was initially used for live shows. It became one of Keansburg's landmarks, and in later years it was used as a skating rink, bowling alley, and arcade before burning down in the 1980s.

The Jack Rabbit, the largest ride ever to operate at Keansburg, opened in 1919. This large wooden roller coaster was designed by John Miller, the most prolific roller coaster builder of the early twentieth century. It was relocated to Keansburg from the nearby town of Long Branch and replaced the Scenic Railway. The ride was so large that its structure crossed over the Beachway, the street running in front of the amusement area. A hole in the structure permitted cars to pass through.

The Roaring Twenties

Keansburg Amusement Park continued to add new features throughout the 1920s. A miniature train ride was built on the steamboat pier to facilitate access between the boats and the amusement area, and attractions such as a whip, airplane swing, and fun house appeared along the Boardwalk. An all-new steamboat, the 250-foot long *City of Keansburg,* was launched in 1926, replacing the original boat that had been destroyed by fire, and a new dance hall was constructed on the former site of the New Point Comfort Hotel, which also was destroyed by fire in 1917. The dance hall was a large steel building that was moved to Keansburg from the 1926 Sesquicentennial Exposition in Philadelphia.

As the country was plunged into the Depression in the 1930s, Keansburg managed to continue growing. In 1930, a 100-by-150-foot, 600,000-gallon swimming pool opened after two years of construction. Toward the end of that year, the massive Gavioli band organ in the carousel building was sent to the Wurlitzer factory near Buffalo, New York, for maintenance work. For reasons that remain unclear, the organ never returned to Keansburg, and Gelhaus leased the empty space to another concessionaire.

That concessionaire walled off the portion of the pavilion that the organ formerly occupied and hired Leon Cassidy, who had founded the Pretzel Amusement Company just a few years earlier, to build a dark ride. Cassidy provided track, cars, and scenery, and in 1931, the Mystery Ride opened. Now known as the Spook House, the ride remains in operation as one of the world's oldest operating dark rides.

The park struggled to survive during the 1930s, but it occasionally managed to add a few kiddie rides, launching its long tradition as having one of the largest kiddie ride collections around. But the troubled economy did catch up with the park. The drop-off in traffic forced the steam-

Opened in 1931, the Spook House is one of the oldest dark rides still in operation.

boat company to scrap two of its ships in 1939, and the Jack Rabbit was demolished. Declining business meant that the roller coaster's owners could no longer afford to properly maintain the ride to the point where occasionally the train would fail to completely negotiate the circuit.

While there were setbacks, Keansburg had become an established summer resort. Stars such as Ruby Keeler and Oscar Hammerstein maintained residences there, and a young crooner from nearby Hoboken named Frank Sinatra performed in the nightclubs along the Boardwalk.

The amusement park was hit with another blow in 1944, when a hurricane devastated the Boardwalk area. Since many of the concession buildings were built on pilings above the water, they were demolished by the surging sea. The Boardwalk was torn up, a number of rides including the Airplane Swing were destroyed, and two of the steamships were severely damaged when the high winds blew one on top of another.

Material shortages were commonplace as a result of World War II, and it became a daunting challenge to get the park back into operation. Ride parts were even fished out of the mud. With lumber in short supply, the Boardwalk could not be reconstructed, and it was replaced by a paved walkway that remains the heart of the park.

Starting in the late 1930s, Keansburg Amusement Park was known for its collection of kiddie rides. Most of the rides shown in this 1947 view are still in operation.

In 1950, William Gelhaus passed away and his son Henry took over the family's operations. It was a decade of challenges for the resort. In 1953, a second hurricane damaged the amusement area, while another one in 1960 destroyed the steamboat pier, severing the water link with New York City. The pier was not rebuilt, signaling the end of steamship service in Keansburg.

There were also positive changes at Keansburg. A number of new rides were added during this period, including a Wild Mouse roller coaster and spinning rides such as the Bubble Bounce, Caterpillar, Loop-O-Plane, Rock-O-Plane, Roll-O-Plane, and Trabant.

In 1969, the Army Corps of Engineers undertook an $8 million project intended to protect the town from further hurricane damage. Sand was pumped in from the bay to widen the beach and create a series of dunes along the waterfront. The amusement park no longer was in danger from surging seas, and a portion of the newly created land became a parking lot between the amusement area and the beach.

Hard Times

The beach expansion was a positive development, but the amusement park was struggling as a result of larger problems plaguing the town as a whole. Throughout the 1950s and 1960s, expressways started criss-crossing New Jersey, making it easier for people to travel to more distant resorts. As a result, the summer bungalows started to be converted to year-round rentals owned by absentee landlords, attracting a low-income population. Former summer boarding homes became halfway houses, downtown businesses starting closing, crime increased, and Raritan Bay became polluted. Naturally Keansburg Amusement Park suffered as fewer vacationers were coming into town.

In 1972, Henry Gelhaus was experiencing health problems. With his children too young to take over the amusement park, he sold it to Grandal Enterprises, a company owned by Al Reid and Tony Cantalupo. In the first years of ownership, Grandal added only a minimal number of rides as they worked to maintain what they had.

By the 1980s, however, Reid and Cantalupo were able to start upgrading the park, adding Paratrooper and Round Up spinning rides and a twin trough water slide to the pool in 1982. They reached a deal to purchase several rides from the 1982 World's Fair in Knoxville, Tennessee, including a Jet 400 roller coaster, log flume, and pirate ship. But the bank that held the loan on the rides folded, and the rides fell into hands of the federal government, which sold them to other parties.

Also during the 1980s, several longtime landmarks such as the former auditorium and dance hall fell victim to a series of fires. In 1984, several priceless figures from the antique carousel were sold to collectors. Much of the money from the carousel sale was put into park improvements. The Wildcat, a new 50-foot-high, 1,837-foot-long steel-track roller coaster was added in 1985, and that same year the owners applied to rebuild the steamship pier that was lost in 1960.

They succeeded in obtaining the needed approvals, although construction was delayed by the U.S. Army Corps of Engineers to relocate an osprey nest that was built on one of the pilings from the original pier. To get the endangered birds to relocate, the Corps built three new nests nearby and succeeded in luring them to one of them. This permitted construction to finally proceed. The 2,178-foot-long pier was complete in 1986.

It was hard to counteract the problems of the town. During the late 1980s, several struggling New Jersey shore towns thought their salvation lay in massive urban renewal projects that would transform their waterfronts into upscale condominium developments. Keansburg was no different.

In 1989, a developer announced plans to transform 80 acres of Keansburg beachfront, including the site of Keansburg Amusement Park, into a $300 million mixed-use development that would feature an artists' colony, entertainment complex, and marina, along with residential, office, and retail space. Grandal reached an agreement to sell the park for $20 million.

The media began covering the pending demise of the amusement park, and local officials seemed resigned to the closure. At the time, Keansburg mayor Honoria Conley told *Amusement Business,* "It's not that the park was ever something bad, but it's time for something different. Times have changed in New Jersey." Just when it seemed that the era of Keansburg Amusement Park had come to a close, the bottom dropped out of the real estate market, the bank financing the development failed, and the deal died.

Keansburg Amusement Park had been saved, but it was not yet a happy ending. The owners seemed to lose interest in the operation and stopped making improvements. In addition, the last remnants of the antique carousel were sold off in 1991, leaving the pavilion empty. The park was dying a slow death.

Back in the Family

The decline of Keansburg Amusement Park was difficult for the Gelhaus family to accept. Henry Gelhaus still maintained an office on the park grounds to manage his remaining businesses, and his son Hank had owned and operated several kiddie rides as a concessionaire at the park for twenty years. Although Henry was reluctant to dive back into the business, Hank approached his brother William, a lawyer, about teaming up to purchase the amusement park and returning ownership to the Gelhaus family. William was enthusiastic about the idea, and soon a deal was reached to acquire the Keansburg Amusement Park from Grandal.

After several years of decline, the amusement park needed a great deal of work. Although they did not have much time to prepare for the 1995 season, they spent $300,000 renovating existing rides and buildings and added two new kiddie rides—a train and Safari Jeeps. In addition, they launched an aggressive leasing program to fill the vacancies that had developed along the midway concession stands.

The first season showed promising results. Business rebounded and vacancies along the midway were replaced by a waiting list of potential tenants. This was the beginning of a comeback not only for the amusement park, but also for the entire town of Keansburg. The same bungalows that gave birth to the community as a summer resort were now finding favor with commuters from New York, who renovated them for year-round housing.

By the end of the 1995 season, the Gelhauses were encouraged by the progress they had made, but they knew they had to send a signal to the community to demonstrate that the amusement park was here to stay. In their initial five-year plan, they had intended to develop a water park

The opening of Runaway Rapids water park in 1996 signaled the rebirth of Keansburg Amusement Park.

on the 2-acre site of the old swimming pool, which had been abandoned for several years. They reached the decision to build the water park in September. Though it would typically take at least two years to plan and develop such a facility, the Gelhauses were set on having the water park open for the 1996 season. They had no plans, permits, or a contractor, but they dove right in. The town rallied behind the proposal, and nine months later, Runaway Rapids water park was ready for business.

The $3.5 million water park featured a wide array of activities to appeal to the entire family, including seven water slides, an 800-foot-long endless river ride, a 10,000-square-foot kiddie play area, and what was billed as the state's biggest hot tub. Runaway Rapids received most of the attention in 1996, yet the amusement park was not forgotten and also received $1.5 million in improvements. These included six new rides: the Pharaoh's Fury swinging ship, the Gravitron spinning ride, a large go-cart track, and three kiddie rides. In addition, the park reintroduced one of its classic kiddie rides. While cleaning up the grounds, William Gelhaus found an old Jolly Caterpillar ride sitting abandoned in the park's junkyard. Remembering the happy memories that the ride had created when it operated in the 1960s, Gelhaus had the ride restored

For a century, this midway has been the heart and soul of Keansburg Amusement Park.

and placed back into operation. In many ways, it has come to symbolize the rebirth of the park. In fact, in the first year of ownership under the Gelhaus brothers, the park had made such progress that they were awarded the Governor's Award for Economic Development by the state of New Jersey.

With Runaway Rapids attracting new visitors to the park, much of the emphasis was placed on improving the worn-out ride lineup. In 1998, the park saw the addition of a new merry-go-round from Chance Rides, and one of the kiddielands was completely renovated. Several new rides were added, including a Frog Hopper tower ride, the Flying Dragon, the Red Baron airplanes, the Sea Serpent, a 400-foot-long kiddie coaster from Miler Manufacturing, and a kiddie flume ride. In addition, many of the vintage kiddie rides, some of which had been at the park since the 1930s, were restored to like-new condition. For instance, the kiddie airplane ride, which had opened in 1937, had sixty years of paint stripped off it and new chrome propellers added.

The 1999 season saw the addition of two new spinning rides, the Chaos and the Tornado. The Double Shot, an air-powered ride that shoots riders up and down a 100-foot-tall tower, made its debut in 2000. Most recently, the water park underwent a major expansion with the addition of the Power Tower, a complex of four different water slides.

By this time, the Gelhauses had replaced twenty of the thirty-five rides they acquired when they purchased the park and renovated the remaining fifteen. Once again in control of the founding Gelhaus family, Keansburg Amusement Park and Runaway Rapids has been reborn.

Keansburg Amusement Park and Runaway Rapids Today

Keansburg Amusement Park and Runaway Rapids combines new and old with its water park and one of the most traditional amusement parks around. Although it occupies just 6½ acres, the park features nearly forty rides and a full-scale water park.

The Beachway is the main street along the waterfront and it bisects the facility. The amusement park and parking lot occupy the north side of the Beachway and lie between the road and the waterfront. Many of the park's larger concessions have entrances from the street.

The amusement park is essentially one long midway lined on both sides by rides and concessions. Entering the amusement park from the east end parking lot (farthest from Runaway Rapids), visitors come upon the first kiddieland. In this area are fifteen kiddie rides, including the Sea Serpent kiddie coaster, kiddie flume, Frog Hopper, Safari Jeeps, and most of the vintage kiddie rides. Farther along the midway are the Wildcat roller coaster, Double Shot, Spook House, bumper cars, and many of the food and game concessions.

Next comes the ride area at the park's western end. Many of the spinning rides, such as Chaos, Tornado, Paratrooper, and Cruisin' (a high-speed tracked circular ride), along with the go-cart track and the remaining kiddie rides, are located here. Access to the pier can also be found at this end of the park.

Across the Beachway from the western end of the amusement park is Runaway Rapids. Immediately inside the entrance is the kiddie play area, with the endless river and many of the slides located to the left. Lockers and changing rooms can be found in the back of the water park.

Clementon Amusement Park and Splash World

OPENED 1907

IN THE LATE 1800S AND EARLY 1900S, THE AMUSEMENT INDUSTRY IN THE United States was undergoing its greatest era of growth. Throughout the country, dozens of amusement parks were opening, many of which were built to serve trolley lines seeking ways to generate ridership on evenings and weekends. There were hundreds of these trolley parks at that time, yet only a dozen are still in existence, including one in New Jersey—Clementon Amusement Park. Even though this park is nearly one-hundred years old, much of it is brand new, thanks to the efforts of its current owners, who saved the park from an almost certain demise.

A Popular Picnic Spot

Clementon Amusement Park is one of the few amusement parks in New Jersey that is not located near the Atlantic Ocean. Rather, it sits in the suburbs of Philadelphia. The 40-acre site includes a 15-acre lake that has shaped much of its history. In 1735, Andrew Newman acquired the parcel to open a gristmill to serve the needs of the growing neighborhood. He dammed a creek that ran through the property to provide power to the mill wheel, thus creating the lake.

The mill operated for more than a century, and in 1872, Theodore Gibbs, a Civil War veteran, purchased the property. Gibbs continued to operate the mill through the late 1800s, when he realized that the lake had become increasingly popular as a site for local picnickers. Gibbs purchased several rowboats to rent to the growing crowds.

Clementon Amusement Park and Splash World
P.O. Box 125
Clementon, NJ 08021
856-783-0263
www.clementonpark.com

In 1907, the nature of his property was changed forever when the local trolley line was extended about 6 miles from Haddon Heights to the sleepy town of Clementon and to Gibbs's property. This gave residents of Philadelphia and Camden direct access to the popular picnic ground. Gibbs seized the opportunity this presented and focused on recreation and entertainment. This marked the official birth of Clementon Amusement Park.

The original Clementon Amusement Park was much like other picnic-oriented trolley parks of the time. It emphasized activities such as dancing, swimming, picnicking, athletic contests, and boating. Attractions included one of the area's first movie theaters, which was housed in a tent, and a penny arcade. There were also two rides: a carousel powered by a steam engine and a contraption known as the aerial wave.

The aerial wave was quite common in amusement parks during the early part of the twentieth century and consisted of a large wooden ring suspended from a pole. Three men pulled on ropes attached to the ring, on which a couple dozen people sat, making it swing back and forth. Although uncomplicated, this device remained a popular attraction at Clementon into the 1920s.

The simple, bucolic atmosphere of Clementon Amusement Park encouraged its growth as a popular destination for people seeking to escape the hot, dirty, crowded conditions of Camden and Philadelphia. Unfortunately,

CLEMENTON LAKE, Clementon, N. J.

In its early years, rowboats were one of Clementon's most popular attractions.

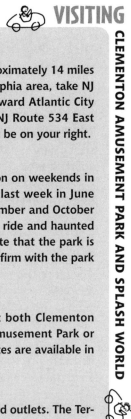

VISITING

CLEMENTON AMUSEMENT PARK AND SPLASH WORLD

LOCATION

Clementon Amusement Park and Splash World is located approximately 14 miles southeast of Philadelphia on NJ Route 534. From the Philadelphia area, take NJ Route 42 South (the North–South Freeway). Follow signs toward Atlantic City and the Blackwood–Clementon exit (NJ Route 534). Follow NJ Route 534 East (Blackwood–Clementon Road) for about 4 miles. The park will be on your right.

OPERATING SCHEDULE

Clementon Amusement Park and Splash World is open at noon on weekends in May, Thursday through Sunday in June, and daily from the last week in June through Labor Day. The park is also open weekends in September and October for their Hallowscreams event complete with a haunted train ride and haunted house. Closing time varies depending on the time of year. Note that the park is closed to the public on selected days for private events, so confirm with the park before visiting.

ADMISSION

Admission of under $30 covers all rides and attractions at both Clementon Amusement Park and SplashWorld. Passes for Clementon Amusement Park or Splash World only are available for slightly less. Discounted rates are available in the evening. Parking is free.

FOOD

Clementon Amusement Park and Splash World features six food outlets. The Terrace Restaurant, located near the waterfront, serves a wide variety of items, including hot dogs, hamburgers, sandwiches, french fries, chicken wings, and salads. Pirates Cove, in Splash World, serves hot dogs, meatball sandwiches, pizza, pretzels, nachos and other snack items. Other food outlets include pizza, ice cream, and candy stands. Food, picnic lunches, coolers, and beverages may be brought into the park's General Public Picnic Area near the Neptune's Revenge flume on a first-come, first-served basis. No food or beverages may be brought into Splash World.

FOR CHILDREN

Clementon Amusement Park and Splash World features a wide variety of attractions for the family. The kiddieland is located in a covered pavilion and features six kiddie rides and a large play area. Other family favorites throughout the park include the merry-go-round, train, Samba Tower, and Showboat.

SPECIAL FEATURES

The Neptune's Revenge log flume is built completely over Clementon Lake. It is likely the only ride of its type in the world.

(continued on page 78)

CLEMENTON AMUSEMENT PARK

VISITING (continued from page 77)

TIME REQUIRED

A visit to Clementon Lake and Splash World can easily occupy an entire day. However, if time is limited, you can enjoy the major rides and attractions in about four hours.

TOURING TIPS

Start your visit with a ride on the Giant Wheel. Located near the entrance, this 100-foot-tall ride provides an excellent overview of the entire park.

The Showboat ride in Clementon Lake is another great way to see the park from a completely different perspective.

Theodore Gibbs did not live beyond the early years to see the success of the park, as he passed away in 1909. But sons Willard and Edgar stepped right in, and Clementon Amusement Park continued to thrive.

Keeping Up

In 1915, the two brothers teamed up with several local businessmen to form the Clementon Park Association. Amusement parks were becoming larger and increasingly sophisticated, and the owners knew that it was crucial for Clementon to keep pace with the competition. They immedi-

The Jack Rabbit entertained riders from 1919 to 2003.

A Philadelphia Toboggan Company carousel was one of the anchors of Clementon Amusement Park's 1919 expansion.

ately kicked off a multiyear expansion program. The first order of business was to take advantage of its greatest asset—the lake—by improving the bathing beach and adding a 10-foot-tall diving tower.

In 1919, the look of the park was totally transformed with the addition of several major attractions, many of which were provided by the nearby Philadelphia Toboggan Company (PTC), the dominant manufacturer of the era. The largest ride was the Jack Rabbit, a wooden roller coaster. While small by today's standards, the $80,000 ride was considered a thriller in 1919, standing 50 feet tall with 1,380 feet of track. It remained in operation until 2003.

PTC also provided a new carousel to replace the original steam-driven model. Representing the latest technology of the era, the ride featured forty-eight hand-carved horses, twenty-eight of which moved up and down, arranged into three rows. It was placed in an elaborate new building along the lakeshore.

Also provided by PTC was the Mill Chute, a forerunner of today's log flume rides. Visitors rode in boats that traveled down a long, wooden, water-filled trough and through a tunnel. At the end of the ride was an incline the boats traveled up before plunging into a pool.

The last major new attraction in 1919 was the Noah's Ark, a fun house that resembled the biblical boat sitting on top of Mount Ararat. Visitors made their way through the dark passages of the mountain, where they encountered a variety of stunts, such as shaking floors and wobbly stairs. The passages then led into the boat, which rocked back and forth. Noah's Ark was just one of two fun houses added to the park during this period. The other, known as the Boo Fun House, featured attractions such as rotating barrels and spinning floors.

The improvements of 1919 made Clementon Amusement Park one of the leading attractions in southern New Jersey, and in 1920 several more rides were installed, including a large Ferris wheel, a whip, and a boat ride in the lake. In addition, twenty new rowboats were purchased, expanding the fleet to 125.

Expansion slowed somewhat during the 1920s. The most notable new attraction was a dark ride from Pretzel Amusements, a fledgling New Jersey ride manufacturer. Clementon's popularity remained strong, because unlike many amusement parks, it was easily accessible for the emerging automobile culture.

The 1930s were a struggle for Clementon. The depressed economy meant that improvements were kept to a minimum. A further blow came in 1935, when bus service replaced the trolley line, and trolley service to the park was stopped. However, the buses only lasted until 1939 due to the popularity of the automobile. But Clementon did what it could to survive. Dance marathons became a popular attraction in the ballroom and kept people coming into the park.

The economy slowly started to improve, and in 1940, the park added a Roll-O-Plane ride. The good times were short-lived, however. Follow-

The 1920s were a prosperous time for Clementon Amusement Park. CLEMENTON AMUSEMENT PARK

Clementon Amusement Park's midway in the 1950s. LAKE COUNTY MUSEUM, CURT TEICH
COLLECTION

ing the 1941 season, the United States entered World War II. Materials
were in short supply, and the park had to maintain its rides and attractions as best it could. Unfortunately, the deteriorating Noah's Ark was
demolished during this period.

America entered a new era of prosperity following World War II, and
Clementon Amusement Park added a number of long-overdue new rides,
including the Crazy Dazy, Flying Scooter, Loop-O-Plane, Train, Twister,
Mirror Maze, and a number of kiddie rides. Also added was the Mystery
House, which gave riders the illusion that they were being flipped upside
down. Between the late 1940s and the mid-1960s, the number of rides
at the park nearly doubled, from twelve to twenty-three. Also new at
this time was Theodore Gibbs's granddaughter, Mildred Eldred, who had
taken over operation of the park.

As the ride lineup grew throughout the 1950s and 1960s, the ballroom also enjoyed renewed popularity as a location for dances hosted by
Philadelphia disk jockey Dick Clark.

But the good times at Clementon were coming to an end. The park's
rides and buildings were aging, and customers were being drawn to the
larger theme parks starting to emerge in the region. It became harder to
maintain the park, and longtime features started to be closed. The 1972
season marked the last time rowboats plied the lake, and swimming was
stopped in 1974.

There was the occasional improvement to the park, such as the opening of the Wacky Shack, a fun house attraction, in 1974. But overall, the park had fallen into such disrepair that customers were staying away. The future looked bleak.

An Experienced Veteran to the Rescue

A new era dawned for Clementon Amusement Park in March 1977, when Abe Baker purchased the dying facility from the Gibbs family. Baker was an industry veteran who had gotten his start in the entertainment business operating a nightclub in Miami during World War II. He soon moved into operating games, and within a few years, he had operations along the New Jersey shore and in Los Angeles. In 1955, Baker purchased Glen Echo Park, a popular amusement park in Glen Echo, Maryland, a suburb of Washington, D.C. He operated the park successfully for several years, but when it closed in 1968, he arranged a land swap with the National Park Service, which converted it into an arts center. Today many of Glen Echo's buildings remain for arts purposes, while its original antique carousel continues as the park's centerpiece.

Baker missed the amusement industry after leaving Glen Echo. Not only did he wish to return, but he also wanted to find a business that he could operate with his three sons, Larry, Jimmy, and Murray. Clementon had a very appealing location in the densely populated Philadelphia suburbs, and Abe Baker knew that with the right amount of tender loving care, it could once again be a successful business. He purchased the park for less than $1 million, sight unseen.

Clementon Amusement Park needed lots of help, and the Bakers had just a few months to prepare for the 1977 season. They immediately undertook a $300,000 improvement program. Many of the needed renovations were invisible to the regular customer, including new foundations for many of the buildings, new electrical wiring and plumbing, renovated restrooms, and new food-service equipment. The Bakers also added a Shooting Gallery, several kiddie rides, and the Indy 500, an electric go-cart ride. Through the late 1970s, many of the old, worn-out rides were replaced by new ones, including the Astroliner, which simulated a trip to the moon, and spinning rides such as the Scrambler, the Spider, and Surf's Up.

Splash Down

By the early 1980s, Clementon was well on its way back from an almost certain demise. While Abe's sons Jimmy and Murray had moved on to other pursuits, Larry gradually took over the operations. He seemed particularly suited to the job, having been introduced to the amusement industry at the age of seven cooking hamburgers at Glen Echo.

With the existing buildings renovated and the ride lineup updated, the Bakers' attention now turned to expansion. They knew that a high-profile attraction was needed to send a message that Clementon Amusement Park had come back and was again a thriving, growing facility.

Fate was on their side. The developers of Little England, a major theme park under construction near Orlando, Florida, had run out of funds. The project was halted, and Intamin, their primary supplier of rides, was stuck with several million dollars' worth of equipment ordered by Little England that they were looking to unload at a substantial discount. Among the rides was a 1,646-foot-long log flume. One of the most popular rides at any amusement park, the log flume was just the ride needed to take Clementon to the next level, and the Bakers quickly reached a deal to purchase it.

The next challenge was finding a place to locate such a large ride. About the only large expanse of property in the park that was not occupied was the lake. It had seen little use since the bathing beach was closed, and Larry initially thought that they would fill in a portion of the lake and build the ride there. But it soon occurred to him that the ride experience would be greatly enhanced if the ride could be built over the lake. The ride took eight months to build. When it was completed, Neptune's Revenge was the only log flume built completely over water. The Bakers spent more on Neptune's Revenge, which opened in 1983, than they had paid for the entire park in 1977, with a final cost of $2 million.

Over the next few years, the ride lineup continued to improve. Older rides were removed, such as the Indy 500 in 1983, the Haunted House dark ride and Wacky Shack fun house in 1985, and the Flying Skooter in 1987. Several modern rides were added, including the Gravitron, a gravity-defying spinning ride (1986); the Thunderbolt, a high-speed Himalaya-type ride (1987); and the Sea Dragon swinging ship and Falling Star (1988).

The 1988 season also marked the start of a five-year process to supplement the amusement park with a full-scale water park. Since 1980, Clementon had successfully operated a water slide as a separate attraction in the parking lot. But with the growth of the park, something much larger was needed.

The new water park represented a new era of growth for Clementon Amusement Park, but it came at a price. In order to help raise the funds for the water park, Baker sold twenty-three of the carousel's original hand-carved horses in 1990 and replaced them with fiberglass replicas.

By the end of the 1992 season, Clementon was ready to begin construction on the water park. Several existing rides and features had to be relocated to make room for the $4.5 million project. The kiddieland was moved to a new location behind the gift shop and placed inside a covered pavilion, and several older structures were removed, including two picnic pavilions and a number of food and game stands. In addition, the original water slide was sold. This created a 4-acre site that became home to Splash World. Among the attractions were Sky River Rapids, a series of elevated pools connected by 12-foot-wide water slides; Black Viper, a 700-foot-long enclosed tube slide; a 1,200-foot-long endless river; a 5,000-square-foot wading pool; and a 10,000-square-foot water play area for kids.

Splash World was well received, and crowds came to the park in record numbers. Over the next several years, Clementon emphasized expanding and improving the ride lineup to handle the larger crowds. In 1995, a new landmark called to passersby in the form of the 100-foot-tall Giant Ferris wheel. The next season, the Flying Pharaoh, a large swing ride, replaced the Scrambler. The remaining portions of the old carousel were sold, and a new merry-go-round took its place. Four water slides were also added to the kids' area of Splash World.

Also in 1996, the elaborate carousel building became home to the Big Cat Encounter, an educational exhibit featuring several African lions, Royal Bengal tigers, and rare white Bengal tigers. A number of the animals were used in a show starring fifth-generation animal trainer Kay Rosaire.

Improvements continued at the park. In 1998, Surf's Up gave way to Chaos, a new-generation spinning ride. The Jack Rabbit received a major facelift for its eightieth birthday in 1999 that included a new train

Splash World water park opened in 1993.

View of Clementon Amusement Park from the Giant Wheel.

and braking system. The 1999 season also marked the final year for two of the park's most enduring attractions, the whip and bumper cars, along with the Astroliner. In their place came a ride package valued at $1.2 million. This included the Inverter, which leaves riders hanging upside down 50 feet in the air, along with two family spinning rides, the Kite Flyer, which opened in 2000, and the 41-foot-tall Samba Tower, 2001. Splash World celebrated its tenth anniversary in 2003 with the addition of Vertical Limit, a six-lane slide where riders race each other traveling headfirst. Also, Sky River Rapids underwent a major overhaul with the addition of a launch system.

The transformation is not yet complete. One attraction Clementon lacks is a signature roller coaster, and the park plans to fix that in 2004 with the addition of a 100-foot-tall, 3,000-foot-long wooden roller coaster, the Tsunami. Built by S&S Power of Utah, the ride will completely encircle the picnic groves and travel over the lake with hills of seventy, eighty, and one hundred ten feet.

Clementon Amusement Park and Splash World Today

Nearly a century old, Clementon Amusement Park and Splash World remains a thriving example of an old-fashioned amusement park combining a variety of new attractions in a traditional atmosphere. The park features more than twenty rides, a full-scale water park, and the Big Cat Encounter.

Upon entering the park, visitors can choose between Splash World, located to the right, and the amusement park, to the left. Splash World is home to six water-based attractions, including the Sky River Rapids, Black Viper, and Vertical Limit slides, as well as the Endless River, a wading pool, and a kids' play area.

Entering the amusement park, visitors are greeted by the Thunderbolt, Inverter, and Giant Ferris wheel. This leads to the main midway, home of the train. Next to the main midway are rides such as the Kite Flyer, Samba Tower, Falling Star, Tilt-A-Whirl, Chaos, and Showboat, along with the Penny Arcade and Big Cat Encounter.

Along the lakefront are the Flying Pharaoh swing ride, Sea Dragon, Neptune's Revenge flume, Tsunami roller coaster, and the picnic shelters. The kiddieland can be found behind the gift shop.

Jenkinson's Boardwalk

OPENED 1928

A DAY AT THE BEACH DOES NOT GET MUCH BETTER THAN A VISIT TO JENKinson's Boardwalk. With its immaculately raked sands adorned with palm trees, carefully maintained boardwalk, amusement park, and large oceanfront pavilion with a restaurant and bar overlooking the beach and cooled by sea breezes, Jenkinson's is a complete experience.

A Simple Beginning

Charles Jenkinson was one of many entrepreneurs who flocked to the Atlantic shore to seek their fortune by catering to the throngs of tourists that came to enjoy the sea air. In the early 1900s, he opened soda fountains in the shore towns of Asbury Park and Ocean Grove. Both stores occupied leased space, and Jenkinson eventually grew tired of the restrictions placed on him by his landlords. As a result, in 1926, he acquired property in the nearby town of Point Pleasant Beach. Its Boardwalk was much quieter than the ones in Asbury Park and Ocean Grove, and he saw an opportunity to have a significant impact. In 1928, Jenkinson's Pavilion opened for business, totally transforming the sleepy Point Pleasant Beach Boardwalk.

Jenkinson erected the Pavilion, a large open-air building on the beach, featuring a candy shop, soda fountain, and refreshment stand. On the opposite side of the Boardwalk from the Pavilion, Jenkinson built a novelty store and a swimming pool.

People flocked to the new operation, and in 1929, Jenkinson expanded the pavilion, adding a

Jenkinson's Boardwalk
300 Ocean Ave.
Point Pleasant Beach
NJ 08742
732-892-0600
www.jenkinsons.com

dance hall. That was soon followed by a miniature golf course near the swimming pool. Despite the effects of the Depression on businesses throughout the country, Jenkinson's was able to thrive, and in 1934, the operation expanded by acquiring the beach as well as a bathhouse and pavilion north of his existing operation at the Inlet, where the Manasquan River flowed into the ocean.

Charles Jenkinson passed away in 1937, but his son Orlo stepped in, and growth continued. Big Band dances featuring the likes of Glenn Miller, Tommy Dorsey, and Sammy Kaye commenced that year and were broadcast through the region on radio. In 1938, the Pavilion was again expanded, and nearly 2,000 feet of beachfront was purchased.

The operation was able to thrive through the 1940s, despite World War II–related materials and travel restrictions. In 1949, Jenkinson's acquired an additional 500 feet of beachfront near the inlet. With operations clustered around the Pavilion and the inlet a half mile away, Jenkinson's opened a miniature train ride along the beach to connect the two areas. It remained a popular attraction until it was retired in 1996. With the additional acreage at the Inlet, Jenkinson's opened a small kiddie park in 1954 that remained popular attraction until it was replaced by a miniature golf course in the mid-1960s.

In 1964, Orlo Jenkinson passed away, and his son took over the business. While Jenkinson's remained a popular destination, without the

Jenkinson's originally consisted of a swimming pool and the pavilion (background).

VISITING

JENKINSON'S BOARDWALK

LOCATION

Jenkinson's Boardwalk is located in Point Pleasant Beach in central New Jersey. Parking is available at local lots for an additional fee.

From the north, take Exit 98 off the Garden State Parkway, and follow NJ Route 34 South to NJ Route 35 South. Cross the Manasquan Inlet Bridge and stay in the left lane. Make the left jughandle turn .25 mile after the Exxon. Complete the turn and head north on NJ Route 35, and make a right onto Broadway (last right before going over bridge). Take Broadway all the way to the end, and follow the right turn lane and make a right onto Ocean Avenue.

From the south, take the Garden State Parkway North to Exit 90. Turn right at the exit ramp and follow to NJ Route 70 to NJ Route 88. Turn right onto Route 88 East and follow to NJ Route 35 North. Turn right on Arnold Avenue (by the train station), and head east to Ocean Avenue.

OPERATING SCHEDULE

The amusement park at Jenkinson's Boardwalk opens at noon on weekends starting in April, is open daily from mid-June through Labor Day, and weekends again from September through mid-October. Closing time varies by time of year. Many of Jenkinson's other attractions, including the Aquarium, Pavilion, and arcades, are open year-round.

ADMISSION

Admission is free, with rides and attractions available on a pay-as-you-go basis. Ride tickets cost about 75 cents each, and rides require from two to seven tickets. The Fun House, beach, Aquarium, and miniature golf each have separate admissions.

FOOD

There are nearly twenty food outlets, ranging from boardwalk concession stands to sit-down restaurants. The Pavilion is the main food outlet, offering the full-service Oceanside dining room, sushi bar, raw bar, and food court with stands serving pizza, grilled items, seafood, and deli sandwiches. Kids' meals are also available in the Pavilion. Also on the Boardwalk are Joey Tomatoes pizza, the Boardwalk Bar & Grill, and Little Mac's near the amusement park with pizza and sandwiches.

FOR CHILDREN

Jenkinson's Boardwalk features fifteen kiddie rides, with favorites including the Dragon coaster, Gators, Convoy, and the fire engines and pony carts, two classics dating from the 1940s. Many of the remaining rides, such as the train, Crazy Bus, and Balloon wheel, can be enjoyed by the entire family.

(continued on page 90)

VISITING (continued from page 89)

SPECIAL FEATURES

Don't miss the Fun House, one of the few large amusement park fun houses to have been built in the past fifty years.

The beach along Jenkinson's Boardwalk is one of the few privately owned beaches in New Jersey and is one of the cleanest and best-maintained beaches in the state.

TIME REQUIRED

The amusement park at Jenkinson's Boardwalk can be enjoyed in about two hours, but to fully experience the facility, plan to spend the day and visit the beach, Aquarium, and Boardwalk.

TOURING TIPS

Visit during the week to avoid crowds. If you come on weekends or other busy days, arrive early to assure a parking space.

hands-on leadership that Orlo had provided, it went into a period of stagnation. In 1975, two separate fires destroyed many of the older buildings along the Boardwalk. Though most of them were not owned by Jenkinson's, their loss nonetheless had a negative impact.

A Shot in the Arm

The Jenkinson's operation was struggling, and new blood was needed to revitalize the Pavilion and Boardwalk. Around this time, Pasquale "Pat" Storino, a jukebox and arcade games dealer, was looking for a new opportunity that would not require so much travel. His family had owned a summer home in Point Pleasant Beach since the 1940s, and he thought the tired old Pavilion would be a great opportunity.

Storino reached a deal to purchase Jenkinson's holdings, which included the Pavilion, swimming pool, miniature golf course, a half mile of beach, the beach train, and the pavilion and bathhouse at the Inlet. He immediately launched a renovation of the Pavilion, creating an arcade, concession stands, games, and a restaurant. In 1978, a dinner theater was added to the Pavilion, and in 1980, a water slide complex replaced the aging swimming pool and miniature golf course.

Storino knew that the long-term future of his business depended on his acquiring control of as much of the Boardwalk as possible so that he could create a multifaceted destination. As part of that strategy, in 1980 he acquired Fun Fair, a small kiddie park that was located across the Boardwalk from the Pavilion. The park, opened in 1954, featured about eight rides, including a merry-go-round and train, both from the Allan Herschell company of North Tonowanda, New York.

The acquisitions did not stop there. In 1983, after two years of negotiations, Storino purchased Holiday Playland, another small amusement park located on the southern end of the Boardwalk. Kiddie rides first appeared at this location in 1945, but Holiday Playland actually opened in 1952. The small park featured about a dozen rides, including an antique carousel manufactured by William Dentzel around 1909, which was relocated to Point Pleasant Beach in the 1960s from nearby Ocean Grove, and the Swiss Toboggan, a unique, compact, roller-coaster-type ride. Also included in the $3 million acquisition was 600 feet of beachfront.

Holiday Playland was immediately renamed Jenkinson's South, and after the 1983 season, the Toboggan and a Swiss Bobs spinning ride were sold to make room for more family-oriented rides. In 1985, the wooden horses on the carousel were sold and replaced by aluminum versions, and the funds immediately put back into improving the operation.

The year 1987 was a critical one for Jenkinson's amusement park operations. At the end of the season, Fun Fair was closed and replaced by an elaborate miniature golf course. Herman's Amusements, an amusement park next door to Jenkinson's South, was purchased. Dating back to

Jenkinson's first amusement area was a small kiddie park that operated near the Inlet from 1954 until the mid-1960s.

Aerial view of Holiday Playland (left) and Herman's Amusements (right) from the 1960s. The two were combined in the 1980s to form the amusement area of Jenkinson's Boardwalk. JERRY WOOLLEY COLLECTION

1949, Herman's featured about ten rides, including a Haunted House dark ride, Scrambler, and Rock-O-Plane, a Ferris-wheel-type ride. As part of the improvement program, the old carousel at Jenkinson's South was sold and replaced by a modern merry-go-round from Chance Rides, while an arcade replaced Herman's Haunted House.

By 1989, Storino was well on his way to realizing his ultimate vision for the Point Pleasant Beach Boardwalk. The southern end was now anchored by a single family-oriented amusement park featuring about two dozen rides, while the northern end featured the Inlet facilities. At the heart of the Boardwalk was the original Pavilion, now supplemented by a new miniature golf course that replaced the Fun Fair and the water slides that replaced the original pool.

But on November 22, 1989, Storino's vision suffered a major setback when a fire broke out in the Pavilion's kitchen, which was closed for the season and under renovation. For three hours, one hundred firefighters fought the blaze in a blinding snowstorm. When it was finally under control, the Pavilion that had given birth to the entire operation was a total loss. Only a friendly wind kept the fire from spreading to the Boardwalk.

But Storino was undeterred and immediately began making plans to replace the Pavilion. Construction was complete on the new cement and steel structure the following May. Like the original, the new twelve hundred-seat Pavilion was the heart of Jenkinson's Boardwalk, featuring a food court facing the Boardwalk and a full-service restaurant in back, along with live entertainment, tropical-themed bars, and a large arcade.

With the Pavilion successfully restored, Storino turned his attention to upgrading the Boardwalk. Throughout the late 1980s, business at the water slides had been declining in the face of the popularity of the beach and competition from nearby water parks. Meanwhile, Storino thought that the park lacked an attraction that would provide something to do on days when the weather was bad. He settled on an aquarium, and in June 1991, Jenkinson's Aquarium was open for business. Built at a cost of $5 million, the two-story facility featured a full variety of marine life, including sharks, penguins, seals, alligators, rays, coral reefs, and a touch tank, which allowed visitors to touch live animals ranging from a sea star to a juvenile shark.

Improvements also continued to be made at the amusement park, the most notable being the addition of the Flitzer, a 25-foot-high, 1,200-foot-long steel-track roller coaster in 1992.

In 1998, Jenkinson's turned back the clock with the addition of a fun house. At one time nearly every amusement park had a fun house, where visitors would encounter a variety of tricks and obstacles, but by the

Jenkinson's features one of the few fun houses found in any amusement park.

1990s they had pretty much disappeared. Located along the Boardwalk near the Pavilion, the 4,000-square-foot, two-story Fun House was designed by Jack Rouse Associates of Cincinnati. Among the features were mazes, "shrinking" rooms, a rotating tunnel, trick mirrors, air blasts, sound effects, black lights, moving floors, a slide, and the Butt Room, a one-of-a-kind attraction that featured images of rear ends on the floor that lit up. When visitors jumped on a lighted image, it made a variety of noises. The Fun House anchored a larger multiyear renovation of much of Jenkinson's Boardwalk that included a new bathhouse, the Sweet Shop, the Boardwalk Bar and Grill, and Joey Tomatoes Pizza.

Jenkinson's Boardwalk Today

From its humble beginnings as an oceanfront pavilion and swimming pool, Jenkinson's Boardwalk had been totally remade into a complete multifaceted destination encompassing most of the waterfront in Point Pleasant Beach. In addition to more than two dozen rides, the complex features an aquarium, fun house, two miniature golf courses, and one of the most attractive beaches on the Jersey shore.

As it always has, the Pavilion remains the heart of the Boardwalk, with its variety of dining options in an oceanfront setting. Across the Boardwalk from the Pavilion is the Aquarium, along with a variety of concessions.

Jenkinson's amusement area is filled with a wide array of family rides.

Strolling down the Boardwalk, visitors come across the Fun House, Island miniature golf, and Boardwalk Bar & Grill. Next come more concessions and the second miniature golf course, which is actually on the roof of an arcade building. The amusement park anchors the southern end of Jenkinson's.

The end of the amusement park closest to the Pavilion is home to most of the kiddie rides, along with the merry-go-round, train, and Dragon coaster. The southern end includes larger rides such as the Flitzer roller coaster, Himalaya, Rock-O-Plane, Bumper Cars, Tilt-A-Whirl, and Spin Out, which replaced the Scrambler in 2002.

Casino Pier and Water Works

OPENED 1932

FOR NEARLY SEVENTY YEARS, THE CASINO BUILDING HAS SERVED AS THE anchor of the seaside community of Seaside Heights. Originally it was the focus of the Casino Pier's operations and contained most of its attractions. As the years passed and the operation expanded beyond the building, it has remained the heart of the facility. Although the building is smaller than it was originally, its importance is not diminished. It is both the link between Casino Pier's amusement park and the Water Works water park, and also the location of the park's most prized possession, an antique carousel.

A Quiet Corner of Town

Today Casino Pier and Water Works is in the heart of an action-packed seaside resort community, but it roots are much more humble. Seaside Heights was a quiet community of small summer homes when Linus Gilbert came to town. Gilbert had recently acquired a carousel and was looking for a place to set it up. He found a commercial fishery with a small fishing pier extending into the ocean at what was then the north end of the town's Boardwalk.

Casino Pier and Water Works

800 Ocean Terrace
Seaside Heights, NJ 08751

732-793-6488

www.casinopier-
waterworks.com

Gilbert purchased the site and in 1932 set up his carousel across the Boardwalk from the beach on the site of the fishery's fishpond. The ride dates back to 1910, when it was assembled from a variety of figures, some dating back to the 1890s, made by some of the leading carvers of the era such as William Dentzel, Charles Looff, Charles

Carmel, and Marcus Illions. Among its fifty-eight animals were thirty-six jumping horses, two camels, a lion, a tiger, and a donkey. The ride originally operated Island Beach Park in Burlington, New Jersey, but was damaged when a fire destroyed the park in 1928. Gilbert had the ride renovated and relocated it along with its ten-sided building to Seaside Heights.

During those first years of Gilbert's operation, the complex consisted solely of the carousel, linked to the Boardwalk by a wooden walkway. Compared to the more established Freeman's Amusements, located on the southern end of the Boardwalk, there was not much to attract vacationers, and the fledgling operation struggled. But Gilbert was not discouraged and in 1937 launched a multifaceted expansion that established it as the leading entertainment complex in Seaside Heights.

Gilbert built a large structure called the Seaside Height Casino around the carousel building. Advertised as the "largest exhibition hall on the Jersey Shore," the Casino contained a variety of diversions such as games, concessions, and a ballroom. Just west of the Casino Building was a huge 165-by-65-foot swimming pool and a roller rink. On the other side of the Casino, on the Boardwalk, a nightclub was constructed over the beach, next to the fishing pier. Originally known as the Bamboo Bar, it was renamed the Parrot Club in 1950 and became quite popular before being demolished in 1971 to make room for other amusements.

The expanded Seaside Heights Casino and Pool, as it was then known, was an immediate success and made the northern end of town a desti-

Casino Pier's carousel. This original ride is a true work of art.

Aerial view of Casino Pier following its 1938 expansion, showing the swimming pool and Casino Building. CASINO PIER AND WATER WORKS

nation in its own right. As traffic grew, additional rides began to appear, including a dark ride in the Casino Building. A couple of spinning rides, such as the Silver Streak, one of the first high-speed circular rides, were erected on a small extension of the Boardwalk, built over the beach. This was the beginning of Casino Pier as it exists today.

In 1948, Gilbert sold the complex to John FitzGerald and John Christopher, real estate speculators with property in New York, New England, and Miami Beach. Christopher took on the role of the hands-on operator, while FitzGerald's role was more passive.

The new owners worked hard to maintain and improve the facility, but expansion took a backseat, with just a few rides being added. One of the largest of these was a new double-decker dark ride located on the pier, replacing the Jungle dark ride in the Casino Building. Opened in 1959, its was the first two-level dark ride built by the Pretzel Amusement Company, the dominant dark ride manufacturer of the era.

Also that year, John Christopher passed away. FitzGerald bought out Christopher's estate and persuaded his family to take a more active role in operating the park. He recruited his son-in-law, Ken Wynne, to take over operations in 1960, giving him an ownership interest. A lawyer and children's television producer, Wynne took to the amusement industry and began a major expansion of the pier.

 **VISITING**

LOCATION

Casino Pier and Water Works is located on the Atlantic Ocean in the heart of the Seaside Heights Boardwalk. Take Exit 82 off the Garden State Parkway to NJ Route 37 East over the Mathis Bridge. Follow the road to the fork, and keep to the left for Seaside Heights. Go around the circle, staying to your right. After the "Welcome to Seaside Heights" sign, make a quick left. Take the second right onto Grant Avenue, and go four blocks to the ocean. Parking is available for an additional fee at the park's lot behind Water Works and at other local lots.

OPERATING SCHEDULE

Casino Pier opens at noon on weekends from April through mid-June, daily through August, and weekends in September. Water Works opens at 9 A.M. on weekends from Memorial Day weekend through mid-June, daily through August and on Labor Day weekend. Closing times vary by season. The Casino Building is open weekends year-round.

ADMISSION

Admission to Casino Pier is free, with rides and attractions available on a pay-as-you-go basis. Ride tickets cost around 75 cents each, and rides require from one to ten tickets. Admission to Water Works is separate. For under $20, visitors can enjoy all of the attractions at Water Works for a two-hour period.

FOOD

Nearly twenty different food concessions offer a wide array of easy-to-eat food, including pizza, subs, sandwiches, pretzels, and ice cream. The food stand near the rear of the Wild Mouse offers indoor seating.

FOR CHILDREN

Casino Pier and Water Works features about eight kiddie rides and a number of other family rides, including the Floyd Moreland Carousel, Big Wheel, Kite Flyer, Speedway, and London Fog and Mardi Gras fun houses.

SPECIAL FEATURES

Don't miss the Floyd Moreland Carousel. Located in the Casino Building, the carousel is the ride that started Casino Pier and Water Works when it came to Seaside Heights in 1932. Dating to 1910, the ride was assembled from some of the best work of the top carvers of the late 1800s and early 1900s.

Casino Pier's miniature golf course occupies the roofs of five concession stands along the Boardwalk and is quite possibly the world's only twenty-five-hole miniature golf course.

(continued on page 100)

CASINO PIER AND WATER WORKS

VISITING (continued from page 99)

TIME REQUIRED

The Casino Building, Pier, and water park can be experienced in about five hours, but visitors should plan to spend the day in Seaside Heights and enjoy the beach, the Boardwalk, and nearby Funtown Pier.

TOURING TIPS

Visit on a Wednesday, when crowds are lighter and it's the only day of the week when a pay-one-price admission is available. For less than $20, visitors can enjoy all of the rides from noon until 6 P.M. In addition, admission to the beach is free on Wednesdays, and there is a fireworks display in the evening.

Don't forget a ride on the Big Wheel. The view of the surrounding area is spectacular.

The Sky Ride is also a great way to check out the action on the Seaside Heights Boardwalk.

Becoming More Amusing

Over the next few years, Wynne added many new rides and expanded the pier toward the ocean a section at a time. Among the first attractions were an Octopus, Chair Swing, and Roll-O-Plane, which at the time were considered some of the most advanced rides available. These were soon joined by Casino Pier's first roller coaster, the Wild Mouse, built around 1962 on a newly constructed section of the pier. The Wild Mouse represented the newest generation of roller coasters, which featured steel rather than wood track. Instead of big drops, the ride emphasized a series of sharp turns that gave the illusion that the car would fly off the track. Its compact track layout was perfect for the amusement pier, where space was a scarce commodity.

Unlike many amusement facilities, Casino Pier itself owned very few attractions. Wynne leased out sections of the pier to various independent businessmen who would bring in rides and concessions. As a result, the next several decades at the pier were highlighted by a constantly changing lineup.

Soon after taking over, Wynne saw an advertisement in an amusement industry trade publication by a Swiss company that wanted to place a ride in the United States. Thinking that a relationship with the company would allow him to introduce some unique rides to the public, he contacted the company and got to know Eddie Maier, a European ride broker who brought America's first Himalaya ride to Casino Pier in 1963.

Now a common sight at most amusement parks, the Himalaya consisted of a series of two-person cars that traveled at high speeds over an undulating track. The entire ride was adorned with thousands of electric lights that, when combined with loud music, immediately made its presence known on the midway. The ride was a huge hit. As part of Maier's agreement with Casino Pier, he would offer the Himalaya for sale at the end of the season and bring in a new one. That way, Casino Pier received six new Himalayas over a ten-year period, each more elaborate than the previous one.

The successful results of the Maier partnership demonstrated to Wynne that establishing relationships with European ride manufacturers would give him something unique to promote his park, and soon he was making annual trips to Europe to scope out rides.

The pier had grown tremendously since Wynne took over, and he decided to install a sky ride in 1964 that traveled from the ocean end of the pier to the pool and back, which gave patrons an overview of the entire complex. The ride was built by Universal Design of nearby Wildwood, New Jersey.

Also around this time, a one-of-a-kind miniature golf course made its appearance at Casino Pier. Since space was always at a premium, the roofs of two concession stands along the Boardwalk were connected, and a golf course was placed on the roof. Today the miniature golf course has been expanded to cover five concession stand roofs and is quite possibly the world's only twenty-five-hole miniature golf course.

By the 1940s, what is now Casino Pier started being developed as a few rides were added to an extension of the Boardwalk.

By the mid-1960s, Casino Pier had grown to become one of the largest amusement facilities in New Jersey, with eighteen major rides and eighteen kiddie rides, nearly double the amount when Wynne took over. A major expansion of the pier was undertaken for the 1965 season. A new section of pier measuring 85 by 320 feet was constructed and the Pretzel dark ride renovated. In addition, several new rides were added, including a Trabant spinning ride and a one-of-a-kind Italian Ferris wheel that not only turned in the traditional manner, but also spun on a horizontal turntable at the same time.

On June 10, 1965, as the season was kicking into high gear, Casino Pier nearly became a memory. Around 2:30 P.M., a fire broke out, apparently started by a discarded cigarette that fell into the boards of the pier. Fanned by easterly winds, one-third of the pier was soon engulfed in flames. Fifteen fire companies fought the fire, and thanks to a shift in the wind, they were able to confine the damage to the eastern third of the pier.

Still, the damage to the pier was extensive, totaling $2 million. Eight rides, including a new Himalaya, the Italian Ferris wheel, Rotor, Scrambler, Sky Ride, and Wild Mouse, were destroyed, and four others were severely damaged. But Wynne did not let the fire defeat him. Workers began clearing the debris the next day, and within a week, contracts were awarded to rebuild the damaged section. The destroyed area was fenced off, and a number of temporary attractions, including a dolphin show, were booked for the remainder of the season. In the true spirit of the industry, other amusement operators also offered attractions to fill in the empty space. Beech Bend Park in Kentucky even loaned a spare Wild Mouse that they had stored at their facility.

The fire inconvenienced not only Casino Pier's owners and customers, but also local fishermen who had long used the pier as a favorite fishing spot. Wanting to miss as few days as possible, the fishermen collectively approached pier management and offered to help rebuild their fishing area. Management provided tools, nails, and lumber, and soon at least the part of the pier used for fishing was back in operation.

Concerned about the possibility of another fire that dry summer, management watered the remainder of the pier for the rest of the season. After closing each evening, the night watchman turned on a backyard lawn sprinkler and moved it around every half hour. The water drenched the Boardwalk surface, saturating any smoldering cigarettes.

Bouncing Back

Casino Pier was ready to go for the 1966 season with $500,000 in new rides. Several of the new rides, such as the Wild Mouse and Himalaya, replaced those destroyed by the fire. But a number of new pieces were also added, including the Sky Diver, a Ferris-wheel-type attraction; the Grand Prix, an electric go-cart ride; a dark ride; a fun house; and three kiddie rides.

In response to the hippie culture of the late 1960s, Casino Pier revamped an existing dark ride in 1968 to give it a "mod" theme. Its eight rooms were filled with a variety of psychedelic effects such as strobe lights, black lights, liquid light projections, and other color and light effects. The dark ride was joined by a psychedelic fun house. The dark ride continued to adapt to changing tastes with many different themes until around 1980, when it was removed.

The Wild Mouse was considered a cutting-edge ride when it was first added to the pier in the late 1950s, but by 1969 it was passé, and Wynne went shopping for a new roller coaster. On one of his European trips, Wynne located a major new roller coaster that he knew would be the perfect addition to Casino Pier: the Jet Star.

The Jet Star was a 45-foot-tall steel-track roller coaster designed by Anton Schwarzkopf, one of the all-time great roller coaster designers. The compact 1,766-foot-long layout featured a series of steep drops into high-speed turns, providing a completely different ride experience than the Wild Mouse.

According to an article in *Amusement Business,* as told by Ken Wynne, installation of the new roller coaster was an interesting challenge. On the day construction started, Wynne marked on the pier where the Jet Star was to be built and left for lunch. But when he returned, Roland Koch, who had sold him the ride, had begun construction in another area of the pier. Wynne told him the ride was supposed to be set up elsewhere, and Koch replied, "This is where the ride goes." Wynne explained that he owned the pier and that it should go wherever he wanted it to. Koch then sternly told him, "You are crazy; this is where it should go, you don't know what you are talking about." Koch prevailed, and the ride remained in the same location for its thirty-year stay at Casino Pier.

In 1971, Casino Pier launched a $2 million renovation program that completely changed the look of the facility. Most of the old rides were sold; two old restaurants on the pier were demolished, including the Parrot Club; and several new rides and a kiddieland were added. The new rides included the Sky Wheel, a double Ferris wheel; and the Orbit, a unique spinning ride. In addition, the Ballroom—no longer popular in the age of rock and roll—was converted into the Italian Village shopping area, with two dozen booths offering craft items.

A wide array of rides rotated through Casino Pier during the 1970s, most of which appeared for a few seasons and moved on. Among the more notable rides were the Utopia 2000 dark ride, located in an air-supported dome, and a 100-foot-wide, 50-foot-deep, Arabian-themed fun house adorned with ten thousand light bulbs. Both attractions debuted in 1972.

In 1973, the pier added one of the country's first Bumper Boat rides. It featured a unique loading system in which a hydraulic grate rose from the bottom of the pool and lifted the boats out of the water, allowing the patrons to walk out of the pool on the grate. In 1975, Casino Pier introduced the Untied States to the Enterprise, a spinning ride that flipped riders upside down. The next year saw the introduction of a Scrambler ride enclosed in a vinyl dome and enhanced by a variety of special effects. The indoor Scrambler has become one of Casino Pier's most enduring attractions, although it has been relocated a number of times and renamed Poltergeist and, most recently, Centrifuge.

In the 1979, the Jet Star was joined by another roller coaster. Called the Luv Bugs, this ride replaced Utopia 2000 and was originally built in 1958 by Mack, a German firm. Just 18 feet tall with a 15-foot drop, the 800-foot-long ride featured a spiral lift hill with most of the ride located indoors. Luv Bugs was originally called the Broadway Trip and operated for a number of years at the legendary Palisades Park in Cliffside Park, New Jersey. After it closed in 1971, the ride was moved to the Canadian National Exposition in Toronto, before finding its way to Casino Pier. In 1988, it underwent a $20,000 renovation, and was renamed the Wizard's Cavern. It was retired in 2003.

The unique Wizard's Cavern indoor roller coaster first opened in 1979 as Luv Bugs and was retired in 2003.

Aerial view of the pier in 1982. THE SCHELLER COMPANY

Ken Wynne gained a new business partner in 1982, when Bob Bennett purchased the FitzGerald family's remaining interest in the operation. Bennett was hardly a stranger to Casino Pier. He had gotten his start in the amusement industry in the summer of 1949 at age seventeen, when he worked at the Casino as a locker room attendant and pool cleaner during the day and monitored the fishing pier at night. After a four-year stint in the Navy, he returned to Seaside Heights in 1956 with plans to open a concession stand along the Boardwalk. Bennett arrived in Seaside around the time the New Jersey legislature outlawed games of chance along the state's boardwalks, and he found many operators who were looking to sell, allowing Bennett to acquire a number of concession stands at bargain prices. The ban was overturned in November 1959, and by the early 1980s, Bennett had thirty boardwalk concession stands, including most of the ones at Casino Pier.

During Bennett's first season as an owner, he added the Ranger, a large looping ride. But there was also a setback: A thunderstorm caused $1 million in damage when it blew the Sky Diver ride onto the Himalaya, destroying both rides. Fortunately the patrons had already taken shelter and no one was injured.

Changing Times

For many years, Ocean Terrace, one of the major north-south streets in Seaside Heights, dead-ended at the Casino Building. The city had long sought to extend the road through the Casino property to link the southern and northern halves of town. Casino Pier's owners had mixed feelings about this plan. While it would split the property in two, separating the pool from the Casino Building and Pier, it would greatly increase the amount of traffic that passed the facility and encourage growth on the northern end of town, putting Casino Pier in the center of the action.

Eventually the positives outweighed the negatives, and the owners agreed to sell the right-of-way to the city. In November 1982, demolition began on a 70-by-200-foot section of the Casino Building. Many of the building's features were lost, including seven games, a shooting gallery, and the ballroom, which had been used as an arcade since 1978, but the carousel was spared. The remaining Casino Building was renovated and given a distinctive facade resembling a castle, complete with several tall turrets, measuring up to 65 feet tall.

The construction also meant the removal of the park's Sky Ride, which was added in the late 1960s as a replacement to the ride lost in the 1965 fire. Casino Pier took the opportunity to add a new version. Unlike the previous Sky Ride, which had traveled from the end of the pier to the pool and back, the new Sky Ride provided transportation 35 feet above the Boardwalk, traveling from the pier to a second station eight blocks to the north.

The 1984 season started on an optimistic note with the expenditure of $3 million to add nine new rides, including a fun house. It was also a year when Casino Pier's most valuable attraction was almost lost. Dur-

The Power Surge was the first ride of its kind in North America when it opened in 1999.

ing the mid-1980s, antique carousel animals became highly sought after by collectors, and amusement park operators came under tremendous pressure to break up their rides and sell the animals individually.

In the summer of 1984, it looked like Casino Pier's carousel might meet a similar fate. Floyd Moreland, a classics professor at the City University of New York, was appalled when he heard the news of the potential sale. Moreland had a special relationship with the ride, having first fallen in love with it as a three-year-old when he rode it while visiting Seaside Heights with his family. As a teenager, he worked at the pier and operated the carousel, and he returned every summer during college, traveling from as far away as California.

Moreland could not bear to see the ride dismantled and wrote a letter to the owners offering to purchase the ride and the Casino Building. When he found out the deal would be beyond his budget, he returned to the pier during the summer of 1984 to operate his beloved ride for one final season. Fate intervened and the planned sale fell through. Moreland believed that the ride was such an integral part of the pier that it should be renovated rather than removed. He approached Wynne with his proposal to restore the ride, and Wynne presented him the key to the building and told him to go ahead.

Throughout the winter, Moreland worked in the unheated Casino Building repainting the carousel frame, restoring the paintings that ringed the top of the ride, and replacing fluorescent light fixtures with twenty-two hundred incandescent light bulbs. The story of one person trying to save this irreplaceable antique struck a chord with the media in the region, and his efforts were profiled in the *New York Times* and by several television networks. The publicity led to a huge increase in visitors to the pier who wanted to ride the carousel, and soon any talk of selling the ride was silenced. Moreland, now retired, has remained at the pier ever since, operating and caring for the ride. The park recognized his efforts by naming the carousel after him in 1986.

Working in an Expansion

Casino Pier continued to expand with the addition of a go-cart track and the Kamikaze, a looping ride, in 1985 and the London Fog fun house in 1986. But now the pier's expansion efforts were focused on the other side of the complex.

For a number of years, the popularity of the aging swimming pool was decreasing in the wake of the growing influence of water slides. In 1978, two water slides were added to the pool, and a third was added in 1982. But by the late 1980s, it was apparent that something more dramatic was needed to take the operation to the next level.

Following the 1986 season, demolition started on the pool to make way for the Water Works, a 2.3-acre, $4.5 million water park. Water Works contained a full day's worth of activities for the entire family, with nine water slides up to 55 feet high, a river ride, and activity pools for kids and adults. Weather-related construction delays kept the Water Works from opening until August, but it was a success from the beginning.

With the opening of Water Works in 1987, Casino Pier was enjoying a level of success it had never before attained. Wynne, about to turn sixty-five, decided it was time to move on and sold his interest in the pier to his partner, Bob Bennett, who continued to expand and improve Casino Pier. It had not had a major dark ride for a number of years, so in 1989, the park purchased dark rides from two defunct amusement parks in Massachusetts and combined them into an all new dark ride, Nightmare Manor.

Through the early 1990s, Casino Pier continued its strategy of rotating rides in and out every few years to continually present a fresh lineup of rides and concessions. A 66-foot-tall Ferris wheel was imported from Italy in 1993 to commemorate the hundredth anniversary of the ride, while a small log flume and the Evolution, a large spinning ride that was the first of its kind in the United States, each made one-year appearances in 1995.

But by the late 1990s, Casino Pier shifted its strategy and started purchasing rides for the pier to provide a more consistent experience to visitors. Given the popularity of the flume that operated at the pier in 1995, Casino Pier purchased a larger flume in 1997. Manufactured by Reverchon of France, the compact ride packed two drops of 30 and 40 feet along a 750-foot-long trough. The following year, a 65-foot-tall Ferris wheel and two spinning rides, the Tilt-A-Whirl and Tornado, along with the Persian Kamel fun house, anchored $1.5 million in improvements.

By 1995, the Wild Mouse roller coaster that Casino Pier had removed as obsolete twenty-five years earlier was discovered by a new generation of riders, as roller coaster manufacturers around the world developed new versions of the ride. One of those was Miler Manufacturing of Oregon, which had introduced a modern version of the Wild Mouse nearly forty years after they stopped manufacturing their original version. Casino Pier stepped up to purchase its first model, and the 35-foot-tall, 1,100-foot-long ride opened for the 1999 season.

The improvements in 1999 included many other new rides as well. Near the Wild Mouse, the pier installed the first Power Surge ride in the United States. Manufactured by the Italian firm Zamperla, the Power Surge was a six-story-tall ride that spun riders on three different axes concurrently. Casino Pier also added family rides including the Frog Hopper and the Speedway, which is a throwback to the classic whip rides.

Casino Pier has rides for everyone.

Anchoring the expansion the next two seasons were the Skyscraper and Slingshot. The Skyscraper consists of a long boom with four seats on each end that rotates at a high rate of speed; the Slingshot is a bungee-style attraction that flings riders into the sky.

As the face of the pier was changing, Bob Bennett decided that he wanted to slow down, and in early 2002, he sold Casino Pier and Water Works to the Storino family, a longtime competitor that owns the nearby Jenkinson's Boardwalk in Point Pleasant Beach. Bennett was not the only Casino Pier institution to retire during this period. After thirty years of service, the Jet Star needed to be replaced, and it was retired after the 2000 season. Given the success of the Wild Mouse, Casino Pier returned to Miler Manufacturing for a new roller coaster similar to the Jet Star, with its twisting drops. Miler responded by designing the Star Jet, a 52-foot-tall, 1,300-feet-long roller coaster that opened in 2002. It was placed in the same location as the Jet Star, at the end of the pier, and featured a section of track towering high above the ocean.

Following in the tradition of Wynne and Bennett, and their own tradition at Point Pleasant Beach, the Storinos launched a major improvement program at Casino Pier for the 2003 season. Many of the park's rides were rearranged, and infrastructure improvements were made. Four new rides were added, and three favorites were rebuilt. Thrill seekers were offered the Rock 'n Roll, a Himalaya type-ride; and Moby Dick, which features fast side-to-side movements. The Hot Tamale kiddie roller coaster and Samba Balloon were added for families. Nightmare Manor was rebuilt as Stillwalk Manor, a new dark ride using the ride system from the former dark ride. The Poltergeist indoor scrambler was converted into the Centrifuge, and the kiddie bumper car ride was rebuilt.

Casino Pier and Water Works Today

Casino Pier and Water Works remains a classic, action-packed New Jersey boardwalk amusement park. The 3½-acre complex consists of three major components. Farthest inland is the Water Works water park. This full-scale water park offers more than twenty attractions, including a wide array of water slides, activity pools for kids and adults, and a quarter-mile-long river ride.

Between Water Works and the Boardwalk is the Casino Building, the oldest existing portion of Casino Pier and Water Works. The turreted Casino Building is home to the park's most prized possession, the Floyd Moreland Carousel. Assembled around 1910, this is Casino Pier's original ride and is still considered the heart of the complex. The Casino is also home to a number of games, a large arcade, and several gift shops and food stands.

On the other side of the Boardwalk is Casino Pier, extending 630 feet over the beach and ocean and featuring more than thirty rides and three fun houses. The entrance of the pier is highlighted by a wide variety of food stands and skill games. The one-of-a-kind miniature golf course is located on the roof of several of these concession stands. Also at the entrance of the pier is the Sky Ride, which provides transportation over eight blocks of the Boardwalk. Past the concession stands are the pier's eight kiddie rides, as well as the Mardi Gras, London Fog, and Persian Kamel fun houses; the Big Wheel; and the Skyscraper.

On the upper level of the pier, closest to the ocean, are most of the larger rides, including the Star Jet and Wild Mouse roller coasters, the Log Flume, the Stillwalk Manor dark ride, the Centrifuge, and the Slingshot.

Playland's Castaway Cove

OPENED 1939

ONE OF THE GREAT JOYS OF STROLLING THE MANY BOARDWALKS OF NEW Jersey is the undiscovered treasures that present themselves if you look closely. Ocean City's Boardwalk is no different. As you walk along, taking advantage of the games, food stands, and taffy shops, you will come across what appears to be a simple arcade adorned with a replica of a pirate ship. It would be a mistake to dismiss this arcade and continue along the Boardwalk, as it's not just an arcade, but the entrance to Playland's Castaway Cove, one of the most action-packed amusement parks on the Jersey shore.

World's Fair Leftovers

While the roots of Playland's Castaway Cove actually date back to 1939, it was 1941 when it truly made its presence known on the Ocean City Boardwalk. As the 1939–40 New York World's Fair was coming to a close, the Bingham family, who owned the fledgling operation, purchased one of the fair's exposition buildings, disassembled it, and transported it back to Ocean City. The building's arched wooden trusses immediately made Bingham's Playland a landmark along the Boardwalk.

Through the 1940s and 1950s, Bingham's Playland was able to succeed by catering to passersby with its assortment of arcade games and kiddie rides. The operation changed hands in 1959, when David Simpson, who had operated several miniature golf courses in the area, purchased the park with partner Fred Tarvas.

Playland's Castaway Cove
1020 Boardwalk
Ocean City, NJ 08226
609-399-4751
www.boardwalkfun.com

With amusement parks around the country adding kiddie rides in the wake of the postwar baby boom, the new owners decided to follow suit and added several new kiddie rides for the 1959 season. Many of these rides, such as the merry-go-round, autos, pony cart, fire truck, Ferris wheel, and boats, were manufactured by the William F. Mangels Company of Coney Island, New York. In addition, a train ride was added that traveled through the building and around an outdoor area in back.

During this time, an ordinance in Ocean City prohibited amusement rides with motors of greater than one horsepower from operating outdoors, severely limiting Playland's expansion options. One ride that Simpson's partner Tarvas briefly added was a steel-track kiddie roller coaster. He was able to erect it outdoors behind the building, but its noisy chain lift and train screeching along the track created a racket. The owner of a neighboring hotel immediately petitioned the city council, which enacted a new ordinance prohibiting roller coasters with chain lifts, and the kiddie coaster's time at Playland quickly ended.

Despite these ordinances, Playland did manage to expand in the early 1960s, emphasizing rides such as the Devil's Den dark ride; King Tut's Tomb and Monster Mansion, two walk-through attractions; and the Mystery Room, an illusion-based attraction that gave riders the impression that they were being flipped upside down.

Because of the restrictions on operating rides outdoors, Playland erected a large metal building behind the original structure in 1964 to accommodate additional rides. One of the new rides was a full-size merry-go-round manufactured by Allan Herschell, although an antique wooden carousel carved by Marcus Illions and M. D. Borelli soon replaced it.

The Elephants were one of Playland's early rides. PLAYLAND'S CASTAWAY COVE

David Simpson bought out his partner in 1970. While the ordinances continued to limit what he could do in terms of expansion, the business remained successful. By the late 1970s, the restrictions began to be lifted, and Simpson started to expand the operation. When he sold the antique carousel following the 1979 season, the proceeds were put back into Playland. Although the park consisted of just 32,000 square feet, the relaxed laws permitted it to expand onto the outdoor portion of its property, and in 1980, Playland increased its number of rides from twelve to eighteen.

In 1985, however, stricter state regulations prompted the removal of the dark ride, which had been rethemed as the Haunted Mansion, as well as the walk-throughs and the Mystery Room. But new rides were added as space permitted, including a Dragon coaster in 1986, a Ferris wheel in 1988, the TV Playhouse fun house in 1993, and the Flitzer, Playland's first full-size roller coaster, in 1994. Manufactured by the German firm Zierer, the Flitzer was a compact 25-foot-tall steel-track ride with 1,200 feet of track.

Triple Play

Fate smiled on Playland in 1995 when a neighboring hotel sold off a portion of its property. Scott Simpson, who had taken over day-to-day operations from his father, quickly moved to purchase the property, increasing their holdings from 1 to 3 acres. This permitted a major expansion of Playland that would increase its ride count from seventeen in 1985 to twenty-nine ten years later. Not only was the ride lineup expanded, but also many of the older rides were replaced. In fact, by the time the expansion was completed, just four rides from the 1995 season, a Giant Slide, the antique cars, the Tilt-A-Whirl, and the Flitzer, still remained.

Five rides were added for the 1996 season, including the Spider, a spinning ride; the Pelican Splash, a kiddie flume ride; and three roller coasters. The largest coaster was the Python, a looping roller coaster from the Italian firm Pinfari that stood 36 feet high and had 1,200 feet of track. At the opposite end of the park and the thrill spectrum was the Sea Serpent, a kiddie roller coaster from Miler Manufacturing.

Simpson also purchased a Wild Mouse roller coaster from Miler that had been in storage. The ride was originally manufactured by company founder Fred Miler in the mid-1950s. After operating it at fairs and carnivals, Miler had placed it in storage in a barn in Oregon in 1959, where it sat until 1995. Simpson immediately jumped on the chance to purchase this barely used ride and brought it to New Jersey. The Wild Mouse rounded out Playland's roller coaster offerings. Standing 33 feet tall, the 900-foot-long ride featured a series of sharp turns that gave riders the illusion that they would plunge over the edge.

LOCATION

Playland's Castaway Cove is located along the Ocean City Boardwalk in southern New Jersey. Take Exit 30 off the Garden State Parkway, and follow NJ Route 52 East over the bridge and into Ocean City. Go to Ocean Avenue and make a right. Travel one block, and Playland's Castaway Cove is on the left at 10th and the Boardwalk.

OPERATING SCHEDULE

Playland's Castaway Cove opens at 1 P.M. on weekends from mid-April through mid-June and in September and October. From early to mid-June, the park also opens weekdays at 6 P.M. Between mid-June and Labor Day, Playland opens at 1 P.M. daily. Closing time varies by time of year.

ADMISSION

Admission is free, with rides and attractions available on a pay-as-you-go basis. Ride tickets cost about 75 cents each, and rides require from two to seven tickets.

FOOD

Two food stands, including a Dairy Queen, are located in the heart of the park near the TV Playhouse and offer pizza, pretzels, ice cream, and other snacks. An ice cream stand is located in the arcade building, facing the Boardwalk. A wide variety of other food options are also available nearby on the Boardwalk.

FOR CHILDREN

Playland's Castaway Cove features eight kiddie rides, with favorites including the Sea Serpent roller coaster and the Pelican Splash flume. Many of the park's other rides, such as the Ferris wheel, train, antique cars, Dizzy Dragons, and Samba Balloon, can be enjoyed by the entire family.

SPECIAL FEATURES

The arcade building that serves as the park's main entrance was originally constructed for the 1939–40 New York World's Fair. It is one of the last surviving remnants of the exposition.

TIME REQUIRED

Playland's Castaway Cove can be enjoyed in about two hours. However, a visit can be a full-day experience when coupled with the beach and nearby Gillian's Wonderland Pier and Gillian's Island water park.

TOURING TIPS

Visit during the week or prior to July 4 to avoid the crowds.

Following the triple roller coaster addition in 1996, Simpson followed up in 1997 with a 90-foot-tall Ferris wheel, a Gravitron spinning ride, and a new train ride from Chance Rides. Although quite popular with the families that frequented the park, putting a train in the tightly packed facility proved to be quite a challenge. Playland had to create eight different railroad crossings and always had a person walking in front of the train to ensure that no one wandered into its path.

Another major expansion took place in 1999, when five new rides made their debut. The expansion that year had a decided thrill ride orientation, including the Double Shot, on which riders were shot up and down a 100-foot-tall tower; the High Flyer, which flipped riders upside down; the Typhoon, with an aggressive side-to-side motion; and the Sea Dragon, a swinging ship.

Almost as if to signify the transformation of the park, problems with the electrical system in the 1964 addition to the original building prompted its demolition following the 1999 season. A new bumper car building took its place for the 2000 season. Also added that year was the High Seas, a log flume with two splash-downs.

Improvements have continued. A new merry-go-round with a variety of different fiberglass animals opened in 2001. The year 2002 saw two new kiddie rides. An elaborate Flying Carousel swing ride and Bulgy the Whale, a vintage kiddie ride, joined the lineup in 2003.

View from the Ferris wheel shows the Python looping coaster nestled among other rides.

Playland's action-packed midway features rides of every description.

Playland's Castaway Cove Today

From its humble beginnings as little more than an arcade with a few kiddie rides, Playland's Castaway Cove has evolved into an action-packed amusement park with a wide variety of rides. As it has been for more than sixty years, the main entrance to the park is through the former exposition building. Originally holding all of the park's operations, the building today houses the park's arcade. Once emerging from the arcade, visitors enter the main part of Playland's Castaway Cove and are greeted by the merry-go-round, bumper cars, Double Shot, and Typhoon. Continuing on, visitors pass the giant slide and Flitzer roller coaster before coming upon the area that features the High Flyer, Python roller coaster, and Graviton.

Playland's main midway begins here and travels through the heart of the park. From the Wild Mouse, visitors pass the TV Playhouse, High Seas flume, and Ferris wheel. Most of the smaller kiddie rides are clustered around the Ferris wheel. Toward the back of the park are the Spider, train, antique cars, Sea Serpent kiddie coaster, and Pelican Splash flume.

Bowcraft Amusement Park

OPENED 1946

ROUTE 22 IS ONE OF THOSE CONGESTED SUBURBAN ROADWAYS THAT ARE commonplace in suburban America. But as cars make their way past the gas stations and shopping centers, drivers can catch a glimpse of a small oasis in the midst of the hustle and bustle. Large trees, colorful rides, iron fences, and brick walkways highlight this oasis—Bowcraft Amusement Park, a community institution since 1946.

Living His Passion

Ted Miller had two passions in life: archery and skiing. Much of his free time in the summer was spent competing in archery tournaments, and his winters were spent plunging down snow-covered mountains. He decided that he wanted to share those passions with others, and on July 1, 1940, he opened a small store offering archery and ski equipment, much of which he made and serviced.

As he worked to build his fledgling business, America was drawn into World War II, and Miller found himself leaving his business to serve his country. While his father filled in for him, Miller served with the 10th Mountain Division in Europe, where his expertise in skiing was put to good use. While in Europe, Miller worked to save as much of his pay as possible so that he could expand the business upon his return. Once the war ended, he returned to New Jersey with $5,000 in savings and married Isabel. In early 1946, he purchased a 7 1/2-acre parcel where he planned to erect a new store, an archery range, and a small ski slope.

**Bowcraft
Amusement Park**

2545 Route 22 West
Scotch Plains, NJ 07076

908-233-0675

www.bowcraft.com

With materials in short supply due to the postwar building boom, the Millers were lucky to obtain enough lumber to start construction. But because of those shortages, theft at the construction site became a problem. As a result, the young couple erected a tent at the site, where they lived while they finished building their new business.

In the spring of 1946, Bowcraft Park was ready for business. During its early years, the park emphasized sports activities, and the Millers were constantly trying to find new activities that would appeal to their customers. Growing from their initial base of the store, archery range, and ski slope, the Millers dammed a stream to create a small pond where they offered canoeing in the summer and ice skating in the winter. Around 1950, a miniature golf course was erected; grass tennis courts soon followed. They proved to be too fragile and were soon converted into cement courts that could also be used as an outdoor roller-skating rink in the summer and an ice-skating rink in the winter. Other attractions included badminton, batting cages, shuffleboard, table tennis, and horseback riding.

A Change in Direction

With business booming, the Miller's acquired additional property, increasing their holdings to 12 acres. But while many of the activities were successful, the ski business was tapering off in the face of increasing competition. Some of their other sports activities were also seeing decreasing popularity, and as a result, the Millers started to look for other attractions to add to increase business during the summer months.

This 1970s view from the Ferris wheel shows some of the early rides.

Around 1969, the tennis courts gave way to a go-cart track, but it was in 1973 that the direction of Bowcraft was changed forever. The Millers' children, who had become involved in the business, thought that the park should add amusement rides to bring in more summer traffic. They forged ahead with the idea and for the 1973 season undertook a major expansion that saw the addition of a number of amusement park rides, including a merry-go-round, Ferris wheel, Paratrooper, Tilt-A-Whirl, and Scrambler.

The rides were a huge success, and soon most of the original sports activities had been replaced by further rides. In 1975, a train was added, soon followed by bumper cars, paddleboats, and the Speedway, a car ride around the pond. By 1984, the park featured seventeen rides.

A Changing of the Guard

Bowcraft Amusement Park continued to thrive into the mid-1990s, but the Millers were aging, and their children were looking for other challenges in life. They decided to put the operation up for sale, and in 1996, they reached an agreement to sell it to the Marke family, which consisted of four brothers who had worked on the Jersey shore for a number of years. Bowcraft was the perfect operation for them. "It's one of the few businesses that's big enough for four brothers to work together,"

The Dragon was Bowcraft's first roller coaster when it opened in 1998.

VISITING

LOCATION

Bowcraft Amusement Park is located in northern New Jersey along U.S. Route 22. From the New Jersey Turnpike, take Exit 14 (the Newark Airport exit). Follow signs for U.S. Route 22 West. Proceed for approximately 10 miles, and the park is on the right after the third traffic light. From the Garden State Parkway, take Exit 140 (or 140A from the southbound Parkway). Follow signs for U.S. Route 22 West and proceed about 7^1/$_2$ miles. Bowcraft is on the right after the third traffic light.

OPERATING SCHEDULE

Bowcraft is open weekends in April and May from 11 A.M. to 8 P.M. and weekdays in May from noon to 6 P.M. The park is open daily from 10 A.M. to 9 P.M. in June, July, and August, and weekends from noon to 6 P.M. in September and October. The arcade is open every day of the year from noon to 8 P.M.

ADMISSION

Admission is free, with rides and attractions available on a pay-as-you-go basis. Tickets can be purchased in packages: twenty tickets for $14, thirty tickets for $19, forty-five tickets for $25, or one hundred tickets for $50. Rides take four or five tickets. A pay-one-price admission is available for under $30.

FOOD

Bowcraft Amusement Park features three food outlets. The Pizza Stand, next to the Paratrooper, serves pizza, calzones, and hero sandwiches. A stand next to the train ride has burgers, hot dogs, cheese steaks, chicken sandwiches, shish kebabs, french fries, onion rings, and pretzels. A third stand near the merry-go-round offers snacks.

FOR CHILDREN

Bowcraft Amusement Park has been built with children from ages two to twelve in mind. The park features about half a dozen kiddie rides and a number of rides for the entire family, including the merry-go-round, Marke Express train, Dragon coaster, and Galleon.

SPECIAL FEATURES

While completely updated, Bowcraft is reminiscent of the kiddielands that dotted suburban America back in the 1950s and 1960s.

TIME REQUIRED

Families with smaller children can easily spend most of the day at Bowcraft Amusement Park. If you are pressed for time, the park can be enjoyed in about three hours.

TOURING TIPS

A ride on the Marke Express Train is a great way to start your visit. It circles the entire park and gives you a great overview of all the attractions.

Bowcraft's ride area sits at the base of a hill.

says Steve Marke, citing the "15-acre backyard" where they could each have their own responsibilities.

The Markes immediately went to work to improve the operation. Much of the pavement was upgraded by adding brick walkways, new buildings were constructed, and many of the older rides were replaced.

Given the park's appeal to smaller children, a 12,000-square-foot birthday party area was constructed in 1998, and four new rides were added, including Bowcraft's first roller coaster—the Dragon. The 1999 season saw the addition of two kiddie rides. Three larger rides—the Barnstormer, the Crazy Sub, and the Convoy—opened in 2000. Other recent additions included the Giant Slide in 2001 and the Galleon swinging ship in 2002.

Having totally remade their ride lineup and renovated much of the park, the Markes realized that one major feature was missing from their park: a water area where kids could cool off on a hot day. Plans are to have the new water park, which will include a 10,000-square-foot water play area, a river ride, and four 14-foot-tall water slides, ready for the 2005 season.

Bowcraft Amusement Park Today

Nearly half a century after opening as an archery range, ski slope, and sporting goods store on a 7 1/2-acre site, Bowcraft Amusement Park has grown into a full-fledged 25-acre amusement park for families with children under age twelve. The park features twenty-three rides, a miniature golf course, and an arcade.

Front and center at the park is the sporting goods store that started it all, long since converted into the park's arcade. To the left of the arcade is a midway leading past the Flying Swings, Barnstormer, and train rides, toward the birthday party building and the miniature golf course. To the right of the arcade sit the Paratrooper, bumper cars, and Dragon roller coaster. Most of the park's rides are found toward the back, including the merry-go-round, Tilt-A-Whirl, Crazy Sub, Galleon, and Speedway.

Land of Make Believe

OPENED 1954

LOCATED IN THE ROLLING COUNTRYSIDE AND FARMLAND OF NORTHWEST New Jersey is the small community of Hope. Founded in 1769 as a settlement of the Moravian religious order, it is the first planned community in the United States. Today the town is known for the sturdy limestone buildings that the Moravians constructed. Despite this staid landscape, the sounds of happy children emanate from the outskirts of town as they enjoy the fun-filled activities offered on the site of a former dairy farm, now an amusement park that for half a century has attracted families from throughout the Northeast.

Founding Father

Hermann Maier was frustrated. A former educator and businessman living in Brooklyn in the early 1940s, he delighted in taking his children to nearby amusement areas such as Coney Island and Jones Beach. But he was dismayed by the fact that most times, he was relegated to the role of a passive spectator, because no children's rides accommodated adults.

"I looked forward to being a father, and I felt gypped," his son Christopher recalls him saying. As a result, turning that frustration into inspiration, he decided to start a place where children and their parents could enjoy attractions together.

After traveling the region for a few years, gathering ideas and making plans, he set out to find an appropriate parcel of land on which to create his dream park. Maier soon found a dairy farm outside Hope, 55 miles from New York City.

Land of Make Believe
P.O. Box 295
Hope, NJ 07844
809-459-9000
www.lomb.com

124

Not only could he make use of the existing buildings, but it also was in a gorgeous natural setting at the foot of Jenny Jump Mountain.

The mountain's unusual name is an integral part of the history of the farm that Maier acquired. In 1748, when this part of New Jersey was the frontier, a Swedish family built a home where Land of Make Believe now stands. One day, the owner's nine-year-old daughter was up on the mountain picking berries when Indians started chasing her. She ran to a rock ledge and shouted to her father standing below. Her father, standing below, told her, "Jump, Jenny, jump." Jenny's fate is not known. In honor of the incident, the state of New Jersey named the mountain and a state park next to Land of Make Believe in her honor.

Though it is not known exactly what happened to Jenny, Hermann Maier was able to confirm that the family did actually exist and lived on the site. The house they occupied still stands as an attraction in the park, with an addition dating from the 1800s being the only major change. In fact, visitors can still operate the well dug by Jenny's family and can hike up the mountain to view the rock and relive the legend.

Hermann Maier bought the property and set out to create his Land of Make Believe. Drawing upon his experience as an educator, he developed attractions that reflected the thoughts and dreams of children. The former dairy barn was converted into Santa's Barn, where children could climb up through the chimney to visit Santa at his summer home in New Jersey.

In front of Santa's Barn, Maier created the Candy Cane Forest, a collection of huge candy canes made from concrete using molds he created. Fifty years later, children still delight in running through the forest of larger-than-life candy.

Another nearby barn was converted into the Haunted Halloween House, a spook house created with kids in mind. The Country Store refreshment stand and Cookie House gift shop were converted from chicken coops.

The Land of Make Believe also featured several new attractions. At the end of the park opposite from Santa's Barn, Maier built a Wild West area featuring Fort Wilderness, a frontier fort constructed using timber harvested from the wooded property, alongside an Indian Village and a Trading Post. There was a large Pirate Ship, which originally was a float used in the 1952 Macy's Thanksgiving Parade, along with a Nativity Chapel. Families could enjoy a petting zoo full of farm animals at Old McDonald's Farm. As a former resident of Brooklyn, Maier observed that it was particularly important to include a place where children could interact with farm animals, as many kids, though familiar with exotic animals at the zoo, didn't know the difference between a sheep and a goat.

Maier also created four rides that could be enjoyed by the entire family: a tractor-drawn hayride called the Alfalfa Express, a horse-drawn hayride, the Pumpkin Coach, and a Fire Engine.

On August 6, 1954, Hermann Maier made his dream come true when he opened Land of Make Believe as the first facility where parents could participate with their kids in all of the activities. As the original park brochure stated, it was a place "Where Songs and Stories Come to Life."

Land of Make Believe was an immediate success, and soon Maier was looking for new ways to entertain his visitors. One of the first attractions added was Colonel Corn, a magical scarecrow that that carried on conversations with visitors. According to legend, Colonel Corn was an ordinary scarecrow in a field until a witch who lived in the Haunted Halloween House thought he would be happier in Land of Make Believe and gave him a ride back to the park on her broomstick. Even today, talking with Colonel Corn is rated by children as one of the most memorable parts of their visit to Land of Make Believe.

Aerial view of Land of Make Believe from the 1950s, showing its original attractions and layout. LAND OF MAKE BELIEVE

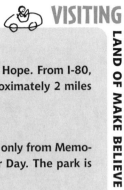

VISITING

LOCATION

Land of Make Believe is located on NJ Route 611, just outside Hope. From I-80, take Exit 12 (NJ Route 521 South), and follow the signs approximately 2 miles to NJ Route 519, then take NJ Route 611 to the park.

OPERATING SCHEDULE

Land of Make Believe is open from 10 A.M. to 6 P.M., weekends only from Memorial Day to mid-June, and daily from mid-June through Labor Day. The park is also open the first weekend after Labor Day.

ADMISSION

Pay-one-price admission of under $20 entitles visitors to all rides and attractions, with the exception of games. Parking is free.

FOOD

Land of Make Believe has eight different food service facilities. Mama Santa's Pizza is located in Santa's Barn and has air-conditioned seating. The Country Store, next to the merry-go-round, serves hot dogs and hamburgers. The nearby Chicken Chalet specializes in chicken nuggets. You may bring food into the park and use the designated picnic area. Glass and grills are not permitted.

FOR CHILDREN

Land of Make Believe was created with the idea that parents and kids should be able to enjoy activities together. As a result, only a few attractions have any height restrictions.

SPECIAL FEATURES

Land of Make Believe is one of the few amusement parks in the country designed for children and their parents to share. Nearly all of the activities can be enjoyed by the entire family. Favorites include the train, Alfala Express hay ride, and Pirate's Cove wading pool.

TIME REQUIRED

Land of Make Believe can easily fill an entire day, especially if you have kids. If time is limited, the park can be enjoyed in about three hours if you skip the water park.

TOURING TIPS

Try to visit on a weekday, when the park tends to be less crowded. A ride on the train is a great way to kick off your visit, as it circles the entire park and gives you a great overview.

Crowds at the water park tend to peak during the middle of the day, when it is hottest. To avoid the rush, visit early or late in the day.

Jet Star

Land of Make Believe Hope, N.J.

Land of Make Believe started installing traditional amusement park rides in 1976. The Star Jet is the last of the original rides still in operation. THE SCHELLER COMPANY

The park remained popular, and Maier continued to make enhancements, although he removed Fort Wilderness in the face of increasing maintenance costs. In the 1970s, the park expanded its appeal to older kids by adding traditional amusement park rides. The first rides were installed in 1976 with the opening of the merry-go-round, Little Dipper roller coaster, kiddie whip, and Star Jet, which remains in operation.

In 1980, the CP Huntington train began operation. Built by Chance Manufacturing of Wichita, Kansas, the train is a miniature replica of one constructed in Patterson, New Jersey, in 1862 and completely circles the park. The train was soon followed by several smaller rides, including a car ride and the Red Baron, an airplane ride that replaced the kiddie whip.

Additions were not limited to rides. In 1982, Christopher Maier, who had by now taken over operation of the park from his father, found the front portion of a DC-3 airplane sitting abandoned behind a barn. An avid pilot, he knew that the relic would be a great addition to the park, allowing the entire family to experience the thrill of sitting in a real airplane cockpit.

Throughout the 1980s, Land of Make Believe grew by adding new rides such as the Dixie Cars in 1986, the Himalaya in 1987, and the Dragon in 1988, a year in which major changes occurred to the park.

Wet and Wild

In July 1988, a record heat wave descended on much of America, with temperatures at Land of Make Believe often exceeding 90 degrees. Not only was the scorching weather hurting business, as most people left by early afternoon, but it was also wreaking havoc on the landscaping.

One sweltering day, Christopher Maier put some sprinklers out to water the grass in an effort to save the lawn. Almost immediately, kids started running through the sprinklers to cool off. "It became the most popular attraction in the park," he recalls. He soon realized that a water park was crucial to the park's long-term success.

After working for nearly three years to obtain the necessary zoning changes, planning began on the new water park. Construction began in December 1991 on Land of Make Believe's largest expansion ever. In keeping with its founding mission, Maier wanted the water park to be a place where parents could interact with their children. As a result, the heart of the area is a 12,200-square-foot wading pool—billed as the world's largest—surrounded by small slides shaped like frogs and seashells, built just for little kids and their parents. In the center of the pool is a lifesize 42-foot-long pirate ship with fountains, slides, and water

Land of Make Believe's water park is one of its most popular features.

cannons. Replacing the Indian Village, Pirate's Cove was an immediate success, and customers flocked to the park like never before.

The Pirate Ship was custom-made for Land of Make Believe by New Brunfels General Store (NBGS), the world's premier manufacturer of water-based attractions. NBGS wanted to sell Land of Make Believe one of its submarine-themed water play areas, but Maier thought the confined spaces would discourage adults from joining their children. The idea of a Pirate Ship appealed to Maier, however, and he worked closely with NBGS to develop one that fit his vision.

For the 1993 season, the park moved in a new direction with the opening of the Middle Earth Theater. Unlike most live entertainment, the parents and children participated in the show, dressing up in costumes and acting out parts together.

By the 1990s, Land of Make Believe's original roller coaster was in need of replacement, and the park purchased a new junior-size roller coaster from the Miler Coaster Company. With a maximum height of 10 feet, the ride accommodates even the smallest rider. In a contest open to visitors, the new coaster was named the Thriller.

With the increasing popularity of Pirate's Cove, expansion in 1995 moved back into the water park with the addition of Blackbeard's Action River. The 800-foot-long attraction has many special features, such as waterfalls, geysers, fountains, and a wave-making machine that accounted for 70 percent of the $1 million construction cost. At 20 feet, Action River is twice as wide as similar attractions at other parks, and the second widest ever constructed. This allows the family to travel down the river together with enough room for a passing lane for those looking to travel faster.

For the visitors, the highlight of the 1996 season was the addition of a Tilt-A-Whirl ride. For the park, however, the most important development of the year was a change in local zoning regulations that permitted Land of Make Believe to build attractions up to 75 feet high.

Since then, Land of Make Believe has alternated between expanding the Pirate's Cove water park and the amusement park side of the operation. In 1997, visitors were introduced to Pirate's Peak, a 40-foot-tall tower with two 400-foot-long water slides.

That was followed in 1998 by the addition of two rides from Sellner Manufacturing: T-Rex, in which riders spun around inside a friendly dinosaur, and the Windjammer, where patrons operated miniature hang gliders. In 1999, the Black Hole opened in the water park. The Black Hole is a completely enclosed water slide in which riders descend in total darkness. When it opened, water slide expert Bill McCartney rated it as the best in the country.

The Red Baron and Tornado are some of Land of Make Believe's newer rides.

In 2000, Land of Make Believe celebrated the new millennium by adding two rides. Since the year was dubbed the International Year of the Carousel by the International Association of Amusement Parks and Attractions, Land of Make Believe replaced its original merry-go-round with a new one manufactured by Chance Rides that features fiberglass replicas of turn-of-the-century carousel figures. Also added was the Frog Hopper, a bouncing tower ride. The next year, the Himalaya was replaced by the Tornado, a high-speed spinning ride, and in 2002, the only Sidewinder in the Eastern United States opened in Pirate's Cove. The Sidewinder is a unique water-based thrill ride in which riders drop into a giant U-shaped structure and slide back and forth. Most recently, a two-story, interactive Pirate Fort water play area debuted in 2003, featuring a giant bucket holding 1,000 gallons of water that tips over at regular intervals, drenching anyone nearby.

Land of Make Believe Today

A half century after its founding, Land of Make Believe remains true to its mission of providing a full day's worth of activities that parents and children can enjoy together. The 30-acre park at the foot of Jenny Jump Mountain now features fifteen rides, a full-scale water park, petting zoo, the Haunted Halloween House, and many other attractions.

Upon entering the park, visitors can enjoy the merry-go-round, Maze, and Candy Cane Forest. Behind the Candy Cane Forest is Santa's Barn. Originally a dairy barn, it now features a gift shop, Mama Santa's Pizza, and the New Jersey home of Santa Claus. Don't miss the fireplace that serves as the entrance to the North Pole.

In the vicinity of Santa's Barn are many of the park's oldest attractions, such as Colonel Corn, the Jenny Jump House, the Haunted Halloween House, and Old McDonald's Farm, in addition to the Train Depot. Past the Train Depot are most of Land of Make Believe's rides, including the Tornado, Windjammer, Red Baron, and Thriller roller coaster.

Next comes the Middle Earth Theater, the DC-3 cockpit, and the entrance to the water park. At the water park, visitors will find the Pirate's Cove huge wading pool complete with the Pirate Ship water play area, Blackbeard's Action River, Blackbeard's Pirate Port, three water slides, and the unique Sidewinder.

Storybook Land

OPENED 1955

STORYBOOK LAND IS AN OASIS ALONG A BUSY SUBURBAN THOROUGHFARE. Nestled in among the shopping centers and motels is a white castle beckoning to passersby. The high board fence in front obscures the delights that await inside. A trip through the castle brings you to Storybook Land and all of its enchanting attractions.

Building the Dream

John and Esther Fricano were like many Americans in the early 1950s. John was a World War II veteran and worked as a house painter while Esther cared for their two children. In the summer, the family would take vacations in their automobile. During one trip, however, the Fricanos became frustrated after a day of driving when there was little for their kids to do to unwind.

The Fricanos thought it would be a good idea to open a small road-side attraction for families to enjoy while driving to vacation spots along the Jersey shore. They wisely selected a wooded 5-acre parcel along Black Horse Pike, just 10 miles west of Atlantic City. At the time, there was little more than a horse-racing track and a couple of restaurants in the vicinity, but the road was the main route connecting the Philadelphia area with the Atlantic coast. Thousands of cars packed with families traveled the road every day.

The Fricanos soon went to work on their new park. John cleared the site by hand and erected all of the attractions himself, while Esther took

> **Storybook Land**
> 6415 Black Horse Pike—Cardiff
> Egg Harbor Township
> NJ 08234
> 609-641-7847
> www.storybookland.com

care of furnishing and decorating the buildings. The Fricanos chose to fill the property with re-created scenes from favorite storybook tales to appeal to a wide audience.

When Storybook Land opened in the summer of 1955, the main attractions were displays of beloved storybook tales. These included Humpty Dumpty, Jack & Jill's Hill, the House That Jack Built, Little Miss Muffet, Little Boy Blue, the Three Bears House, the Old Woman's Shoe, and the Little Red School House with Mary's Little Lamb, which remains as Storybook Land's last original structure. Many of the attractions were built at the Fricanos' house in Vineland, New Jersey, and hauled to the site piece by piece, where they were erected by a homemade crane made out of telephone poles.

There were two rides in Storybook Land: a genuine 1929 fire engine that was adapted to give rides around the grounds and the Jolly Trolley, a trackless train ride. Fricano discovered the train while it was being used as a promotional vehicle by the Baltimore Orioles. A luncheonette was built to serve as both the entrance to the park and also as a snack bar for passing motorists.

The simple little park went over well with vacationing families. By the late 1950s, the luncheonette was replaced by a new entrance and gift shop that resembled a castle, which is a local landmark today. Other attractions were built as additional acreage was acquired, including a Pumpkin Coach ride straight out of Cinderella and the Tin Lizzys, several antique-looking kiddie cars that Fricano modified for Storybook

Storybook Land featured this simple front entrance when it opened in 1955.
STORYBOOK LAND

VISITING

LOCATION

Storybook Land is located 10 miles west of Atlantic City on Black Horse Pike (U.S. Route 40/322). From the west and north, take Exit 37 off the Garden State Parkway. Turn right and follow signs to Route 40/322 West. The park entrance is two miles on the left. From the south, take Exit 36 off the Garden State Parkway. Turn left at traffic light, then left on Tilton Road, then left on Route 40/322 West (approximately three miles).

OPERATING SCHEDULE

Storybook Land is open weekends from mid-March until the beginning of May, daily from May through August, and weekends in September and October. Opening time varies from 10 A.M. to 11A.M. and closing time from 3 P.M. to 5 P.M., depending on the time of year.

The park is open for the Christmas Fantasy with Lights celebration on weekends from mid-November through Thanksgiving and daily from the Friday after Thanksgiving until the end of December, with opening times ranging from 2 P.M. to 4:30 P.M.

ADMISSION

Admission of under $20 covers all rides and attractions. Parking is free.

FOOD

Storybook Land has two food outlets. The Gingerbread House serves Mother Goose meals for kids, cheese steaks, burgers, hot dogs, chicken nuggets, grilled cheese, french fries, and ice cream. The Snack Station offers up pizza, hot dogs, chicken nuggets, french fries, popcorn, and nachos. Both have indoor and outdoor seating. You can bring your own food into the park. A picnic pavilion is available.

FOR CHILDREN

For nearly fifty years, Storybook Land has focused on children ages ten and under and their families. As a result, the entire family can enjoy nearly all of the attractions at the park.

SPECIAL FEATURES

Few parks in the country are as immaculately cared for as Storybook Land. With its spotless walkways, carefully tended gardens, and rides that look almost new, the care put into the operation is evident throughout the park.

Storybook Land is full of displays re-creating beloved storybook tales. Among the best is the Three Bears House. The animated bears retelling the story mesmerize kids of all ages.

Don't miss Alice in Wonderland, one of the most creative family-oriented walk-through attractions found in any amusement park.

(continued on page 136)

VISITING (continued from page 135)

TIME REQUIRED

Families with smaller children can easily spend most of the day at Storybook Land. If you are pressed for time, the park can be enjoyed in about three hours.

TOURING TIPS

A ride on the Candy Cane Express or J&J Railroad is a great way to start your visit. They both circle the entire park and give you a great overview of all the attractions.

The park offers a number of special features in October, including fall flowers, Elmer's Hay-Mazin' Maze, pumpkin decorating, hayrides, and trick-or-treat weekend, when kids can go through the park and receive treats.

Land. When Storybook Village, a nearby competitor, closed in 1962, Storybook Land was able to expand further with the acquisitions of the Sleeping Beauty Castle, the Crooked House, and a picnic pavilion shaped like a giant birthday cake.

The Fricanos have long been collectors, and over the years, they have used this interest to fill the park with unique attractions. In the early 1960s, they brought the Chapel of Peace to the park from Vineland. The 15-by-20-foot chapel was originally constructed in 1885 by eighteen-year-old Andrew Cresci as a gift for his parents, and even includes stained-glass windows that Cresci created. Nearby is an authentic, full-size railroad caboose. "It was something we had to have," says Fricano. The family had found it in

The Jolly Trolley was one of Storybook Land's original attractions. STORYBOOK LAND

The Alice in Wonderland walk-through is one of Storybook Land's most distinctive attractions.

Vineland, where it was used as a railroad office. They purchased it and moved it to the park to use as a party room. Several other artifacts are scattered throughout the grounds, including antique cars, exotic birds, and a clock from the 1920s that once adorned the city of Vineland. Even the fire truck remained on display after it was retired as a ride.

By now the operation had greatly increased in size, and in 1969, the Fricanos' two children, JoAnne and John Jr., became involved with the operation.

Storybook Land's other original ride, the Jolly Trolley, was replaced in 1971 by the Happy Train, another trackless train ride that was built by Fricano. In the early 1970s, Storybook Land added what has since become one of its most popular features—Alice in Wonderland. This walk-through attraction allows visitors to relive the beloved story, wandering into the rabbit hole, with more adventurous visitors going down a slide, and then traveling through a cave where enchanting displays tell the tale. When visitors emerge from the cave, they navigate a maze of giant playing cards to exit the attraction.

Expanding the Season

One of the park's most beloved traditions debuted in 1980, when the park first opened during the holiday season for the Christmas Fantasy with Lights. For years, Santa Claus had made occasional appearances at

Storybook Land's landmark castle front entrance is a key feature during the park's annual Christmas Fantasy with Lights. STORYBOOK LAND

the park during the summer season, and a corner of the park featured Santa's House, Santa's Reindeer, a Christmas Shop, and the North Pole, a pillar of ice that provided a cool diversion on the hottest of days.

For the Christmas Fantasy with Lights, the entire park was decorated with fifty thousand lights, and Santa emerged from the chimney every night to "flip the switch" and illuminate the park. The Christmas Fantasy with Lights has grown every year, and there are now five hundred thousand lights adorning the park, with more added each year.

The Christmas Fantasy with Lights kicked off a new era of growth for Storybook Land. Starting around 1980, several new mechanical rides were added, including the Flying Jumbos elephant ride and the Groovy Cars bumper car ride, and in 1982, the Rock, Spin & Roll. The following year, a merry-go-round that was manufactured in 1954 by the Allan Herschell Company made its debut. In 1984, a kiddie Ferris wheel opened, and the Happy Train was retired and replaced by the Candy Cane Express, another trackless train ride that was purchased from the defunct Paradise Lake theme park in Ohio.

A Storybook Land icon also made its debut in 1984, when a 25-foot-tall statue of Mother Goose was installed just inside the front gate. The statue also came from Paradise Lake but actually began life in 1957 at Fantasyland, a theme park in Gettysburg, Pennsylvania.

Storybook Land's expansion continued in 1986 with the addition of the Old Tymers, an antique car ride purchased from New York's Roseland Park when it closed. Other new attractions followed, such as the Flying Dragons in 1990; the Big Foot truck ride in 1992; the Sun and Moon, a replacement Ferris wheel, in 1993; and the Up, Up and Away balloon ride in 1994.

Another park staple arrived at Storybook Land in 1996 with the opening of the J&J Railroad. Named after the Fricanos' two grandchildren, Jessica and John III, the train was originally manufactured 1964 by Chance Rides of Wichita, Kansas. The Fricanos purchased it used and completely rebuilt it for the park. The Tin Lizzys, one of the park's most enduring attractions, was retired to make room for the new train.

Storybook Land had now grown to 20 acres in size. Following the 1998 addition of a whimsically themed Tilt-A-Whirl called the Turtle Twirl, the park still lacked one key attraction: a roller coaster. That was taken care of in 2001, when the park contracted with Miler Coaster of Portland, Oregon, to custom build a roller coaster. Storybook Land's primary customers are children under age ten, so it was important that the ride not be too intimidating or too rough. The result was a 15-foot-tall ride with a train resembling a happy dragon, named Bubbles, the Coaster, because of its happy connotation. A bubble machine was installed at the bottom of the first hill so that riders traveled through a cloud of bubbles. Every season, the park goes through 450 gallons of bubble solution to keep the machine stocked.

Bubbles, the Coaster, opened in 2001.

Storybook Land continues to improve and update the attractions. A new Fantasy Ferris wheel replaced the Sun and Moon wheel, and a newer version of the Flying Jumbos was installed in 2002. The original Three Bears House display was updated in 2003. Now the bears occupy a charming log cabin, and animated versions of Mama, Papa, and Baby Bear and Goldilocks relive the classic story.

Storybook Land Today

Since Storybook Land opened nearly a half century ago, it has developed into a charming, beloved New Jersey tradition. Under its lush canopy of trees, visitors will find a dozen rides, more than two dozen displays of enchanting childhood stories, live animals, and several historical displays scattered throughout the impeccable, lovingly maintained grounds.

The park is laid out roughly in an oval. From the entrance, visitors are greeted by the giant Mother Goose statue, the Little Red School House with Mary's Little Lamb, and rides such as the Fantasy Ferris wheel, merry-go-round, and Candy Cane Express. Walking around the oval, visitors will find the Happy Dragon ride, Little Red Riding Hood's House, Sleeping Beauty's Castle, and the Old Tymers cars. Bubbles, the Coaster, the Turtle Twirl, and live animals are next. Closing the loop are the J&J Railroad, Big Foot, Flying Jumbos, caboose, antique car display, the Christmas area, the Chapel of Peace, and the Three Bears House.

At the center of the oval are many of the earlier storybook displays, including Humpty Dumpty, the Jack and Jill Slide, Snow White's House, the Old Woman's Shoe, and Cinderella's Coach (now retired as a ride), along with the Alice in Wonderland attraction, Up, Up and Away Balloon ride, and the exotic bird aviary.

Funtown Pier

OPENED 1957

AT FIRST THE SOUND CAN BE DISCONCERTING. IN THE MIDST OF FUNTOWN Pier, all of a sudden, a crash can be heard beneath your feet. Again you hear the sound, and soon you realize that it is the sea crashing up against the underside of the pier. It's just another part of this seaside amusement park experience.

Born of Disaster

The roots of the current Funtown Pier lie within the oldest amusement facility in the boroughs of Seaside Heights and Seaside Park. In 1915, Joseph Vanderslice of Philadelphia came to this fledgling resort intent on opening a place to entertain the growing crowds. He built a pavilion on the Boardwalk and opened a gasoline-powered merry-go-round. The venture failed after a single season, but Frank Freeman saw opportunity in the shuttered venture.

Freeman acquired the pavilion, expanded it, and brought in an all-new electric-powered carousel manufactured by the Dentzel Carousel Company of Philadelphia. This endeavor was much more successful than Vanderslice's. Through the 1920s and 1930s, Freeman expanded the facility, building an outdoor deck for a few rides. In the 1940s, the operation passed into the hands of J. Stanley Tunney, who was also the mayor of Seaside Heights.

By now the park, called Freeman's Amusements, served as the southern anchor for the bustling Boardwalk. But it was almost lost. At 6 A.M. on June 9, 1955, a fire broke out. Fifty mile-

Funtown Amusement Pier
1930 Boardwalk
P.O. Box 248
Seaside Park, NJ 08752
732-830-PIER (7437)
www.funtownpier.com

per-hour winds fanned the flames, spreading the fire throughout the surrounding neighborhood. By the time it was extinguished, four blocks of the Boardwalk, housing fifty concessions along with Freeman's Amusements, were lost.

Most distressing was the loss of the carousel, which had become a beloved Boardwalk landmark. Tunney, who had a lifelong affection for carousels, immediately found another machine to operate on a temporary basis while a more permanent replacement was located. He located a carousel for sale at Coney Island, the renowned New York amusement resort, and purchased it for $22,000. He then spent another $20,000 to relocate and renovate it, painting many of the animals himself.

The ride was truly something special. Carved in 1917 by Marcus Illions, who was known for manufacturing elaborate carousel animals, the machine featured sixty-four animals arranged in four rows, fifty-six of which moved up and down. To make the ride unique, Tunney replaced some of the Illions figures with richly jeweled animals carved by Charles Carmel and M. D. Borelli from the temporary machine. This carousel remained a Boardwalk favorite until it was broken up and sold to collectors in 1990. A modern fiberglass machine from Chance Rides now turns in its space.

Although Tunney quickly rebuilt Freeman's Amusements, the fire inspired him to grander visions. With Casino Pier on the north end of the

Funtown Pier grew out of the ashes of the fire that destroyed Freeman's Amusements in 1955. This picture shows Freeman's in the 1940s.

VISITING

FUNTOWN PIER

LOCATION

Funtown Pier is located in central New Jersey, straddling the boundary between Seaside Heights and Seaside Park. From the New Jersey Turnpike, take Exit 11, Garden State Parkway South, and take the Parkway to Exit 82. Follow NJ Route 37 East to the Mathis Bridge to the fork. Keep to the right for Seaside Park, and look for the Giant Wheel and the Tower of Fear. Parking is available for an additional fee in the lot at Porter Avenue and Boardwalk and at numerous other local lots.

OPERATING SCHEDULE

Funtown Pier is open weekends at noon, from Easter weekend through mid-June and in September. From mid-June through Labor Day, the park opens daily at noon. Closing time varies by the time of year.

ADMISSION

Admission is free, with rides and attractions available on a pay-as-you-go basis. Ride tickets cost about 75 cents each, and rides require from four to fourteen tickets. A pay-one-price admission is available on Wednesdays, entitling visitors to all rides.

FOOD

About half a dozen food stands offer a variety of traditional snacks such as hot dogs, pretzels, and lemonade. Many other food options are also available on the nearby Boardwalk.

FOR CHILDREN

With about fifteen kiddie rides, Funtown Pier has one of the heaviest concentrations on the Jersey shore. The park also has a number of rides for the entire family, including the merry-go-round, Giant Wheel, Under the Sea dark ride, and Raiders and Ice Age fun houses.

SPECIAL FEATURES

Funtown Pier features one of the tallest Ferris wheels in the state of New Jersey. Its placement close to the oceanfront provides a spectacular view.

TIME REQUIRED

Funtown Pier can be experienced in about three hours, but you should plan to spend the day in Seaside Heights and enjoy the beach, Boardwalk, and nearby Casino Pier and Waterworks.

TOURING TIPS

Visit on a Wednesday. Crowds are lighter, and it is the only day of the week when a pay-one-price admission is available. For less than $20, you can enjoy all of the rides from noon until 6 P.M. In addition, admission to the beach is free on Wednesdays, and there is a fireworks display in the evening.

Funtown Pier's Wild Mouse was the first roller coaster to operate in the towns of Seaside Heights and Seaside Park.

Boardwalk now growing into a competitor, Tunney wanted to build a major amusement destination at the southern end. He combined efforts with other businessmen in the neighborhood to develop much of the burnt-out area into a new amusement facility, constructing a new pier straddling the line between the bustling Seaside Heights Boardwalk and the more sedate Seaside Park Boardwalk. Construction began in 1956, and in the spring of 1957, Funtown USA was open for business.

Funtown's owners operated the new business as landlords, renting out much of the space to concessionaires who would bring in rides, games, and food stands. Among the early rides at Funtown were a Rocket Ship swing; the Sun Valley, with cars that traveled over a circular, undulating track; a Roto Jet; Fly-O-Plane; Tilt-A-Whirl; Haunted Castle dark ride; a train; and the Wild Mouse, the seaside resort's first roller coaster.

Flagship Attractions

Funtown built one of its most distinctive rides in 1961, with the addition of the Sky Ride. It was developed by the Allan Herschell Company of North Tonowanda, New York, and represented a new type of sky ride in which riders in four-person cars traveled on an elevated rail. Funtown purchased Herschell's first version of the ride for $50,000 and erected it over the pier. At 1,500 feet long, it traveled 14 feet above the ground and became an immediate hit, attracting more than 71,000 riders in its first five weeks of operation at 35 cents per ride.

Funtown USA was now firmly established as a major amusement facility. As a result, the park teamed up with surrounding concessions to create the Funtown USA Association, a marketing group that coordinated promotional efforts for the southern end of the Boardwalk.

Another unique prototype ride made a brief appearance at Funtown in 1965, with the opening of the Moon Shot. The ride consisted of a series of nine tubs on a circular track that riders were able to spin. Riders tried to maneuver a miniature missile attached to each car so it came in contact with one of two overhead targets.

Through the 1970s, a wide array of rides were featured at Funtown. In 1970, a fun house was added, and the Supersonic roller coaster, a compact steel-track roller coaster from Pinfari, an Italian manufacturer, debuted in 1973. By now the pier had become a major showcase of imported European rides, including spinning rides such as the Polyp, Bayern Kurve, Telecombat, Rotor, and Himalaya.

In 1977, Funtown Pier, under the ownership of Mike Brown, undertook its largest expansion ever and added the biggest ride to appear in the Seaside Heights–Seaside Park area. Built at a cost of $2 million by Arrow Manufacturing, the new ride was one of the largest log flumes ever constructed, measuring 2,060 feet long. It occupied two-thirds of

Funtown Pier's Sky Ride was the first of its kind when it opened in 1961.

Funtown Pier's log flume was one of the largest ever built when it opened in 1977.
OWEN KANZLER AERIAL PHOTOGRAPHY, LINDEN, NEW JERSEY

the pier and featured two splash-downs and a lengthy section that traveled high above the pier. In addition to the flume, the Jet Star, a steel-track roller coaster, and a haunted house were also added. To make room for the new attractions, the Sky Ride and a number of other larger rides were removed.

Throughout the 1980s, most of the remaining thrill rides gave way to family rides, and Funtown Pier promoted itself primarily as a kiddie park in addition to being home to one of the world's biggest log flumes. A 35,000-square-foot addition to the pier in 1982 allowed the kiddie park to double in size. Three water slides also anchored the end of the pier opposite from the flume.

A Change of Pace

In 1989, Bill Major purchased Funtown Pier and started an improvement program that continues to this day. First, he added two major rides: the Giant Wheel, a 120-foot-tall Ferris wheel purchased for $500,000, and the Roller Coast Loop, a 48-foot-tall, 1,831-foot-long looping roller coaster. Manufactured by Pinfari, an Italian firm, the Roller Coast Loop was erected right at the edge of the pier overlooking the ocean.

In 1993, a new light show was placed on the Giant Wheel in honor of the one hundredth anniversary of the opening of the original Ferris wheel.

While the flume remained a popular ride, the fact that it took up so much space on the pier precluded any meaningful expansion. As a result, it was removed in 1997. Over the next few seasons, a number of new rides took its place, including a large go-cart track, bumper cars, and the Raiders fun house in 1998; and a Himalaya and Go Gator kiddie coaster in 1999.

The pier received a new trademark ride for the 2000 season with the opening of the Tower of Fear. Built by S&S Power of Utah, the Tower of Fear used compressed air to shoot riders up a tower at high speeds. The 225-foot-tall ride was and still is the tallest amusement ride on the Jersey shore. But the Tower of Fear was not the only new addition that season. Kids benefited from the addition of a junior-size flume ride, a kiddie swinging ship, and their own version of the Tower of Fear, the Jumpin' Star. The next year saw the addition of the Under the Sea kiddie dark ride and kiddie go-carts.

The 2003 season saw a series of concession buildings demolished to increase the amount of space available for rides by 25 percent. A number of kiddie rides were added, including junior go-carts, bumper cars, flying elephants, and airplanes, along with the Hip Hop, a smaller version of the Tower of Fear, and a large Haunted House walk-through attraction.

Roller Coast Loop was added in 1989.

Funtown Pier today features a wide array of rides.

Funtown Pier Today

Funtown Pier has grown to be one of the largest amusement piers in New Jersey, featuring a constantly changing variety of more than thirty rides and numerous other attractions. Entering the park from the Seaside Heights Boardwalk, visitors will pass the Carousel Family Entertainment Center, the original Freeman's Amusements building, with its merry-go-round and large game arcade. At this end of the park are attractions such as the Haunted House, Big Wheel, and Tower of Fear.

Continuing along the midway, rides such as the Roller Coaster Loop, Arctic Circle Himalaya, go-carts, and Chaos can be found. The remainder of the pier is home to most of the kiddie rides. Along the Boardwalk are kiddie rides such as the merry-go-round, Himalaya, train, Go Gator coaster, elephants, Safari Jeeps, and pirate ship. At the far end of the park are the Under the Sea dark ride, Raiders, kiddie go-carts, and kiddie flume.

Wild West City

OPENED 1957

A DUSTY MAIN STREET STRAIGHT OUT OF THE OLD WEST IS NOT EXACTLY something you would expect to find in New Jersey. But this street is different. It's Wild West City, a northern New Jersey institution since 1957.

The Wild West Comes to the East

The late 1950s were a time when the new suburban automobile culture of America was seeking out diversions for weekend drives. Throughout the country, entrepreneurs responded by opening a variety of amusement attractions. Seizing upon the trend of Westerns on television and the movies, Wild West parks were popular, with three opening in New Jersey alone.

In northern New Jersey, a group of five investors led by Justus Nienauber formed the Enterprises for the Preservation of Old Americana to construct a Wild West park. They decided to model the facility after Dodge City, Kansas, of the 1880s and spent a year researching the town, even sending their architect to Kansas to study the town's archives.

In the fall of 1956, construction began on the $150,000 project, and by the following spring, the town was completed. Wild West City featured twenty-one buildings clustered around a 400-foot-long dirt street. There was a church, marshall's office, jail, saloon, and blacksmith shop. A train, stagecoach, and ponies offered rides.

While Wild West City was initially a success, around 1960, the owners leased the park to an operator who ran it into the ground and never

Wild West City
P.O. Box 37
Route 206 North
Netcong, NJ 07857
973-347-8900
www.wildwestcity.com

paid rent. According to one of the current owners, Michael Stabile, Nienauber and several of his friends showed up one day to evict the leaseholder, marching up Main Street to confront the operator. "It was a lot like a High Noon battle," recalls Stabile. Nienauber succeeded in evicting the leaseholder, but several employees trashed the park and it was closed. It appeared that Wild West City would join New Jersey's other Wild West parks as a ghost town.

Saved by the Good Guys

Wild West City's "hero in the white hat" was Michael Stabile Sr., a World War II veteran, Pearl Harbor survivor, truck driver, and car wash owner. Stabile and two investor friends purchased the park in 1963 and reopened it the next spring. "The place was in pretty rough shape," remembers his son Michael Jr. "It needed lots of TLC."

As Wild West City was resurrected, Stabile realized that his family of six could provide traditional family entertainment for other families. The Stabiles' most significant addition during those early years was a program of continuous live entertainment that takes place throughout the day along the main street. Twenty-two different shows were presented each day that reflected life in the Old West, such as the pony express delivery, a cowboy competition, the persistent undertaker, live

The Wild West comes alive in suburban New Jersey at Wild West City.

 **VISITING**

WILD WEST CITY

LOCATION

Wild West City is located 55 miles from the George Washington Bridge and 35 miles west of Newark, just off Exit 25 of I-80. From the exit, follow U.S. Route 206 North three lights to Lackawanna Drive, and turn right. Wild West City is up the road on the right.

OPERATING SCHEDULE

The park is open daily from mid-June through Labor Day, and weekends in May, September, and early October. Wild West City offers a living-history program for school groups and the general public in which daily life on the frontier is enacted by a blacksmith, schoolmarm, mountain man, and camp cook during the season.

ADMISSION

Admission of under $10 gains access to all of the live shows, exhibits, parking, picnic area, and gold panning. Rides, miniature golf, and souvenirs are extra.

FOOD

Four food stands are available, including the Silver Dollar Saloon, offering hot dogs and nachos, and the Golden Nugget Saloon, with hot dogs, sandwiches, burgers, grilled cheese, and ice cream. A picnic grove is also available.

FOR CHILDREN

Kids love the wide variety of live entertainment, in particular the stagecoach hold-up, where children are deputized and asked to help apprehend the bad guys.

SPECIAL FEATURES

Wild West City represents one of the few remaining examples of a classic 1950s roadside attraction. It is a throwback to the 1950s as well as to the 1880s.

TIME REQUIRED

With a wide array of live entertainment, a visit to Wild West City can occupy several hours.

TOURING TIPS

Try to get a seat on one of the main street's covered porches. It's a great place to view the shows that take place along Main Street.

country-western entertainment, and a stagecoach holdup in which kids were deputized, given badges, and asked to help apprehend the bad guys. The shows were very well received and continue to this day.

There were setbacks, however, such as a 1967 fire that destroyed several buildings including the jail and Marshall's office. But the Stabiles immediately rebuilt and continued to make improvements. A new stagecoach was added in 1967. The Surrey Shop, a western wear store, debuted in 1970, and a petting zoo and the Golden Nugget Saloon soon followed. Over the years, more attractions were added so that visitors could pan for gold (1982), play miniature golf (1994), experience life in a one-room schoolhouse (2000), or try their luck on Roller Roper, a device used to train cowboys how to rope calves (2001).

Wild West City Today

Today Wild West City remains an excellent, well-preserved example of the roadside attractions that dotted America in the 1950s and 1960s. Michael and Mary Stabile's children, Mary and Michael Jr., who grew up at Wild West City, now run the facility. The park features three rides (a stagecoach, train, and ponies), continuous live entertainment, fifteen Old West exhibits, miniature golf, panning for gold, and a unique attraction called a Little Bit of the Old West, an engineering masterpiece of small, hand-carved, animated wooden figures depicting life on the frontier.

Wild West City continues to be a Western film location for movies, commercials, music videos, and corporate promotional segments. The park's chapel has hosted many weddings, and the Ten Commandments chiseled in stone are on display. A weekend special events calendar includes acts such as a trick horse, Native American dancers, chuck wagon cooking, Civil War encampments, mountain man rendezvous, medicine man shows, fiddlers, and ventriloquists.

Gillian's Wonderland Pier

OPENED 1965

ANYONE WHO HAS BEEN TO OCEAN CITY, NEW JERSEY, WILL KNOW WHAT you are talking about if you tell them to meet you at the spinning W. For nearly forty years, ten spinning blocks, each one adorned with a letter spelling out W-O-N-D-E-R-L-A-N-D, have adorned the Ocean City Boardwalk, welcoming passersby to the entrance of Gillian's Wonderland Pier.

A Family Tradition

The story of Wonderland Pier actually predates its 1965 opening by half a century. In 1914, musician David Gillian arrived in Ocean City to get a job with an orchestra at Hippodrome Pier, the largest theater in town. He spent his summers playing at the pier, and during the winter he lived in Philadelphia, where he played with hotel orchestras. But in 1927, the Hippodrome burnt down, and Gillian found himself out of a job.

The amusement industry had been in Gillian's blood since he was a boy growing up in Easton, Pennsylvania. Some of his first jobs were at local amusement parks, and he promised himself that one day he would own a merry-go-round. That dream became a reality when he talked to Mr. Otis Townsend, who operated a miniature golf course along the Boardwalk, and convinced him to lease Gillian space to operate a merry-go-round. He purchased a used merry-go-round that was manufactured in 1925 by Spillman Engineering of North Tonowanda, New York, and opened it on Townsend's property in

Gillian's Wonderland Pier
6th St. & Boardwalk
P.O. Box 365
Ocean City, NJ 08226
609-399-7082

Gillian's Island
Plymouth Place & Boardwalk
P.O. Box 1186
Ocean City, NJ 08226
609-399-0483

www.gillians.com

1930. That was the beginning of Gillian's Fun Deck. The success of the merry-go-round prompted him to add a Ferris wheel in 1931. By 1945, the business had grown to the point that Gillian was able to purchase the property from Townsend. By now, the Fun Deck also featured a Tilt-A-Whirl and three kiddie rides.

Although the operation was modest in scope, it quickly became one of the most popular destinations on the Boardwalk and provided Gillian with the means to support his family. Two of his sons, Bob and Roy, were particularly enamored with the business and started working there. In 1953, Roy, who started working on the merry-go-round at age twelve, returned from the Army to work full time at the Fun Deck. As he became more experienced, Roy caught the attention of Bud Hunt, who was developing his own amusement pier in nearby Wildwood. He offered Roy a job managing his new pier. David Gillian figured that if Roy was worth that much to Hunt, then Gillian should make the same opportunity available to Roy. In 1957, David retired and sold the operation to Roy and his brother.

Running the Fun Deck with his brother was a fulfilling career, but Roy Gillian wanted something more. Just a few blocks down the Boardwalk from the Fun Deck was the former site of Stainton's Playland, an amusement park that burned down in 1955. The land had sat vacant since then, so Roy approached Howard Stainton, who still owned the site, and asked what he planned to do with it. Stainton told Roy Gillian, "You

226   The "Fun Deck" Plymouth Place and Boardwalk, Ocean City, N. J.

Gillian's Fun Deck was one of the first amusement facilities in Ocean City when it opened in 1930.

LOCATION

Gillian's Wonderland Pier and Gillian's Island water park are located along the Ocean City Boardwalk. Take Exit 30 off the Garden State Parkway, and follow NJ Route 52 East into Ocean City. Wonderland is located between Fifth and Sixth Streets; Gillian's Island is located off Plymouth Place. Parking is available for an additional fee at independently owned lots throughout town.

OPERATING SCHEDULE

Gillian's Wonderland operates weekends from Palm Sunday weekend through May, from 1 P.M. to 11 P.M. From the first Friday in June through mid-June, Wonderland is open weekdays from 6 P.M. to 11 P.M. and weekends from 1 P.M. to 11 P.M. Between mid-June and Labor Day, operating hours are 1 P.M. to 11 P.M. daily. The park is then open weekends from 1 P.M. to 11 P.M. through October, and weeknights during the first three weeks of September.

Gillian's Island is open daily from 9 A.M. to 5 P.M. from Memorial Day weekend to mid-June, and from 9:30 A.M. to 6:30 P.M. from mid-June through Labor Day.

ADMISSION

Admission to Gillian's Wonderland is free, with rides and attractions available on a pay-as-you-go basis. Ride tickets cost 75 cents each, and rides require from one to four tickets.

Admission to Gillian's Island is separate. An all-day pass to the water park costs under $25, and two- and three-hour passes are available for less.

FOOD

Gillian's Wonderland Pier has three food stands that serve traditional amusement park fare such as hot dogs, cotton candy, and popcorn. All of the food stands are located in the main building, facing the Boardwalk. Gillian's Island also has a refreshment stand. A wide variety of food outlets also can be found along the Boardwalk.

FOR CHILDREN

Wonderland Pier offers two kiddie ride areas. The larger of the two is located in the main building and features five kiddie rides and six additional rides, including an antique carousel and monorail that can be enjoyed by the entire family. The second kiddie area is located in the Fun Deck section and includes seven kiddie rides, along with the Raiders and Glass House walk-through attractions.

Many of the other rides, including the Giant Wheel, Crazy Dazy, and Galleon, can be enjoyed by most members of the family.

SPECIAL FEATURES

Gillian's has one of only three antique carousels in the state of New Jersey, and the only one carved by the Philadelphia Toboggan Company. It is a true classic and not to be missed. (continued on page 156)

VISITING (continued from page 155)

TIME REQUIRED

Gillian's Wonderland Pier can be enjoyed in about two hours, with an additional two hours needed for Gillian's Island. However, a visit can be a full-day experience when coupled with the beach and nearby Playland's Castaway Cove.

TOURING TIPS

About a third of Wonderland Pier's rides are located in the large Boardwalk-side building, so don't let inclement weather spoil your day.

A ride on the monorail is the perfect way to get an overview of the park and is a great way to start your visit.

The Giant Wheel is one of the tallest Ferris wheels along the Atlantic coast, and the view it affords of the surrounding area is spectacular.

Since 1972, Gillian's has been celebrating the start of its season by having a half-price ticket sale on Palm Sunday and Easter weekends. If you're in the area, it's a great way to save money by stocking up for the coming season.

should have it." Roy quickly jumped on the proposal, but his brother Bob thought it was too risky and wanted out.

In 1964, Roy Gillian signed a thirty-year lease purchase agreement with Stainton, sold his interest in the Fun Deck to his brother, and went to work building his dream. At the time, zoning regulations in Ocean City prohibited the operation of amusement rides with motors of one horsepower or more on an outdoor deck. Gillian decided to bring his park indoors and built a 22,500-square-foot, 24-foot-tall building to contain his rides. Built along the Boardwalk, the building served as an inspiration for the park's name. Gillian had seen a unique entrance sign at Hunts Pier in nearby Wildwood, where spinning blocks spelled out the name of the pier, and he wanted to do something similar at his new operation. One of his employees noted that there were ten support columns running along the Boardwalk and that the name Wonderland had ten letters. The name was adopted, and Gillian put up ten spinning cubes at the entrance to the pier spelling out W-O-N-D-E-R-L-A-N-D. This quickly became a local landmark.

Many people in the industry were impressed with Roy Gillian's ambition and provided him rides with no money down, allowing him to start the park with just $1,000 of his own money. The Philadelphia Toboggan Company provided a Crazy Dazy teacup ride, Lusse Brothers furnished bumper cars, and the Eli Bridge Company sold him a Scrambler. Gillian was also able to work out a deal with the defunct Forest Park in Hanover, Pennsylvania, to install several of their rides, including an antique carousel carved by William Dentzel and four kiddie rides. Rounding out the initial ride lineup was a custom-built monorail ride that encircled the inside of the building.

The ten-ride park had a very successful first season and was able to add a Loop-O-Plane ride for 1966. Gillian also replaced the carousel. The old ride was not as popular as it should have been, since the animals did not move up and down. Gillian sold the forty-five-horse carousel and acquired a modern version featuring fiberglass animals made by the King Amusement Company of Michigan.

The new merry-go-round still did not satisfy Gillian. While the fiberglass merry-go-round was popular with the children, it was not elaborate and lacked the personality of the antique ride that he had sold. In 1972, Gillian discovered that Rolling Green Park in Selinsgrove, Pennsylvania, had closed and was selling its antique carousel. The ride had been carved in 1926 by the Philadelphia Toboggan Company and had operated at Rolling Green Park since 1946. It was just the ride that Gillian wanted for his park, featuring forty-eight horses, twenty-eight of which moved up and down.

Gillian was an amateur pilot, so over the period of several weeks, he flew up to Selinsgrove every day to dismantle the ride and load it on a truck for the trip down to Ocean City. He left behind the old drive motor, thinking that a new one would be more reliable. But when Gillian contacted John Allen at the Philadelphia Toboggan Company for a replace-

The spinning letters in front of Gillian's Wonderland Pier have been a local landmark since 1965.

The large building at Gillian's holds many of its rides, including the antique carousel.

ment, he was told to go back and get his, as they didn't build them like that anymore. So he retrieved the motor, and it remains on the carousel to this day.

A New Era of Growth

By the 1970s, the restrictions on operating rides outdoors were being lifted, and Wonderland began installing larger rides in an open area behind the building. A Trabant ride was installed in 1972. This was followed in 1974 by the Super Cat, a Himalaya-type ride in which cars traveled around an undulating track at a high rate of speed, and the Flying Comet in 1975.

In 1977, when water slides were just starting to appear in the country, Wonderland added one of the first water slide complexes ever constructed, with two runs and standing 30 feet tall. The water slide industry was still in its infancy, so Gillian hired Gil Ramagosa of Wildwood, New Jersey, in tandem with John Allen of the Philadelphia Toboggan Company, who was better known as a roller coaster designer, to create his.

An unusual addition in 1977 was an ice rink, which was meant to provide revenue during the winter. But Ocean City in the winter was just not the draw it was in the summer, and the ice rink lasted only until 1981.

Also in 1977, Roy Gillian's brother Bob, who had continued to operate the Fun Deck after Roy opened Wonderland, decided to retire. Roy bought out his brother and once again found himself owner of the Fun

Deck. The much smaller Fun Deck was pretty much filled in terms of rides, but expansion continued at Wonderland in 1978 with the addition of the Sky Diver, a Ferris-wheel-type ride.

By 1978, Gillian determined that the park had grown to the point where a roller coaster should be added. Zoning regulations prohibited roller coasters with chain-driven lifts, which essentially ruled out nearly every roller coaster being manufactured at the time, but Gillian located a roller coaster operating at Salisbury Beach, Massachusetts, that had a spiral lift powered by electric motors on the trains to haul the riders to the top. The roller coaster was called the City Jet and was 36 feet high with a compact 1,362-foot long layout, making it perfect for Wonderland. It had originally opened at Atlantic City's Steel Pier in 1976 and moved to Salisbury Beach the following year.

The City Jet launched a new era of growth for Gillian's operations. In 1985, a Tilt-A-Whirl, Galleon swinging ship, Zugspitze Himalaya ride, and walk-through Mirror Maze were added. A chair swing ride replaced the Flying Comet in 1986. Also that year, the monorail, Wonderland's last original attraction, was extensively renovated. New trains were acquired and 600 feet of track added. The monorail now traveled outside the building and above the outdoor portion of Wonderland. While new attractions were added, others were removed, with 1986 being the

The City Jet roller coaster anchors the outdoor portion of Gillian's Wonderland Pier.

last season for Ghost Creek Caverns, a dark ride that had operated at Wonderland for nearly twenty years.

The next year was a pivotal one in Gillian family history. A referendum overturned longtime blue laws in Ocean City, allowing amusements to open on Sundays for the first time. With the growth of Wonderland and the increasing popularity of water parks, Roy's son, Jim, who managed the Fun Deck, determined that the small, old-fashioned park's future was limited.

The Next Generation

Gillian closed the Fun Deck after the 1987 season and auctioned off its nine rides, including the Spillman carousel that had started everything. But the sale did not mean that the 275-by-130-foot parcel had been retired from use in the amusement industry. Bob Gillian, who owned the land, sold it to three of Roy's sons, Jim, Steve, and Jay, so that they could develop a water park.

The result of their effort was Gillian's Island, a $2.5 million water park that opened in 1988. Gillian's Island had four different water slide complexes and a lazy river. In 1994, the water park added L'il Buc's Bay, a 19,000-square-foot kiddie play area.

Although attention in 1988 was focused on the water park, Wonderland was not forgotten. The 1977 vintage water slides were removed, and a Matterhorn ride was added.

During the 1989 season, the look of Wonderland was transformed with the addition of seven new rides. The highest-profile addition was a Giant Ferris wheel purchased from Boardwalk & Baseball, a theme park in Florida. The 140-foot structure towered over the park and was visible from the Garden State Parkway 5 miles away, serving as a beacon to people who had never before heard of Wonderland. Other new additions included spinning rides such as the Paratrooper, Scrambler, and Balloon Race; kiddie rides such as the Mini Scooter and Flying Elephants; and Raiders, a walk-through attraction.

Wonderland opened the 1992 season with the addition of Canyon Falls, a $1.4 million, 35-foot-tall, 940-foot-long log flume along the backside of the park where the water slides used to be. The following year was a sad time for the Gillian family, as patriarch David Gillian passed away at the age of 102.

Improvements at the park continued in the late 1990s with the addition of several new rides. In 1997, the park replaced the Matterhorn, Tip Top, Trabant, Balloon Race, and Flying Dragon rides with the Twister, which flipped riders in several different directions, as well as the Alpine Bobs,

Crazy Sub, NASCAR Raceway, Samba Balloon, and a kiddie train. In 1998, the City Jet was joined by the Miner Mike, a small roller coaster for kids.

When Wonderland started running out of space to grow, it started expanding upward. In 1999, Gillian's constructed a $700,000 deck above the bumper cars and Canyon Falls flume, where many new rides could be added. Several kiddie rides in addition to the Raiders and Glass House walk-throughs were relocated to the deck, creating a second kiddie area. To honor the family's original operation, the area was called Gillian's Fun Deck. Moving many kiddie rides to the new deck created additional space in the main park area, where several new rides were added, including a Trabant, the Tornado, and a kiddie tower ride.

Upgrading of the park's rides has continued. The Sizzler and Music Express replaced the Scrambler and Zugspitze in 2000, and the 1989 Giant Wheel and Sky Diver were replaced by a new 148-foot-tall Giant Wheel and an Inverter in 2001. The most recent additions (2004) include the Slingshot tower ride and Alien Invasion, the park's first dark ride since 1986.

Gillian's Wonderland Today

From the beginning, the spinning blocks have remained a constant attraction, surviving renovations to the original building that included a new castle-style facade in 2002. Today the 120,000-square-foot amusement park features thirty-four rides, including thirteen for kids, and two walk-through attractions, the Raiders and the Glass House. The large Wonderland building remains a dominant feature on the Ocean City Boardwalk and serves as Wonderland's main entrance. Inside are eleven rides, including the antique carousel, monorail, and several family and kiddie rides.

Beyond the main building is the midway, the location of the City Jet roller coaster, swings, and Galleon. Next comes the lower lot, home to the Giant Wheel, bumper boats, Inverter, Canyon Falls flume, and bumper cars.

Above the bumper cars and Canyon Falls flume is Gillian's Fun Deck, where visitors find seven kiddie rides, including the Miner Mike kiddie coaster and a kiddie train, as well as the Raiders and the Glass House walk-throughs.

Gillian's Island water park is just a short walk down the Boardwalk. Included at the water park is Adventure Golf, a Gillian-owned miniature golf course.

Morey's Piers

OPENED 1969

CHANGE IS ONE THING YOU CAN COUNT ON EVERY YEAR AT NEW JERSEY'S seaside resorts. Along the Boardwalk, new concessions replace old ones. Amusement piers add new rides. And entrepreneurs are constantly dreaming up new ways to cash in on the crowd. While change is constant at every resort throughout the Jersey shore, the Wildwoods, a collection of three towns in the far southern reaches of the state—Wildwood, North Wildwood, and Wildwood Crest—are blessed by another constant change: the beach keeps getting bigger. Thanks to strong currents, the ocean increases the width of Wildwood's beach by approximately 50 feet annually. In some places, it is now a quarter mile wide.

Not only does this growing beach attract millions of vacationers annually, but it also allows the towns' amusement piers to constantly grow as the "riparian" rights granted to them permitted the pier owners to continually expand to the ocean. As a result, Wildwood's piers are highlighted by constant growth. This expansion is the hallmark of Morey's Piers, the largest amusement complex along the American coastline, Atlantic or Pacific.

Today what is collectively known as Morey's Piers is actually a collection of four different amusement piers strung along Wildwood's five-mile-long boardwalk. They are, from north to south:

- *Morey's Piers–25th Avenue.* This is the company's first pier. It was originally known as Surfside Pier and later renamed Morey's Pier, the name now given the entire operation. In addition to rides, it is home to one of Morey's Piers' two Raging Waters water park complexes.

Morey's Piers
3501 Boardwalk
Wildwood, NJ 08260
609-522-3900
www.moreyspiers.com

- *The former Hunt's Pier.* Located next door to Morey's Piers–25th Avenue, this pier is home to a couple go-cart tracks and other concessions.

- *Morey's Piers–Schellenger Avenue.* Located in the heart of the Boardwalk, this pier opened in 1931 as Marine Pier and was later known as Mariner's Landing. It is home to the second Raging Wagers water park, along with a wide array of rides.

- *Morey's Piers–Spencer Avenue.* The southernmost of Morey's Piers, this pier originally opened as Fun Pier but was rebuilt as Wild Wheels Raceway and Adventure Pier before being given its current name. It is the location of the largest roller coaster on the Jersey shore, the Great White.

Looking at this huge operation today, it is hard to believe that less than forty years ago, it had such a humble beginning.

A Chance Encounter

In the 1950s and 1960s, brothers Bill and Will Morey were both successful entrepreneurs. Bill operated concessions along the Boardwalk in Wildwood, while Will had a successful construction business that took advantage of the construction boom in Wildwood in the 1950s and 1960s, changing the face of the town.

Using skills he inherited from his father, Louis, a carpenter for the Coast Guard, in 1953 Will built the Fantasy Motel in Wildwood for a client. The Fantasy, inspired by the flamboyant architecture of Miami Beach, became a local landmark with its neon lights, colorful decor, sundeck, swimming pool, and on-site parking, a concession to the growing use of the automobile. Known as the Doo Wop style of architecture, this type of hotel dominated development in the town over the next fifteen years, and Morey built nearly thirty of them, including the Flagship, Satellite, Sea Crest, Carousel, and Pan American.

A life-changing event for the brothers occurred in 1968, when Bill traveled to Florida to visit Will, who was living there for the winter. Driving along Highway A1A near Fort Lauderdale, the brothers spotted a giant, twelve-lane fiberglass slide operating near a shopping center. These slides were popular roadside attractions during this period and were springing up throughout the country.

The brothers knew that such an attraction would be a successful addition to the Wildwood Boardwalk, and they started making plans to acquire one of their own. Given the size of the slide, the brothers could find only one location large enough to accommodate it: a struggling restaurant and miniature golf complex located on the Boardwalk. The complex was actually two small piers separated by a swath of municipally owned land. The town also owned the Boardwalk frontage but permitted access to the piers via 20-foot-wide catwalks. Though it was not the ideal location, especially in comparison with the large amusement complexes with which they would be competing, the Moreys knew the slide would be a success and pressed forward, purchasing the property for $345,000.

The slide, which they named the Wipe Out, was erected over the miniature golf course, which occupied the larger, 130-by-400-foot pier. The pier occupied by the restaurant was leased out to another party.

The fledgling operation, which was named Surfside Pier, was initially met with skepticism by the more established operations along the Boardwalk. They considered it unwise for the Moreys to occupy so much valuable pier space with the large slide, which also blocked the view of any future attractions they would add to the pier. But people flocked to the slide, and as if to vindicate their decision, two competing giant slides were constructed along the Boardwalk the following season.

Their success continued through the 1970 season, and by 1971, they started adding mechanical rides to the pier, including a small monorail ride. They also decided to demolish the restaurant to accommodate additional attractions, the most notable being the King Kong ride, which consisted of a 40-foot-tall fiberglass statue of King Kong around which airplanes circled. At the base of the attraction was the Moreys' first go-

In its early years, Morey's Pier was known for its Wipe Out slide and King Kong airplane ride.

LOCATION

Morey's Piers are located along the Boardwalk in Wildwood and North Wildwood, New Jersey. To reach Wildwood, take the Garden State Parkway to Exit 4B into town. Parking is available at pay lots throughout the area.

OPERATING SCHEDULE

Morey's Piers is open weekends from mid-April through May, daily from Memorial Day weekend through Labor Day, then weekends until mid-October. Opening time varies between 11 A.M. and 1 P.M., although the park opens at 6 P.M. on certain off-peak days. Morey's Piers–Spencer Avenue pier tends to open later than the 25th Avenue and Schellenger Avenue piers.

The two Raging Waters water parks, located at the 25th Avenue and Schellenger Avenue piers, are open weekends only from Memorial Day weekend through mid-June, and daily from mid-June through Labor Day. Opening time varies from 9 A.M. to 11 A.M., depending on the time of year.

ADMISSION

Admission to Morey's Piers is free. Visitors have the option to pay by the ride or purchase an all-day ride pass for about $40 that allows access to all rides except for attractions such as the Skyscraper, Sky Coaster, Spring Shot, Helicopter, and Climbing Walls.

Raging Waters offers several admission plans, including an all-day pass for under $30 and a three-hour pass for under $20.

Combination passes for under $50 are available for the three amusement piers and Raging Waters water parks. All-day ride passes and combination passes are both discounted on weekdays.

FOOD

Each pier has its own selection of food, emphasizing easy-to-eat food that is part of the Boardwalk experience.

The 25th Avenue Pier has about ten food stands, including Curley's Fries, a Boardwalk tradition since 1975. It's famous for its fresh-cooked french fries, fresh-squeezed lemonade, orange juice, and funnel cakes. Beach Grille, in the water park, also has a wide array of items, including breakfast sandwiches.

The Schellenger Avenue pier has about eight food outlets, the largest being Jumbo's Seafood & Pizza Eatery. Located right along the Boardwalk, Jumbo's offers fresh seafood, pizza, sandwiches, hamburgers, and hot dogs. Wrecker's Grille, in the water park, also has a wide array of items, including breakfast sandwiches. This pier also has a Curley's Fries outlet.

Food service at the Spencer Avenue pier is more limited in scope, emphasizing snacks such as Kohr Brothers frozen custard.

(continued on page 166)

VISITING (continued from page 165)

FOR CHILDREN

All three Morey's Piers feature a wide variety of family attractions. The 25th Avenue pier has about eight kiddie rides and popular family attractions such as the double-deck merry-go-round, Demolition Derby, Fire Chief, and Flitzer. At Raging Waters is Banzai Beach, a kids' water play area.

The Schellenger Avenue Pier has about a dozen kiddie rides, along with a double-deck merry-go-round, Kite Flyer, Balloon Race Ferris wheel, and Sky Ship monorail.

The Spencer Avenue pier has a variety of family rides, such as the merry-go-round, Wacky Whip, Jersey Junkyard dark ride, and Snake Slide.

SPECIAL FEATURES

Morey's Piers has the largest selection of amusement rides of any park along any seashore in the United States. With three piers containing nearly seventy-five rides and two full-scale water parks, there is something to appeal to everyone.

Don't miss the 150-foot-tall Giant Wheel for a spectacular view of town and the ocean.

The Great White is the largest oceanfront roller coaster in the country. The 100-foot plunge down to the beach is a one-of-a-kind experience. The piers' six other roller coasters offer a wide variety of riding experiences: the Great Nor'easter, whose trains travel beneath the track; the forward- and backward-looping Sea Serpent; the twisting RC-48; the Doo Wopper, with its sharp, quick turns; and the family-oriented Rollie's Coaster and Flitzer.

TIME REQUIRED

A visit to the seaside resort of Wildwood can form the basis of an entire vacation. The piers themselves require at least one day to fully experience, although the major attractions can be enjoyed in about six hours.

TOURING TIPS

Try to visit Morey's Piers on a weekday, particularly before mid-June, when the piers tend to be less crowded.

The water parks always open before the amusement piers, so start your visit there.

The Sightseer trams have been traveling along the Boardwalk since 1949 and are a great way to get from pier to pier. The trams are not owned by Morey's Piers and thus are not included in any of their ticket plans.

Wildwood is one of the largest resorts on the Atlantic shore and has countless other activities to occupy your day, including the Splash Zone water park, Sportland Pier go-carts, the Den of Lost Thieves and Zombie World dark rides on the Boardwalk, and an aquarium.

cart ride. King Kong became such a well-known landmark that the pier was more widely known as King Kong Pier.

With business booming, the Moreys also began negotiations in 1971 with the city to acquire the land that separated their two small piers. The owner of the neighboring Sportland Pier, Gil Ramagosa, fought the transaction, as he was concerned about his aggressive new neighbors, leading to a lengthy legal battle. But the behind-the-scenes trouble did not deter the Moreys from growing the business. In 1972, the larger pier was expanded to make room for a huge walk-through Haunted House, a Himalaya, and several kiddie rides.

One of the key reasons for the early success of the Morey operation was the complementary talents of the two brothers. Will, given his construction background, was adept at dealing with bankers, lawyers, and other behind-the-scenes issues, while Bill, with his experience operating concessions along the Boardwalk, was an accomplished hands-on manager. As a result, in 1973, Bill and his wife, Dolores, became full-time managers of the pier. Initially they moved into a trailer behind one of the rides. The spartan accommodations were not appealing to Dolores, who told her husband, "Build me an office or I'm not coming back!"

By the end of the 1973 season, the legal battle over the city-owned land had reached a climax with the decision to put the parcel up for public auction the following spring. The future of the Moreys' operation was contingent on winning the auction, as the winning bidder could cut off access to their complex from the Boardwalk. In a spirited round of bidding, the rival pier owner offered more than $700,000 for the parcel, but with a bid of $756,000, the Moreys won out, and at last the two parts of the operation could be unified.

With the summer fast approaching, a crew of fourteen carpenters was put to work filling the 160-foot gap along the Boardwalk as soon as the papers were signed. The completed pier totaled 80,000 square feet, stretching 400 feet from the Boardwalk toward the ocean. This allowed what was now called Morey's Pier to launch a major expansion. Several new kiddie rides were added, along with the Safari dark ride and five games buildings. In addition, Dolores and the rest of the management got a three-level office located under the slide.

The expansion firmly established Morey's Pier on the Wildwood Boardwalk. At the time, this was one of the most competitive amusement park markets in the world, with five different operators fighting for the summer tourist trade. The Moreys sought to stand out by developing several one-of-a-kind attractions, working with Fred Mahana, who designed a number of unique rides along the Atlantic coast. In

Planet of the Apes was one of the unique rides that operated at Morey's Pier.
WILDWOOD HISTORICAL SOCIETY

response to the popularity of disaster movies, in 1974 the park developed a walk-through attraction based on *The Poseidon Adventure,* which later was converted into a *Jaws* theme. In 1975, Morey's opened the In Concert and Planet of the Apes rides. On In Concert, a group of riders sat on a large disk, themed as a record album, and attempted to stay on as it spun faster and faster. Planet of the Apes started with a ride on a spaceship. During the journey, apes took over the spaceship and landed it on their home planet. From there, visitors were led through a walk-through depicting life on the planet. Reflecting changing tastes, the ride was later converted into a *Star Wars*–themed attraction.

Another unusual attraction was the Airplane, a homemade simulator. The Moreys had located a twin-engine Martin 404 aircraft sitting abandoned in a nearby airport and moved it to the pier, where it was mounted on a series of hydraulic actuators that moved the plane in conjunction with a movie shown inside.

In the fall of 1975, the Morey brothers traveled to the Octoberfest in Germany for the first time. They were fascinated by the flashy European rides and knew that many of these rides, which were not yet commonplace in the United States, would help further solidify their pier's position. One ride in particular caught their attention—the Jumbo Jet, a 56-foot-high, 2,854-foot-long roller coaster designed by Anton Schwarzkopf, one of the greatest designers of steel-track roller coasters. The brothers knew it was the perfect high-profile attraction for their pier. They immediately made a deal to purchase the ride for $400,000. To make room, the pier had to be lengthened by 250 feet for the 1976 season, but the effort was worth it. The Jersey shore had never seen anything like the Jumbo Jet, with its spiral lift hill and steeply banked high-speed turns. As a result, Morey's Pier became one of the top attractions on the shore. It also established the pier as a place to enjoy some of the latest rides from Europe, and within years, the Moreys' operations sported rides from France, Germany, Holland, Italy, and Switzerland.

Landing an Expansion

As the 1976 season wound down, the Moreys heard that one of their longtime competitors, Marine Pier Amusements and Playland, was for sale. Located at the heart of the Boardwalk, it was the largest amusement complex in Wildwood, with rides and attractions spread across a 500-foot-long amusement pier on the east side of the Boardwalk (Marine Pier) and an entire city block on the western side of the Boardwalk (Playland).

This complex was also the oldest amusement facility in Wildwood, dating back to 1918, when a carousel was built on a small parcel on the west side of the Boardwalk between Cedar and Schellenger Avenues. Then called the Amusement Center, the carousel was joined the next

The Moreys acquired Marine Pier in 1976 and converted it into Mariner's Landing.

season by large wooden roller coaster called the Jack Rabbit, an Old Mill boat ride, and several smaller rides.

By late 1920s, the Amusement Center had grown to the point where it was pressed for space. As a result, Marine Pier was constructed in 1931. In addition to a miniature railroad and miniature golf course, Marine Pier's central attraction was a 90-foot-tall Ferris wheel purchased from Carsonia Park in Reading, Pennsylvania. Over the next several decades, much of the facility's growth occurred on the pier. By the late 1950s, the pier was lengthened and a number of rides, including a Wild Mouse roller coaster, were added. In late 1960s, the Zyclone, a steel-track roller coaster standing 40 feet tall, had replaced the Wild Mouse, but it was becoming harder for the Marine Pier and Playland complex to keep up with the aggressive new competitors, such as Morey's Pier, that were lining the Boardwalk.

Though the Moreys were not looking to expand onto another pier at the time, the complex's location at the heart of the Boardwalk was too good to pass up. The asking price for the entire facility was too large for their budget, however, so they struck a deal to purchase just the Marine Pier portion. Playland was sold to other operators (in 2000, it was converted into the Splash Zone water park).

While the purchase of Marine Pier represented an important development in the growth of the business, the new owners had their work cut out for them. The pier had been deteriorating for years and had just twelve rides. As a result, a renovation program costing in excess of $1.5 million was launched for the 1977 season. About half the rides, including the Ferris wheel, were considered beyond repair and were scrapped. An elaborate new front entrance was built along the Boardwalk, and several flashy new rides from Europe were added, including the Enterprise, Pirate Ship, and Wave Swinger. Since theme parks were in vogue, the pier's name was changed to Mariner's Landing and given a nautical theme. While Mariner's Landing and Morey's Pier were marketed as a single attraction, each one had a different target market, with Mariner's Landing emphasizing families and Morey's Pier focusing on teenagers.

During the late 1970s, a new type of amusement attraction was introduced to the country: the water slide. The Moreys were not ones to miss out on a new trend, so in 1978, they spent $1.5 million to add three water slides at each pier. To make room, each pier was lengthened by 200 feet. Some observers were initially skeptical that people would be interested in water slides so close to the ocean, but once again the Moreys had made the right call, and the water slides became some of the most popular attractions in Wildwood.

Just two years after taking over the old Marine Pier and renaming it Mariner's Landing, the Moreys had succeeded in reestablishing the facility as a major force along the Boardwalk. As a result, in 1979, they spent $1 million to construct a 217-by-100-foot addition to the pier and add several new rides, including the Polyp and Music Express, two spinning rides, and the Astroliner, a simulated trip to outer space in a rocket ship.

But the most elaborate ride added was Hitchcock Manor, a $120,000 dark ride custom built by Fred Mahana. The ride looked to the stories of Alfred Hitchcock for inspiration. Among its scenes were several rooms done completely in black and white, artificial rain, an expanding room, nearly nine hundred stuffed blackbirds, and a re-creation of the shower scene from *Psycho.*

In 1980, Morey's Pier was able to acquire a 70-by-700-foot parcel immediately adjacent to their existing facility, permitting another major expansion. An animated Bear Show replaced the Safari dark ride. Manufactured by Creative Engineering, it was just the second sale for the company that later went on to supply the Showbiz pizza restaurants. Also added was an elaborate new $125,000 dark ride, Dante's Inferno, which was imported from Germany. In addition, Morey's Pier offered rides on the beach in real dune buggies. Unfortunately, one of the pier's most distinctive landmarks, King Kong, no longer towered over the Boardwalk. The park had hoped to renovate the statue, but when the big gorilla was being hoisted onto a flatbed truck, the deteriorated inner supports gave out, and it collapsed under its own weight.

But Morey's Pier continued to expand. Skeeter Boats and Bumper Boats opened in a 70-by-225-foot aboveground pool in 1980, followed in 1981 by a Sea Dragon swinging ship. Toward the end of the season, however, Mariner's Landing, which had become increasingly successful in its own right, suffered a setback when a fire broke out in a neighboring restaurant on the Boardwalk. High winds pushed the flames into Mariner's Landing, and before they were extinguished, the pier suffered $1 million in damage. Lost were the office building, two food stands, a gift shop, and Hitchcock Manor. But Mariner's Landing quickly bounced back, opening the 1982 season with four new rides and a Ripley's Believe it or Not attraction.

Expansion the following season focused on Morey's Pier with the addition of the Flitzer, a $150,000 family roller coaster imported from Germany, standing 25 feet high and 1,200 feet long. The pier also added the first Gravitron ride ever constructed. This was a high-speed ride that gave riders the sensation that they were defying gravity while the spinning action pressed them into the walls.

By the early 1980s, the Moreys' combined operations had become the dominant amusement enterprise in Wildwood, and it was time to add a signature attraction to Mariner's Landing, much as they had at Morey's Pier in 1976 with the Jumbo Jet. Since looping roller coasters were the rage, it was decided to add one. Finding the right type for the densely packed environment of the amusement pier meant that they had to find a ride that packed the maximum amount of thrills into a minimum amount of space. They found such a ride from Vekoma, a Dutch ride manufacturer. Named the Sea Serpent, the $1.4 million ride was the first of its kind in the United States. The train was hauled backward up a 125-foot-tall incline. It was then released and traveled back through the station into a twisting "boomerang" that flipped riders upside down two times and then through a vertical loop before traveling up another 125-foot-tall incline. The train then reversed and went through everything again backward. In all, riders were turned upside down six times along just 875 feet of track.

The debut of the Sea Serpent took the entire operation to a new level, and the Moreys were intent on riding this positive momentum into 1985 by launching their largest expansion ever. A total of $5 million was spent to add new signature attractions to both piers. Mariner's Landing was

Mariner's Landing added the Giant Wheel and Raging Waters water park in 1985.

lengthened by 95 feet to accommodate a 160-foot-tall Ferris wheel that immediately became a local landmark. In addition, the old water slides were replaced by a 2½-acre water park at the end of the pier called Raging Waters with a wide array of waterslides and other activities.

Meanwhile, the look of Morey's Pier was totally transformed. While many older attractions such as Star Wars, In Concert, Poseidon Adventure/Jaws, and the Haunted House were removed, several major new rides were added. At the center of the expansion was the Zoom Phloom, manufactured by O. D. Hopkins of New Hampshire, a $1.5 million log flume with two 40-foot drops into pools of water and 1,774 feet of trough that wound over and under the pier and many of the other attractions. The ride was so large that the pier had to be widened by 30 feet to accommodate it.

But Morey's Pier did not stop there. Also added was a new fun house; the Schlittenfahrt (German for Sleigh Express), a high-speed spinning ride; and the first Katapult to operate in the United States, a rollercoaster-type ride imported from Germany that was essentially a motor-driven train traveling around a circle and through a vertical loop.

Expanding the Fun

By now Morey's Pier and Mariner's Landing had become so dominant that many of the competitors that had doubted the Morey's staying power in the early years were starting to fall by the wayside. One of these competitors was Fun Pier, located next to Mariner's Landing.

Fun Pier had been built in 1927 as the city's convention center, with a 5,000-seat auditorium and a shopping arcade constructed over the beach. In 1957, Joe Barnes took over the now run-down pier. He demolished many of the old structures and added several rides and a miniature golf course. In 1964, he tore down the old convention hall, and through the 1960s, he added a number of high-profile rides, including a large monorail that traveled over the beach, a Sky Ride, and an observation tower.

By the 1980s, however, Fun Pier was in decline. The Sky Tower was abandoned, and the monorail and Sky Ride were scrapped. In 1984, the pier was hit by two separate fires that destroyed 200 feet of pier and a number of its most popular attractions, such as the Haunted House, Lost World dark ride, Jet 400 roller coaster, and water slides. The pier managed to limp on for a couple more seasons, but in 1987, it was placed on the market.

Knowing the problems that an aggressive upstart competitor could cause, the Moreys moved quickly to purchase Fun Pier. Given the deteriorated state of the pier, the Moreys realized that its days as a major amusement pier were over, and they booked in a circus and other concessions while they determined its long-term future.

In 1987, the Moreys acquired the shuttered Fun Pier, shown here in the 1950s.

While 1987 was a critical year for the Moreys, with the addition of the former Fun Pier to their holdings, it also marked the end of an era as the aging Jumbo Jet roller coaster was dismantled and sold to a business contact in Germany. The contact subsequently bartered the ride to Gorky Park in Moscow for two freight car loads of ketchup, as the ruble was not valid for foreign exchange at the time.

But the loss of the Jumbo Jet was just the start of a long planning process to add a new landmark roller coaster to Morey's Pier. To make up for the loss of the Jumbo Jet, a number of attractions were added to Morey's Pier for the 1988 season. These included the Zyclone, a 33-foot-tall, 1,100-foot-long family roller coaster that made a two-year appearance; and the Condor, a spinning ride in which twenty-eight gondolas revolved in a circle while climbing a 115-foot-tall tower. In addition, with the popularity of Raging Waters at Mariner's Landing, a second $5 million Raging Waters was constructed at Morey's Pier. To make use of the water parks in the evening after they had closed for the day, the Moreys experimented with allowing visitors to kayak down the river rides in each water park.

A number of new attractions were added to both Morey's Pier and Mariner's Landing over the next two seasons. At Morey's Pier, the Katapult was replaced in 1989 by the Breakdance, a high-speed spinning ride, along with a two-level maze attraction. The 1990 season saw the introduction of a miniature golf course.

Meanwhile, Mariner's Landing added an elaborate Teacup ride in 1989, followed by several kiddie rides in 1990, including a 40-foot-high Parachute Tower and the Seal Boats, a flume ride for small children.

After spending several years studying alternative uses for the former Fun Pier, the Moreys decided to take advantage of the increasing interest in participatory attractions and redevelop the pier for 1993 as Wild Wheels Raceway and Adventure Pier. The pier had a totally different persona than Morey's Pier or Mariner's Landing, with three go-cart tracks, bungee jumping, rock climbing, helicopter rides over the ocean, and boat tag, in which riders piloted small boats around a pool and shot tennis balls at other boats. The revitalized pier also featured the first ejector seat attraction in the United States, which strapped passengers into a seat that was catapulted upward. Over on Morey's Pier that season, a 40-foot-high, 1,766-foot-long roller coaster, the Jet Star, was acquired from Knoebel's Amusement Resort in Elysburg, Pennsylvania.

With the popularity of the Raging Waters water parks increasing, the Moreys spent the 1994 season expanding them. Morey's Pier received Hydroworks, a 3,000-square-foot interactive attraction for kids that was surrounded by large rock formations that were actually seating areas for parents. Over at Mariner's Landing, Shipwreck Shoals, another new kiddie area, was constructed. The 5,000-square-foot area drew upon regional history for inspiration for its two main attractions. In the middle of a large wading pool was a large ship that kids could climb through and slide down that was themed after the brigantine *Nancy*, which was involved in a naval battle off the coast of Wildwood in 1776. Nearby, a small water slide complex was themed after Mosquito Point, a fort that stood in western New Jersey in the eighteenth century.

In 1995, the Moreys' eight-year quest to build a new signature roller coaster was at last realized. Seeking something that would truly stand out, they reached an agreement with Vekoma to build the Great Nor'easter, a 115-foot-tall, 2,150-foot-long steel-track roller coaster in which riders were suspended below the track. Installing the $6 million ride on the tightly packed pier was a challenge in and of itself, and Vekoma had to work carefully to thread it over the water slides, under Zoom Phloom, and above the Breakdance ride. In many places there were only a few inches of clearance, but in the end, only one water slide support had to be moved to accommodate the new roller coaster.

The Great Nor'easter took the entire Morey empire to a whole new level, making it even more of a regional draw. Seeking to capitalize on this momentum, it was decided to add another roller coaster and at the same time create a signature attraction for Wild Wheels Pier, much in the same way that the Great Nor'easter and Zoom Phloom anchored

Morey's Pier and the Sea Serpent and Giant Wheel defined Mariner's Landing. Given that a wood-track roller coaster had not operated in Wildwood since 1988, it was a natural choice. The Morey's contracted with Custom Coasters, the leading manufacturer of wooden roller coasters during the 1990s, to design and build the $3.6 million ride.

The new roller coaster, the Great White, became an instant landmark along the Wildwood Boardwalk, standing 100 feet tall with 3,300 feet of track. The ride began with a 20-foot dive out of the station into a tunnel that traveled underneath the pier. To accommodate the Great White, the pier was lengthened by 400 feet to 1,000 feet. Unlike most wooden roller coasters, the Great White had a support structure of galvanized steel to better withstand the elements.

The improvements at Wild Wheels Pier continued, as a 100-foot-tall Sky Ride was erected over the Great White, and a number of traditional amusement park rides such as a merry-go-round and the Jersey Junkyard dark ride were constructed.

By now the Morey brothers' business had grown far beyond their dreams. They were the dominant amusement park operators not only in Wildwood, but along the entire Jersey shore, and as a result, in 1997 their disparate holdings were combined under one holding company: the Morey Organization. Their major addition for the year was a double monorail ride encircling much of Mariner's Landing and its Raging

Morey's Piers–25th Avenue today.

Morey's Piers–Spencer Avenue is highlighted by the Sky Ride over the Great White.

Waters water park. The twin-level track consisted of the Sky Ship on the upper level, with fifteen self-propelled fiberglass boats, and the Sky Cycle on the lower track, with fifteen giant fiberglass seagulls that were powered by the riders using pedals much like a bicycle.

Doo Wop

As the scope of the Morey Organization had grown over the years, the family's livelihood and the fortunes of the town of Wildwood became closely intertwined. Seeing the decline that had plagued several resort towns in northern New Jersey, the Moreys realized they needed to develop a strategic plan not only for their piers, but for the resort as a whole. They knew that their future rested not in competing with theme parks, but in playing up the unique ambience of Wildwood's Boardwalk, their piers, and the community as a whole.

Still scattered throughout the community were the little Doo Wop style hotels such as the Ala Moana, Aquarius, Bel Air, Caribbean, Ebb Tide, Grecian Gardens, Lollipop, and Satellite, many of which Will Morey had launched his career by building. Just a few years before, these hotels with their flamboyant architecture, sundecks, and plastic palm trees were considered dated. But now they represented the future of the resort much in the same way the restored Victorian buildings of Cape May, New Jersey, and the Art Deco style hotels of Miami Beach, Florida, revitalized those communities.

To help formulate a strategy, Will Morey's son, Jack, founded the Doo Wop Preservation League to encourage the preservation, restoration, and expansion of the Doo Wop style of architecture throughout the resort. A six-month study was conducted by a group of college architecture students and professors to locate the remaining Doo Wop style buildings, identify refurbishing and restoration projects, and develop plans to preserve the fifty remaining motels from the Doo Wop period.

The 1998 season began on a down note, as Will Morey passed away. Despite this setback, expansion of the piers continued. The largest addition was the construction of Doo Wopper, a new roller coaster on Wild Wheels Pier. In keeping with the emerging Doo Wop spirit of the town, the 35-foot-tall, 885-foot-long steel-track ride was themed as a 1950s drive-in restaurant. The ride cars resembled 1950s automobiles, complete with headlights, front grilles, and tail fins, while flashy signs advertising menu items adorned the structure.

Another key development during 1998 was the retirement of the separate names for each pier. From now on, the piers would be marketed under the Morey's Piers name. The original Morey's Pier was renamed Morey's Piers–25th Avenue; Mariner's Landing became Morey's

Piers–Schellenger Avenue; and Wild Wheels Pier was called Morey's Piers–Spencer Avenue.

The Schellenger Avenue Pier was the recipient of most of the attention in 1999, with the addition of Rollie's Coaster, a 33-foot-tall, 1,100-foot-long roller coaster that replaced the Zyclone; the Storm, a turbulent rotating ride; and Jumbo's, a new seafood restaurant. And yet again, Morey's Piers was given the opportunity to take over another former competitor, the former Hunt's Pier, located next to Morey's Pier–25th Avenue.

Dating back to 1957, Hunt's Pier had established a reputation in the 1960s and 1970s as the place to go for its creative, high-quality rides. The Flyer, a family-size wooden roller coaster, was one of its original attractions, and others soon followed. The Jungleland ride, based on the famous Disneyland ride, opened in 1959. The Golden Nugget Mine ride, a one-of-a-kind dark ride through a man-made mountain, debuted in 1960, and a large Pirate-ship-themed fun house opened in 1962. A log flume and Wacky Shack dark ride were added in 1970. By the early 1970s, Hunt's Pier's reputation was such that *Amusement Business* dubbed it a "miniature Disney World." But the pier began to decline under new owners during the late 1980s, and by 1991 it had closed. Hunt's Pier sat vacant for four years before being partially reopened in 1995 and redeveloped into Dinosaur Beach, a $10 million theme park, in 1996. By this time, however, the competition was too stiff, and Dinosaur Beach closed in 1998.

With more than seventy rides in operation on three piers, the Moreys did not feel that the town needed another amusement pier, and as a result, they devoted most of Hunt's Pier to support facilities for the other piers, such as storage areas and maintenance shops. However, the portion closest to the Boardwalk was filled with concessions, along with two go-cart tracks and the Skyscraper, which resembles an out-of-control Ferris wheel.

The parade of new roller coasters marched up the Boardwalk to the 25th Avenue Pier in 2000. The aging Jet Star was replaced by the RC-48, a 54-foot-tall, 1,510-foot-long roller coaster characterized by its highly banked turns. The $2.5 million improvement program did not stop with the RC-48, as nine additional new spinning rides were scattered among the three piers. The two largest were added to the Schellenger Avenue Pier: Moby Dick, a fast side-to-side ride, and the Maelstrom, a multiaxial spinning ride that replaced the Enterprise.

As part of the Doo Wop revitalization strategy, the Moreys acquired the 1952-vintage Wingate Hotel in 2000. They renovated it into the Starlux, a celebration of Doo Wop architecture with pastel colors, neon signs, plastic palms, and a glass lobby with futuristic angular architecture.

The piers continue to evolve. Camp Kid-Tastrophe, $1.3 million water play area with a 1,000-gallon water bucket, water cannons, and fountains, debuted at the Raging Waters at Morey's Piers–Schellenger Avenue in 2001, while the Rock 'n Roll, a high-speed spinning ride with cars resembling 1950s automobiles, replaced the Schlittenfahrt on Morey's Piers–25th Avenue Pier. In 2002, the 25th Avenue Pier completed a $600,000 renovation of its kids' area in Raging Waters, while the Fireball Express, a large looping ride, replaced the Storm on Schellenger Avenue.

Morey's Piers Today

Today Morey's Piers is the embodiment of the seashore experience. Consisting of four piers extending from an action-packed Boardwalk, offering more than seventy rides, including seven roller coasters, Morey's Piers is a unique destination.

Morey's Piers–25th Avenue is the northernmost pier and is where the Morey empire got its start. Located in the town of North Wildwood, Morey's Piers–25th Avenue offers about thirty rides, including the Great Nor'easter, RC-48, and Flitzer roller coasters; Zoom Phloom; Dante's Inferno dark ride; Condor; Formula One Racers, a go-cart ride under the pier; and the Wipeout, the giant slide that started it all. Also found on this pier are a double-decker maze, miniature golf course, and one of two Raging Waters water parks.

The Great White now dominates the skyline of the Wildwood seashore.

Next door is the former Hunt's Pier. While not a full-blown amusement pier, it is home to two go-cart tracks and the Skyscraper ride.

Morey's Piers–Schellenger Avenue is located at the heart of the Boardwalk and offers about thirty rides, including the Sea Serpent and Rollie's Coaster roller coasters; the Giant Wheel; the Pirates of Wildwood dark ride; paddle boats; and the Sky Ship and Sky Cycle monorail attractions. Also found here are a miniature golf course and the second Raging Waters water park.

Just south of the Schellenger Avenue Pier is Morey's Piers–Spencer Avenue which offers about fifteen rides, including the Great White and Doo Wopper roller coasters; Sky Ride; Grand Prix Raceway; Jersey Junkyard dark ride; Curse of the Mummy 3-D walk-through; and helicopter rides over the beach. This pier also features a number of participatory activities, such as batting cages and boat tag, where riders pilot small boats around a pool and shoot balls at other boats.

Six Flags Great Adventure

OPENED 1974

AT SIX FLAGS GREAT ADVENTURE, NOTHING IS SMALL. ON 2,200 ACRES OF property, the park is the second-largest entertainment resort in the world and boasts the biggest drive-through animal park outside Africa. Few parks have more rides, and Great Adventure's seventy rides include thirteen roller coasters, the most in the eastern United States, among them Nitro, the tallest and fastest roller coaster east of the Allegheny Mountains. Its grand scale has guided Six Flags Great Adventure's development from the beginning.

One Man's Vision

Six Flags Great Adventure was the vision of Warner LeRoy, who came from a strong show business pedigree. He was the son of Mervin LeRoy, director of movies such as *The Wizard of Oz* and *Mister Roberts,* and great-nephew of Jack Warner, founder of the movie studio. Warner LeRoy himself was a successful show producer and restaurateur when he developed the concept of a complete entertainment complex serving the densely populated area around New York City and Philadelphia. Included in his plans were a theme park, wild animal park, ocenarium and aquatic park, shopping, hotels, and a sports complex.

In the early 1970s, he developed a partnership with the Hardwicke Companies, which operated safari parks around the world, and soon acquired an expansive site in central New Jersey, midway between New York City and Philadelphia. Loca-

**Six Flags
Great Adventure**

P.O. Box 120
Route 537
Jackson, NJ 08527-0120
908-928-1821
www.sixflags.com/parks/
greatadventure/

tion was not the only appeal of the site, as it was covered with dense forest and had fourteen lakes.

In a 1974 interview with the *New York Times,* LeRoy described his vision for the park: "You want to blend the natural elements and the animals with a sense of the fantastic. A fantasy world with its roots in nature. When we do a roller coaster, it's not only a thrill ride, it goes along the lake into the trees, it's an experience in nature. I wanted to bring back a sense of spectacle."

LeRoy and Hardwicke moved quickly to turn the dream into reality. LeRoy took great pains to preserve as many trees as possible. In fact, he posted notices around the construction site stating: "The most valuable assets of Great Adventure are the trees on the land. They are absolutely priceless. It has taken 300 years for these trees to reach their magnificence." The notice then instructed construction workers not to touch any trees without first checking with the on-site horticulturist. It turned out to be a wise move, and the towering canopy of trees remains one of the park's most distinctive features.

Construction was delayed by a dispute over a portion of the land, but within six months, what was then known as Great Adventure had become a reality, and the $65 million project celebrated its grand opening on July 4, 1974.

Great Adventure opened with two major components: the animal safari and the theme park, then called Enchanted Forest. The safari, covering 350 acres, held more than a thousand animals from around the world, including lions, tigers, elephants, giraffes, and bison. The 4½-mile road through the property permitted the animals to walk right up to visitors' vehicles and gave them contact closer than in any zoo.

The theme park, laid out along the shore of one of the lakes, featured eighteen rides in six themed areas: Dream Street, Strawberry Fair (both now part of Fantasy Forest), Rootin' Tootin' (now Frontier Adventures), Woodland Gardens (since replaced), Aqua Spectacle, and the Bandstand (both now part of the Lakefront area).

Dominating the skyline was a 154-foot-tall Ferris wheel billed as the world's largest. The ends of the park were connected by a large Sky Ride that had originally operated at the 1964 New York World's Fair, while a steam train took visitors through the woods. Roller coaster riders could enjoy the 69-foot-high, 2,444-foot-long Runaway Train, which traveled partially over a lake. The 2,170-foot-long Saw Mill Log Flume, one of the longest ever built, provided a cooling diversion. Even the bumper car ride was promoted as the largest in the world.

One of the grandest attractions was the carousel. It was originally carved in 1881 by Frederick Savage, who is widely credited with developing the carousel as it is known today, including inventing the device that makes the horses move up and down. LeRoy purchased the carousel in England from the Patrina Williams Traveling Circus and had it fully restored. Rich in ornamentation, the ride featured twenty-four hand-carved horses, as well as twelve chickens seating two riders each. The original steam engine was converted to compressed air to power the ride, which was placed in an ornate building resembling a sultan's tent.

Supplementing the larger attractions were a number of flashy rides imported from Europe, including an elaborate swing ride called the Flying Wave, the Polyp, the Matterhorn, the Swiss Bobs, and the Grand Prix. There were also five kiddie rides.

Great Adventure was not just about rides. Live entertainment filled the park. The six thousand-seat Great Arena featured jousting, chariot races, circus acts, and sky diving. There were dolphin shows, diving acts, and continuous musical entertainment in the twelve hundred-seat Bandstand. Another unique attraction was the Garden of Marvels. Built at a cost of $1.5 million, the garden featured highly detailed 1/25-scale models of seventy-six famous European buildings nestled among forty thousand flowers.

Great Adventure's 154-foot-tall Ferris wheel was billed as the world's largest in 1974.

LOCATION

Six Flags Great Adventure is located in the center of the state on County Route 537, just off Exit 16A off I-195 East or Exit 16 off I-195 West.

OPERATING SCHEDULE

Six Flags Great Adventure is open weekends from early April through mid-May, daily from late May through Labor Day, and weekends through October. The park opens at 10 A.M., with closing times varying by season.

The Wild Safari is open from 9 A.M. to 4 P.M. on weekends from late March through mid-May and in September, and daily from mid-May through Labor Day. The safari also is open at 10 A.M. on weekends in October.

Hurricane Harbor opens Memorial Day weekend and operates weekends through mid-June. It is open daily from mid-June through Labor Day and the first weekend in September. Opening time is 10 A.M. most days.

Six Flags Winter Lights—Drive Thru Adventure, the holiday light display, operates evenings from mid-November until one week past New Year's Day. The theme park attractions and the Wild Safari are *not* open during Winter Lights.

ADMISSION

Pay-one-price admission of under $50 entitles visitors to all rides and attractions, with the exception of games and attractions such as the Dare Devil Dive, the Great American Road Race, Turbo Bungy, and Eruption. The safari park is also included, although Hurricane Harbor is extra. Parking costs extra. Multiday and combination tickets with the water park are also available. Discounted tickets can be purchased via the Internet on the park's website.

FOOD

About seventy different food outlets range from sit-down restaurants to strolling vendors. Major food outlets, many of which are air-conditioned, include the Great Character Café in Fantasy Forest for burgers and chicken sandwiches; Best of the West in Frontier Adventures for barbecue ribs and chicken; Granny's Country Kitchen in Fantasy Forest for fried chicken; Mamma Flora's for Italian food; Jamaican Callaloo for Jamaican food; and Wok and Roll along the Lakefront for Chinese food. Other stands offer deli sandwiches, Nathan's hot dogs, fish and chips, and cheese steaks.

Outside food and beverages are not permitted in the park. Shaded picnic areas are available adjacent to the theme park bus parking lot and near the exit to Wild Safari. There is a small, nonshaded picnic area just outside Six Flags Hurricane Harbor.

FOR CHILDREN

Six Flags Great Adventure has two distinct areas just for kids. Bugs Bunny Land is a great place for beginners and contains more than a dozen smaller rides, as well

(continued on page 186)

VISITING (continued from page 185)

as numerous other attractions and a stage show. The most popular attractions are the Bugs Bunny Great Western Railroad, Tweety's Round Up merry-go-round, and Looney Tunes Log Jam bumper car ride.

Looney Tunes Seaport offers eleven rides, most of which can be enjoyed by the entire family, including Road Runner Railway, a roller coaster; Taz's Tornado, a swing ride; Taz's Seaport Trucking Co.; and Yosemite Sam's Seaplanes. Also, don't miss the Fun Factory, where the family can send thousands of foam rubber balls through a variety of apparatuses.

SPECIAL FEATURES

Six Flags Great Adventure is one of the largest theme parks in the world, and its size and scope make it a unique experience. With around seventy rides and two kids' areas, there is an extensive variety of attractions for the entire family.

The park's collection of thirteen roller coasters is among the most diverse found anywhere. From the 15-foot-high Road Runner Railroad to the 230-foot-tall Nitro, there is a roller coaster to appeal to anyone. Among the variations found are inverted (dangling below the track, Batman the Ride), floorless (dangling above the track, Medusa), flying (under the track, Superman—Ultimate Flight), indoor (Skull Mountain), shuttle (forward and backward on the same track, Batman & Robin: The Chiller), and multilooping (Great American Scream Machine). Six Flags also has a great assortment of tamer roller coasters, including the kiddie-size Road Runner Express, the slightly larger Blackbeard's Lost Treasure Train, and the Runaway Train.

Don't miss the Wild Safari. Six Flags Great Adventure is the only theme park in North America with its own drive-through animal park. It offers the opportunity to get closer to the animals than in any zoo and provides a great chance to witness more natural behaviors. A trip through the safari is included in theme park admission.

TIME REQUIRED

With all of its rides and attractions, in addition to the Wild Safari and Hurricane Harbor, Six Flags Great Adventure is a vacation unto itself. Plan two to three days to enjoy the theme park, safari park, and water park, with at least one full day set aside just to see the theme park. If you are pressed for time and can visit on a day when crowds are light, the major attractions can be enjoyed in about six hours.

TOURING TIPS

Try to visit Six Flags Great Adventure on a weekday, particularly before mid-June, when the park tends to be less crowded.

Arrive just before the park opens. Start in the one of the areas in the back of the park, such as Looney Tunes Seaport or the Nitro or Medusa roller coaster, as crowds tend to reach these areas last.

(continued on page 187)

Consider participating in Fast Lane, Six Flags' ride reservation system. For an extra fee, you can rent an electronic device that saves you a place in line at the park's thirteen most popular rides. The Fast Lane rental station is located next to the Flying Wave in Fantasy Forest.

A drive through the safari park is a great way to rest and cool off in the middle of the day, when the park is most crowded. But eat first, as the only food there is from vending machines.

Six Flags offers VIP Tours that provide a behind-the-scenes look at the park and special access to selected rides and attractions for an extra charge. The Wild Safari also offers VIP tours that provide special insight into the attraction's animals.

LeRoy had quite a sense of spectacle, so he filled the theme park with "oversize toys" to create childlike wonder in its visitors. The Yum Yum Palace restaurant (now the Great Character Café) looked like the world's biggest ice cream sundae. It cost $2 million to construct. A huge stockade fort dominated the Rootin' Tootin' section and housed the Runaway Train and Sky Ride. Riders of the Log Flume boarded in an oversize sawmill. A gift shop was housed in a 70-foot-high tepee, and a gigantic Conestoga wagon served as a snack bar. Above all of this, a 110-foot-tall hot-air balloon, billed as the world's largest, floated over the park and served as its trademark.

The Garden of Marvels contained miniature replicas of seventy-six European buildings.

Given that Great Adventure had opened in a region that had seen its largest amusement parks close in recent years, there was a huge demand for amusement-park-style entertainment. As a result, the park found itself overwhelmed by visitors, with traffic backing up for miles and long lines developing at the ticket booths, food stands, and restrooms.

By the end of the first season, the creditors and management determined that Great Adventure needed several million dollars in upgrades to handle the huge crowds. To provide the needed capital, the Pritzker family of Chicago, best known for their Hyatt Hotel chain, acquired a 55 percent interest in the fledgling operation, with the remainder being acquired by the First National Bank of Chicago. Hardwicke continued to serve as manager.

The new owners immediately went to work expanding the operation for the 1975 season with a $10 million improvement program. The number of food outlets was doubled, the parking lot enlarged, and additional restrooms constructed. Most significant, however, was the debut of eight new rides, including several in a new six-acre section called Fun Fair (now part of Movietown). Since the Saw Mill Log Flume was by far the most popular ride during the first season, the largest addition was a second $2.2 million flume ride. Named the Moon Flume (now called Poland Spring Plunge), the 1,600-foot-long flume shared the woods with the train ride. Other new rides included two steel-track roller coasters: the Jumbo Jet, a 56-foot-high, 2,854-foot-long roller coaster that appeared

The fanciful Yum Yum Palace cost $2 million to construct.

The Jumbo Jet made a one-season appearance at Great Adventure in 1975. SIX FLAGS
GREAT ADVENTURE

for only one season; and the Big Fury, a smaller roller coaster. A second
bumper car ride was also added, as well as the Panorama Wheel, an 80-
foot-tall Ferris wheel, and several additional spinning rides imported
from Europe. The improvements were very well received, and attendance
doubled over the 1974 season.

Aiming to continue its momentum, an additional $5 million was spent
on improvements for the 1976 season. A new main entrance area greeted
visitors with an early American theme in honor of the country's bicenten-
nial. A high-speed roller-coaster-type ride called the Alpen Blitz debuted
in the Fun Fair and lasted through the 1978 season. Younger guests could
enjoy the new Kiddie Kingdom area, where the park's original kiddie
rides were relocated and supplemented with the Screamer kiddie roller
coaster, as well as a petting zoo.

Management also responded to the continuing popularity of the flume
rides by testing a take-a-number system that allowed people to reserve
a place in line. The experiment was short-lived, but it marked the first
time a theme park ever attempted a ride reservation system, something
that gained popularity in the industry in the late 1990s.

Great Adventure supplemented its antique carousel in 1977 with the Spinning Top Gondola ride. Also manufactured by Frederick Savage in 1881, the ride featured eight hand-carved gondolas that traveled along an undulating track. Unfortunately, the ride never enjoyed the popularity of the other carousel and lasted only a few seasons.

Flying the Flags

By the late 1970s, Great Adventure had established itself as the leading theme park in the northeastern United States, attracting the attention of Six Flags, Inc., which purchased the park in the fall of 1977. Great Adventure was the fifth theme park in the Six Flags chain and fit into its expansion strategy perfectly by giving it a presence in the northeastern United States.

Six Flags' origins dated back to 1961, when Texas real estate developer Angus Wynne opened a theme park to anchor the Great Southwest Industrial District, a 5,000-acre development located in Arlington, Texas, halfway between Dallas and Fort Worth. During this period, developers throughout the United States were trying to duplicate the success of Disneyland, which changed the industry when it opened in 1955. All previous attempts had failed.

The park's six areas were themed after the countries Texas had once been part of—the Confederacy, France, Mexico, Spain, Texas, and the United States—leading to the name Six Flags Over Texas. By pioneering such concepts as the pay-one-price admission and introducing rides such as the Runaway Mine Train and log flume, Six Flags Over Texas succeeded where others had failed. Soon its successful concept was expanded to new Six Flags theme parks in Atlanta and St. Louis.

Throughout the 1970s and 1980s, Six Flags expanded by acquiring parks throughout the United States, including Great Adventure. In 1985, the Looney Tunes characters, such as Bugs Bunny and Daffy Duck, became the chain's official ambassadors, and in the 1990s, through an affiliation with Time Warner (which owned the chain for a period), a series of innovatively themed rides and attractions were added.

In 1998, Six Flags was acquired by Premier Parks, a publicly traded company that had an established reputation of acquiring and aggressively improving troubled amusement parks. Premier's name was changed to Six Flags, Inc., and a new era of growth was launched. The Six Flags concept of world-class thrill rides and well-known characters was added to many of its existing parks as far away as Mexico and Europe. Today Six Flags, Inc., is the largest regional theme park chain in the world, operating thirty-nine amusement parks throughout North America and Europe.

The twin-track Lightning Loops was the first major attraction added by Six Flags after it purchased Great Adventure.
SIX FLAGS GREAT ADVENTURE

After purchasing Great Adventure, Six Flags, like its previous owners, believed in continuous improvement and kicked off the park's 1978 season with a $6 million expansion that included a 1,400-seat theater building and two roller coasters. The first, Wildrider, was a small, steel-track roller coaster that replaced Big Fury and operated for just a few seasons. The second was the much larger Lightning Loops, costing $2.7 million and representing one of the most advanced roller coasters built at that point. The ride had two separate tracks that launched the trains from a platform through a loop and then back again. The two loops interlocked with each other, providing close interaction for the riders.

Lightning Loops was followed in 1979 by another unique twin-track roller coaster, the $5 million Rolling Thunder. While every other racing roller coaster built up to then was essentially two identical rides running alongside one another, each track on Rolling Thunder had its own set of hills. The 96-foot-high, 3,200-foot-long ride was designed by Bill Cobb, the leading roller coaster designer of the time. Also that year, a new section was added to the safari featuring Australian animals such as kangaroos and ostriches.

As the 1980s dawned, Six Flags saw demand for water rides increasing, and the park responded by replacing the train with Roaring Rapids, the second river rapids ride ever built. Constructed on a 5 1/2-acre site near the Lightning Loops, the $5.5 million ride sent twelve passenger boats down a quarter-mile-long simulated river where 1.5 million gallons of water soaked riders.

Great Adventure's expansion continued unabated through the 1980s. The skyline changed in 1983 with the addition the 130-foot-tall Freefall and 250-foot Parachuter's Perch, still the tallest ride in the state. In

Frontier Adventures is Six Flags Great Adventure's largest area. The oversize tepee and stockade can be seen in this photo. Rolling Thunder, the park's wooden roller coaster, is to the left. SIX FLAGS GREAT ADVENTURE

1984, the Sarajevo Bobsleds, a roller coaster whose cars freewheeled down a trough much like bobsleds, was added. To celebrate the opening of the $3.8 million attraction, Great Adventure offered free-opening-day admission to anyone who showed up with a snowball. Over nineteen thousand people responded, more than double the number expected.

Tragedy struck the park in May 1984, when a fire broke out in the five-year-old Haunted Castle attraction, killing eight people. The fire was started by a guest using a lighter to find his way through the attraction. Six Flags responded by spending $5 million to upgrade and expand fire protection systems throughout the facility.

Another unique roller coaster arrived at Great Adventure in 1986 when the Ultra Twister opened. The only one of its kind in the United States, the ride started by hauling six passenger cars straight up to the top of a 97-foot-tall hill. The cars then plunged straight down, crested a second hill, and traveled through a 360-degree spin. The cars were then transferred to a lower set of tracks, where they went backward through two additional 360-degree spirals. During this time, the Six Flags theme park chain rotated rides among their various theme parks to give patrons a greater variety of rides on a more frequent basis. So after two seasons, Ultra Twister was relocated to Astroworld in Houston, another Six Flags park, to make way for new attractions.

The park addressed audiences other than thrill-seeking roller coaster riders over the next two seasons. Splashwater Falls, a new-generation water ride in which twenty-passenger boats plunge down a 50-foot hill into a 400,000-gallon pool, opened in 1987.

In 1988, Bugs Bunny Land was developed for the park's younger visitors. Located in the former Kiddie Kingdom area, Bugs Bunny Land offered more than a dozen renovated attractions for children themed after favorite Looney Tunes characters. New features included the Bugs Bunny Western Railroad, a train that replaced the petting zoo, and three new play areas totaling 15,000 square feet.

Riding the Rails

As the 1980s came to a close, the race to build the tallest and fastest roller coaster started anew. Six Flags Great Adventure jumped into the fray in 1989, when the Great American Scream Machine replaced the Sarajevo Bobsled, which was relocated to Six Flags Great America in Illinois. The new ride was built by Arrow Dynamics and opened as the largest looping roller coaster in the world, standing 173 feet tall and featuring seven inversions at a top speed of 68 miles per hour. The ride included three of the tallest vertical loops in the world, standing 136, 107, and 97 feet high.

The 1989 season also marked the debut of a new tradition at Six Flags Great Adventure, when the park stayed open for two weekends in Octo-

The Great American Scream Machine was the world's largest looping roller coaster when it opened in 1989.

ber for Halloweekends. This celebration transformed the park into a Halloween wonderland complete with several custom-built haunted houses erected for the event. Today known as Fright Fest, the event now encompasses the entire month of October.

Great Adventure benefited from the ride rotation program in 1990, when the Shockwave, a steel-track roller coaster, was moved to the park from Six Flags Magic Mountain in California. Riders negotiated the 90-foot-high, 2,300-foot-long track in special trains on which they stood for the entire journey. Shockwave was erected on the site of a miniature golf course that had replaced the Garden of Marvels in 1979. The ride operated through the 1992 season, when it was relocated to Astroworld.

Six Flags Great Adventure celebrated the 1991 season by adding a completely new 15-acre themed area called Adventure Rivers. Billed as "two million gallons of fun," the $4 million project was built in response to the increasing popularity of water rides and consisted of thirteen water-based attractions named after the world's rivers, "from Amazon to Zambezi." The new area incorporated two of the park's existing water attractions: Roaring Rapids, which was renamed Congo Rapids, and the Moon Flume, which became the Irrawaddy Riptide. Adventure Rivers had ten new water slides ranging from 235 to 690 feet long, each providing a different ride experience.

Unlike slides typically found in water parks, these were designed so that guests could enjoy them in their street clothes. While other parks had added slides like this in limited quantities, nothing of this scale had

Adventure Rivers was home to thirteen water-based attractions between 1991 and 1998.

even been attempted before. Rounding out the attractions was a half-acre water play area for children called Koala Canyon.

Another significant development in 1991 occurred when media company Time Warner acquired an interest in the Six Flags chain. This provided Six Flags access to the company's wide array of characters and guided expansion through much of the 1990s.

One of the first characters utilized was Batman, with the introduction of a Batman stunt show for the 1992 season. But things really kicked into high gear in 1993, when Batman the Ride replaced Lightning Loops. Batman the Ride was a roller coaster, designed by the Swiss firm of Bolliger & Mabilliard, that represented a totally new generation of steel-track roller coasters in which riders were seated in trains suspended underneath the track with their feet dangling as on a ski lift. Dubbed an "inverted" coaster, the new ride stood 105 feet tall with 2,693 feet of track and five inversions. Batman the Ride not only was groundbreaking for the way people rode it, but also was one of the first in a new generation of totally immersive rides.

As guests approached the attraction, they entered Gotham Park, an elaborately landscaped "city park" with a fountain, forty-three trees, and almost a thousand shrubs. As riders moved through the line, they ventured into the seamier side of Gotham City, with chain-link fence, exposed pipes, a junkyard, graffiti, and a police car that had crashed into a gushing fire hydrant. This led to the Batcave, where the ride was boarded.

The construction of Batman the Ride prompted the conversion of the surrounding area into Movietown. Buildings were given a Hollywood backlot theme, and the existing rides were given movie names. Splashwater Falls became the Movietown Water Effect, the Freefall became the Stuntman's Freefall, and the Panorama Wheel became Phileas Fogg's Balloon Ride.

Robert Pittman, CEO of Six Flags at the time, described their new strategy: "Our focus is on increasing the fantasy and entertainment level in the park with quality theming." This strategy continued the following season, when an entire corner of the park was converted into a replica of a 1940s Air Force Base for the addition of The Right Stuff Mach 1 Adventure, a 16,000-square-foot simulator attraction. The Right Stuff projected a movie on a 50-by-66-foot screen while riders sat in one of a hundred seats whose movements were synchronized to the action on the screen.

Great Adventure strived to add a diverse assortment of attractions, but the continuing public demand for roller coasters prompted the park to augment its coaster lineup over the next three years. The 1995 season saw the addition of Viper, a one-of-a-kind steel-track roller coaster from Togo of Japan. The 89-foot-tall ride occupied a 3¹/₂-acre site elabo-

Batman & Robin: The Chiller is a one-of-a-kind twin-track roller coaster.

rately themed to resemble a southwestern ghost town and featured a "heartline" spiral roll along its 1,670 feet of track. Viper was followed by Skull Mountain, a 41-foot-tall, 1,377-foot-long steel-track roller coaster completely enclosed inside a 65-foot-high "mountain."

New roller coaster tracks adorned the skyline of Six Flags Great Adventure for the third consecutive year in 1997, as Batman & Robin: The Chiller was built in Movietown. To make room for the new coaster, Six Flags removed Phileas Fogg's Balloon Ride and relocated the twelve-year-old Space Shuttle, a ride that flipped riders head-over-heels.

Batman & Robin: The Chiller was another one-of-a-kind roller coaster that had two separate tracks of 1,137 and 1,229 feet, named Batman and Robin, respectively. Trains were shot out of the station using linear induction motors. Batman was sent through a 139-foot-tall "top hat" inversion, while Robin went through a double-inversion "cobra roll." The two tracks then traveled side by side through a spiral to a 200-foot-high summit, where they reversed and went through everything backward.

Creating a Super Park

Over its first twenty-five years in business, Six Flags Great Adventure had become one of the most popular theme parks in the country. But despite a constant expansion program, guests still found long lines on busy days. Six Flags decided to attack this problem head-on in 1999 with the largest single-year expansion that any theme park had ever undergone. CEO Kieran Burke proclaimed: "We declare war on lines. Our guests will have more rides to ride and with the increased capacity, will be able to more fully enjoy the park's extensive entertainment presentation. The scope of the overall expansion is nothing short of spectacular."

A total of $42 million was spent to increase the park's capacity by 50 percent by adding twenty-four rides. There was something new for everyone, from hard-core thrill seeker to the smallest child. Anchoring the expansion was Medusa, a huge $15 million steel-track roller coaster with the world's first floorless roller coaster trains, in which riders sat propped on top of the track in open cars with no sides or floors. Standing 142 feet tall, the ride featured seven inversions along its 3,985 feet of track, negotiated at speeds of up to 61 miles per hour.

At the opposite end of the park and the thrill spectrum was Looney Tunes Seaport. Replacing Adventure Rivers, the 6-acre seaport contained a dozen attractions that children could enjoy with their parents. Located in this area were the Road Runner Railway, a scaled-down roller coaster, and the Fun Factory, a large room filled with thousands of foam balls that could be used in a variety of activities, including cannons and vacuum hoses.

Other new attractions throughout the park included Blackbeard's Lost Treasure Train, an 1,164-foot-long family roller coaster; Houdini's Great Escape, a themed illusion ride; the Great American Road Rally go-carts; and a number of spinning rides, including Chaos, Rodeo Stampede, and Pendulum. Even the existing kiddie area, Bugs Bunny Land, received two new rides.

With the theme park at Six Flags Great Adventure now firmly entrenched as one of the world largest, attention in 2000 was focused on expanding the resort as a destination with the addition of Six Flags Hurricane Harbor, a 15-acre water park. Themed as a remote island that had been struck by a hurricane, attractions included thirteen water slides; the Blue Lagoon, a 1 1/2-acre, 1-million-gallon wave pool; Taak It Eez Ze Creek, a 2,150-foot-long adventure river; and a special area just for kids.

The park's roller coaster lineup reached new heights with the opening of Nitro in 2001. Towering 230 feet tall, the ride was and still is the tallest and fastest roller coaster in the eastern United States, with a top speed of over 80 miles per hour. The bright yellow ride made its presence known, with many of its seven hills poking above the trees. Along its 5,392 feet of track were several highly banked turns and a high-speed spiral.

Fright Fest had by now become an established tradition, and Six Flags decided to expand its season yet again in 2002 with Six Flags Winter Lights—Drive Thru Adventure, a holiday season display of more than a

Nitro, the largest roller coaster in New Jersey, towers above Six Flags Great Adventure's dense canopy of trees.

million lights adorning nearly two hundred exhibits erected along 2½-mile route through the parking lot.

Most recently, the park continued its tradition of presenting unique roller coasters when it brought Superman—Ultimate Flight to the park for the 2003 season. Designed by the Swiss firm of Bolliger & Mabilliard, the 115-foot-tall, 2,759-foot-long ride featured trains where riders dangled underneath the track flying "Superman-style," traveling on their stomachs for much of the ride.

Six Flags Great Adventure Today

Today there are few theme parks that can match the size and scope of Six Flags Great Adventure. The park has nearly seventy rides, including thirteen roller coasters, among the most of any park in the world.

Visitors enter the park through the Main Street area, which contains an array of shops with an early American theme. Main Street leads to the Freedom Fountain, a popular meeting place, and into the Fantasy Forest section, home to the Big Wheel, Carousel, Houdini's Great Escape, and Sky Way. Beyond Fantasy Forest is the Lakefront area, where many of the live entertainment venues are located, including the Fort Independence aqua theater, the Great Lake Grandstand, and the Bandstand by the Lake. Also in this area are the Skull Mountain and Blackbeard's Lost Treasure Train roller coasters.

Turning right at the Freedom Fountain leads visitors to the Old Country, location of several spinning rides, and Movietown, themed like a Hollywood backlot. At Movietown can be found Batman & Robin: The Chiller, Batman the Ride, and Nitro, along with the Stuntman's Freefall and Movietown Water Effect.

Beyond Movietown is Looney Tunes Seaport. In addition to Congo Rapids and the Poland Springs Plunge flume, this nautically themed area has a number of family and kiddie rides, including the kid-size roller coaster Road Runner Railway and Koala Canyon, a water play area just for kids.

Turning left at Freedom Fountain leads visitors to the Boardwalk, reminiscent of Coney Island or the Jersey shore. This section is home to the Great American Scream Machine and Superman—Ultimate Flight roller coasters, the Parachute Tower, The Right Stuff Mach 1 Adventure, and a wide variety of skill games. Next to the Boardwalk is Bugs Bunny Land, with thirteen kiddie rides and a wide array of attractions for kids to climb on, in, and through.

Beyond Bugs Bunny Land is Frontier Adventures, the park's largest area. Major attractions here include the Runaway Train, Rolling Thunder, Viper, and Medusa roller coasters, as well as the Saw Mill Flume, which provides a relaxing ride along the lakefront. The area is also home to the Northern Star Arena, location of concerts and special events.

Fantasy Island

OPENED 1985

EVERY BEACH RESORT IN NEW JERSEY HAS ITS OWN PERSONALITY, BUT Long Beach Island stands alone. The 18-mile-long island is accessible only by a single road, so it has a much more peaceful atmosphere. There is no boardwalk. Few concessions compete for the tourist dollars, and the beach is quieter than those found elsewhere. Even Fantasy Island, the resort's amusement park, is different. Located between the ocean and the bay, the park has a unique feel lacking in the action-packed piers found elsewhere, and the brick walkways, Victorian-style street lamps, and plentiful park benches evoke nostalgia for a simpler time.

The First Attempt

Fantasy Island opened in 1985, but the site's roots as an amusement park date back much further. In 1960, the Hartman family opened Hartman's Amusement Park on what had been a turnaround for the trains that once served the island. The park was a relatively simple operation consisting of twenty-two rides in a gravel lot. Most of these were kiddie rides, although there were also a go-cart track, a giant slide, and a small steel-track roller coaster.

One of Hartman's most unusual attractions was Big Chip, a two-story-tall robot sculpture constructed out of full-size auto bodies and parts. The sculpture originally played the role of "zookeeper" in the Chrysler Pavilion at the 1964–65 New York World's Fair, where he oversaw a barnyard of animals made of auto parts.

Fantasy Island
320 Seventh St.
Beach Haven, NJ 08008
609-492-4000
www.fantasyislandpark.com

The Hartman family created a moderately successful park, but by the 1970s, they were ready for something else and put the facility up for sale. The park drew a number of interested bidders, but upon discovering that a vacant strip of land not owned by the Hartmans ran through the middle of the park, their interest faded. That was until Ed Florimont came along. Florimont knew that a high-quality amusement park in Beach Haven would be a huge success, given the lack of competition and the fact that the weekly population each summer could swell to two hundred thousand.

Florimont was convinced that he needed to obtain the extra parcel of land to make the amusement park a unified site. To persuade that parcel's owners to sell, Florimont constructed a model of an amusement park that showed a very tall wall surrounding the separate parcel. The owners realized that their land would have little value if Florimont's plans went through, and they decided to sell.

Ed Florimont came to Beach Haven as an experienced amusement industry veteran. His father, an amusement park game inventor and concessionnaire, had introduced him to the industry as a boy. By the time the opportunity to acquire Hartman's Park came along, Florimont had a successful career operating game concessions in nearby Seaside Heights. In an intensely competitive market, he differentiated himself by charging a higher price for the game but offering department-store-quality prizes in an upscale atmosphere characterized by plush carpeting and Tiffany chandeliers. Customers flocked to his games.

Fantasy Island's predecessor, Hartman's Park, was known for its Giant Slide. FANTASY ISLAND

But to maintain that success, Florimont was putting in more than a hundred hours a week during the busy season. Eventually he decided he needed to slow down. He thought that opening an amusement park would allow him to slow down but still remain in the industry, as well as give him a way to keep longtime employees. "This is a retirement project," says Florimont.

A Commitment to Quality

Once the deal to purchase Hartman's Park and the extra parcel was sealed, Florimont and his partners, Gary Philips and Tom Frey, went to the town council to obtain the approvals to build his new amusement park. He impressed them with his vision for bringing a high-quality facility to town, and the council approved the project in January 1985. With Memorial Day rapidly approaching, the new owners had their work cut out for them converting the tired facility into the quality operation they envisioned.

The entire site was leveled to improve drainage and covered with Z-brick pavers that not only were aesthetically pleasing, but also allowed the park to dry more quickly after a rainstorm. The grounds were adorned with custom-made Victorian-style streetlamps, entrances were marked by elaborate arches, and buildings had stained-glass windows. Approximately half of Hartman's rides were sold, including the worn-out giant slide, go-cart track, Caterpillar, Teacups, and roller coaster. A number of buildings were renovated for new uses. The former arcade was converted into a game building, and the maintenance shop became an ice cream parlor.

Several new features were also added, including an elaborate miniature golf course. Given the time constraints, the contractor constructed it in just three weeks. In fact, the work was done so quickly that the cement truck drivers would stop and watch the activity.

The new owners retained and extensively renovated ten rides from Hartman's, including the bumper boats, bumper cars, a merry-go-round, Scrambler, Tilt-A-Whirl, and four kiddie rides. They added five new rides, including the Dragon Coaster, Himalaya, a fun house, and a play area purchased from the 1984 New Orleans World's Fair.

One of the new park's most distinctive features was the 7,000-square-foot arcade building. Drawing upon his many years of experience, Florimont created an arcade that resembled a casino more than an amusement park penny arcade. It included plush carpeting, custom-built Tiffany chandeliers, and subdued lighting and was filled with four hundred games for the entire family, ranging from simple video games to skeeball to slot machines.

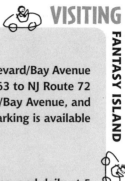

LOCATION

Fantasy Island is located at the intersection of Long Beach Boulevard/Bay Avenue and Seventh Street. From the Garden State Parkway, take Exit 63 to NJ Route 72 East to Long Beach Island. Turn right on Long Beach Boulevard/Bay Avenue, and go south 6.5 miles. Fantasy Island is on the right-hand side. Parking is available in streetside spaces and local lots.

OPERATING SCHEDULE

The park opens weekends at 2 P.M. from mid-May until late June, and daily at 5 P.M. from late June through Labor Day weekend, except on Fridays, when the park opens at 2 P.M. for pay-one-price day. Closing time varies between 11 P.M. and midnight. The Casino Arcade opens at noon daily during the summer and is open weekends in the winter.

ADMISSION

Admission is free, with rides available on a pay-as-you-go basis. Ride tokens are available for around 75 cents each, and rides require from three to eight tokens.

FOOD

There are three food outlets. The Food Court near the back of the park has burgers, hot dogs, cheese steaks, pork roll sandwiches, and french fries. The Ice Cream Parlor, near the carousel, sells ice cream, frozen yogurt, and funnel cakes. The Sugar Shack offers cotton candy and popcorn.

FOR CHILDREN

Fantasy Island's mission is to be a safe, family-oriented amusement park. The park features nine kiddie rides, and most of the larger rides can be enjoyed by the entire family.

SPECIAL FEATURES

The park's Casino Arcade resembles an Atlantic City–style casino more than an amusement park penny arcade. The Casino Arcade has family-oriented casino-style games, Tiffany lamps, and plush carpet. Players can collect points and redeem them for one of three thousand different prizes, ranging from typical knickknacks to fine collectibles, sports memorabilia, and the season's hottest merchandise. It is probably the only arcade around where the prizes are guaranteed for life.

TIME REQUIRED

With the rides and arcade, Fantasy Island takes several hours to enjoy, although families with small kids will likely want to stay longer.

(continued on page 204)

VISITING (continued from page 203)

FANTASY ISLAND

TOURING TIPS

Every Friday is pay-one-price day. The park opens at 2 P.M., and until 7 P.M. visitors can enjoy all the rides for a single price.

A rotating schedule of live entertainment is offered nightly.

Long Beach Island is a well-rounded seaside resort. Combine a trip to Fantasy Island with a visit to the beach and the other attractions that dot the island for a full-day outing.

Amazingly, the $2 million park, now called Fantasy Island, was ready for business on Memorial Day weekend, as promised. Interestingly, a gazebo in a city park approved at the same January town council meeting was not completed until September.

The quiet beachside community responded well to the new facility, and improvements continued. A Gravitron ride made a one-year appearance in 1987. A new carousel was added in 1988, replacing the fun house and a smaller merry-go-round that remained from Hartman's Park. The 36-foot ride was manufactured by Chance Rides and featured thirty horses, each a reproduction of an animal carved at the turn of the century.

In 1989, the Sea Dragon, a large swinging ship ride, replaced another Hartman's holdover, the bumper boats. Two kiddie rides, the Rio Grande Train and Mini Swing, joined the lineup in 1990.

Fantasy Island's carousel is the heart of the park.

View of Fantasy Island from the Giant Wheel.

The miniature golf course initially enjoyed great popularity when the park opened, but by 1994, business was waning. When the owner of the neighboring water park expressed an interest in installing a miniature golf course, Fantasy Island made an agreement whereby it would remove its miniature golf course in exchange for a promise by the water park never to add amusement park rides.

The space occupied by the miniature golf course was filled with two kiddie rides, the Convoy and the Teacups, along with the Giant Wheel, a 66-foot-tall ride adorned with ten thousand light bulbs, which made it an instant landmark on the island. A ride of this magnitude presented Fantasy Island with many challenges. It cost $500,000, and its large size required a foundation made from 150 tons of concrete. Perhaps most challenging of all was locating a local resident fluent in Italian to serve an interpreter between the Italian engineer and American construction workers.

The arcade was hugely popular, and Fantasy Island decided to double its size in 2000, at a cost of $1 million. In 2002, the Drop Zone, a drop tower ride, joined the lineup.

Fantasy Island Today

In less than twenty years, Fantasy Island has become a beloved landmark on Long Beach Island, featuring nineteen rides, the Casino Arcade, and nightly live entertainment all summer long. The park's main entrance and Casino Arcade face Long Beach Boulevard/Bay Avenue, the island's main street. Just inside the main entrance are the Giant

Wheel, Convoy, Teacups, and live entertainment stage. The carousel occupies the heart of the park and is surrounded by rides such as the Drop Zone, Himalaya, Tilt-A-Whirl, and Sea Dragon. The backside of the park is dominated by the Bumper Cars, Scrambler, and Dragon Coaster.

Drawing on his years of industry experience, Florimont has created an operation focused on quality and attention to detail. The grounds are spotless, the rides are maintained in top-notch condition, and it is a rare occasion when a customer spots a burnt-out light bulb. "They know if we take care of the little things, we are taking care of the big things," says Florimont.

Blackbeard's Cave

OPENED 1989

NED BEVELHEIMER MISSED THE AMUSEMENT INDUSTRY. HIS ORIGINAL facility, Sportsland, was condemned in 1974 to make way for the Giants football stadium in Meadowlands, New Jersey. He had kept himself busy in the construction and restaurant businesses, but he missed being able to entertain people. The amusement industry finally called him back in 1989, when he teamed with some partners and purchased a wooded 21-acre parcel in Bayville in central New Jersey. At the time, the industry was seeing the growth of a new type of facility, the family entertainment facility, which emphasized participatory activities. Responding to this trend, Bevelheimer opened Blackbeard's Cave in 1989 with an elaborate miniature golf course and batting cages.

The Park Grows

The park was favorably received, and it grew rapidly. A golf driving range was added in 1991, followed by a quarter-mile go-cart track in 1992, an archery range in 1994, and an arcade, jousting competition, and bumper boats in 1995. The jousting competition was an unusual game in which two players tried to knock people off a platform with padded poles. The bumper boat ride was also no ordinary ride. To enhance the experience, Bevelheimer added underwater explosions and places where observers could shoot water balloons at the boats.

The growing operation opened the CB Huntington restaurant in 1996, a full-service family

Blackbeard's Cave

136 Route 9
Bayville, NJ 08721

732-286-4414

www.blackbeardscave.com

restaurant filled with model train layouts. Bevelheimer also added the aptly named Psycho Swing, where riders could try to swing themselves in a complete loop. A climbing wall opened in 1997.

Kiddie Park

Bevelheimer had established Blackbeard's Cave as a successful family entertainment center, but he realized that there was not much for smaller children to do. He addressed that need in 1998 with the opening of the Adventure Station kiddie park. Initially, Adventure Station contained seven rides for young kids, including a Crazy Bus and Lolli Swing, along with kiddie canoe and train rides that were carefully laid out through the woods. With 300 feet of track, the train was twice as long as similar rides elsewhere.

Adventure Station was a huge success, and for the next several years, expansion focused on that area. A kiddie Ferris wheel joined the line up in 1998, and a giant slide was added in 1999. Two rides were added in 2001, including the Dino Den, a kiddie jeep ride through the woods, and the Dragon Coaster. The Dragon Coaster was acquired from Adventureland, East Farmingdale, New York, and replaced the Crazy Bus. It was the perfect size for Adventure Station's primary customers, standing 12 feet tall with about 300 feet of track. Most recently, a large paintball area called the Splatter Zone made its debut in 2003.

The Adventure Station kiddie area was added to Blackbeard's Cave in 1998.

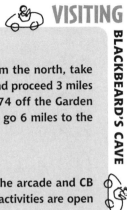

LOCATION

Blackbeard's Cave is located on U.S. Route 9 in Bayville. From the north, take Exit 80 off the Garden State Parkway to U.S. Route 9 South, and proceed 3 miles to the park, which is on the right. From the south, take Exit 74 off the Garden State Parkway. Follow Lacey Road to U.S. Route 9 North, and go 6 miles to the park, which is on the left.

OPERATING SCHEDULE

Blackbeard's Cave is open daily, from 10 A.M. to midnight. The arcade and CB Huntington restaurant are open year round, and the outdoor activities are open March through November, weather permitting.

ADMISSION

Admission is free, with all activities available on a pay-as-you-go basis. Tickets cost 50 cents each, and rides and activities require from two to eleven tickets.

FOOD

CB Huntington is a full-service restaurant open for lunch, dinner, and late night snacks. Two small food stands are available near the miniature golf course.

FOR CHILDREN

Adventure Station, with its selection of family-oriented rides, is the place where most children will want to spend their time.

SPECIAL FEATURES

Blackbeard's Cave features a bumper boat ride in which riders are doused by underwater explosions and water balloons shot by bystanders. Also unique are the jousting competition and Psycho Swing.

TIME REQUIRED

With an array of entertainment options along with the CB Huntington restaurant, a visit to Blackbeard's Cave can occupy several hours.

TOURING TIPS

Blackbeard's Cave is a great place to spend an evening. Start off with a visit to Adventure Station and the go-cart track, enjoy dinner at CB Huntington, and cap off your visit with a round of miniature golf.

Blackbeard's Cave Today

Today the park features eleven rides, including go-carts, bumper boats, the Dragon coaster, and the Dino Den jeeps. There is also a wide array of participatory activities, such as miniature golf, batting cages, a driving range, climbing wall, jousting competition, archery range, and Splatter Zone paintball arena.

Other
Amusement Facilities

- *Blast Fun Park,* 208 Route 9 South, Forked River. Features adult and kiddie go-carts, miniature golf, and an arcade. 609-242-7580. www.blast funpark.com.

- *Camden Children's Garden,* 3 Riverside Drive, Camden. Located in front of the New Jersey State Aquarium. Offers merry-go-round and train rides and themed gardens to explore. 856-365-8733. www.camden childrensgarden.org.

- *Funtime America,* 111 Highway 35 South, Aberdeen. Indoor facility with six rides, laser tag, play area, and a large arcade. 732-583-4600. www.funtimeamerica.com.

- *Jeepers!,* Jersey Gardens Mall, 1000 Kaplowski Road, Elizabeth. Indoor kiddie park featuring five rides, kiddie play area, and an arcade. 908-289-9466. www.jeepers.com.

- *Mountain Creek Waterpark,* 200 Route 94, Vernon. One of the country's largest water parks, with nearly two dozen water slides, three river rides, a wave pool, water play areas, Tarzan swings, and a wading pool. 973-827-2000. www.mountaincreekwaterpark.com.

- *Picadilly Playland,* 597 Route 9, Staffordville. Family entertainment center with kiddie and adult go-carts, bumper boats, a train, batting cages, miniature golf, and a driving range. 609-978-1818

- *Rex Plex,* 1001 Ikea Place, Elizabeth. Five-acre indoor sports and recreation center featuring three rides; laser tag; skate park; fitness center; and facilities for basketball, volleyball, flag football, paintball, and roller and dek hockey. 908-629-1300. www.rexplex.com.

- *Splash Zone,* 3500 Boardwalk, Wildwood. Oceanfront waterpark featuring nine water slides, a river ride, and a water play area. 609-729-5600. www.splashzonewaterpark.com.

- *Sports World,* 200 Route 17 North, Paramus. Indoor facility with four rides, kiddie play area, large arcade, laser tag, and miniature golf. 201-262-1717. www.sportsworld17.com.

- *The Funplex,* 182 Route 10 West, East Hanover. One hundred thousand-square-foot indoor family entertainment center offering go-carts, five other rides, batting cages, laser tag, and a play area. 973-428-1166. www.sngfunplex.com

- *Thundering Surf Waterpark,* Bay and Taylor Avenues, Beach Haven. Water park featuring six water slides, a river ride, water play area, and two miniature golf courses. 609-492-0869. www.thunderingsurf waterpark.com.

- *Tomahawk Lake,* Tomahawk Trail, Garfield. Water park with six water slides, kiddie water world, and an 18-acre lake with white sand beach. Other attractions include bumper boats, paddleboats, and miniature golf. 973-398-7777. www.tomahawklake.com.

INDEX OF MAJOR RIDES
IN OPERATION
IN NEW JERSEY

Roller Coasters
WOOD TRACK

Tsunami, Clementon Amusement Park and Splash World, opened 2004.
Great White, Morey's Piers–Spencer Avenue, opened 1996.
Rolling Thunder, Six Flags Great Adventure, opened 1979.

STEEL TRACK

Dragon, Blackbeard's Cave, opened 2001.
Dragon, Bowcraft Amusement Park, opened 1998.
Hot Tamale, Casino Pier and Water Works, opened 2003.
Star Jet, Casino Pier and Water Works, opened 2002.
Wild Mouse, Casino Pier and Water Works, opened 1999.
Roller Coast Loop, Funtown Pier, opened 1989.
City Jet, Gillian's Wonderland Pier, opened 1978.
Miner Mike, Gillian's Wonderland Pier, opened 1998.
Flitzer, Jenkinson's Boardwalk, opened 1992.
Sea Serpent, Keansburg Amusement Park and Runaway Rapids,
    opened 1998.
Wildcat, Keansburg Amusement Park and Runaway Rapids, opened 1985.
Thriller, Land of Make Believe, opened 1994.
Flitzer, Morey's Piers–25th Avenue, opened 1981.
RC-48, Morey's Piers–25th Avenue, opened 2000.
The Great Nor'easter, Morey's Piers–25th Avenue, opened 1995.
Rollie's Coaster, Morey's Piers–Schellenger Avenue, opened 1999.
Sea Serpent, Morey's Piers–Schellenger Avenue, opened 1984.

Doo Wopper, Morey's Piers–Spencer Avenue, opened 1998.

Flitzer, Playland's Castaway Cove, opened 1994.

Python, Playland's Castaway Cove, opened 1996.

Sea Serpent, Playland's Castaway Cove, opened 1997.

Wild Mouse, Playland's Castaway Cove, opened 1996.

Batman the Ride, Six Flags Great Adventure, opened 1993.

Blackbeard's Lost Treasure Train, Six Flags Great Adventure, opened 1999.

Great American Scream Machine, Six Flags Great Adventure, opened 1989.

Medusa, Six Flags Great Adventure, opened 1999.

Nitro, Six Flags Great Adventure, opened 2001.

Road Runner Railway, Six Flags Great Adventure, opened 1999.

Runaway Train, Six Flags Great Adventure, opened 1974.

Skull Mountain, Six Flags Great Adventure, opened 1996.

Superman—Ultimate Flight, Six Flags Great Adventure, opened 2003.

The Chiller: Batman, Six Flags Great Adventure, opened 1997.

The Chiller: Robin, Six Flags Great Adventure, opened 1997.

Viper, Six Flags Great Adventure, opened 1995.

Crazy Mouse, Steel Pier, opened 1999.

Little Leaper, Steel Pier, opened 1994.

Name not announced, Steel Pier, opened 2004.

Bubbles, the Coaster, Storybook Land, opened 2001.

Wooden Carousels

Casino Pier and Water Works, manufactured in 1910 by Dentzel-Looff-Illions, installed 1932.

Gillian's Wonderland Pier, manufactured in 1926 by the Philadelphia Toboggan Company, installed 1972.

Six Flags Great Adventure, manufactured in 1881 by Savage, installed 1974.

Dark Rides

Stillwalk Manor, Casino Pier and Water Works, opened 2003.

Spongebob Under the Sea, Funtown Pier, opened 2001.

Alien Invasion, Gillian's Wonderland Pier, opened 2004.

Spook House, Keansburg Amusement Park, opened 1931.

Dante's Inferno, Morey's Piers–25th Avenue, opened 1980.

Pirates of Wildwood, Morey's Piers–Schellenger Avenue, opened early 1990s.

Jersey Junkyard, Morey's Piers–Spencer Avenue, opened 1996.

Houdini's Great Escape, Six Flags Great Adventure, opened 1999.

Den of Lost Thieves, Wildwood Boardwalk, opened 1998.

Zombie World, Wildwood Boardwalk, opened 2000.

Walk-Throughs and Fun Houses

Mardi Gras, Casino Pier and Water Works, opened late 1990s.

Persian Kamel, Casino Pier and Water Works, opened 1998.

Haunted House, Funtown Pier, opened 2003.

Ice Age, Funtown Pier, opened early 2000s.

Mirror Maze, Gillian's Wonderland Pier, opened 1985.

Fun House, Jenkinson's Boardwalk, opened 1998.

Haunted Halloween House, Land of Make Believe, opened 1954.

Space Maze, Morey's Piers–25th Avenue, opened 2002.

Chamber of Checkers, Morey's Piers–Spencer Avenue, opened late 1990s.

Curse of the Mummy, Morey's Piers–Spencer Avenue, opened early 2000s.

TV Playhouse, Playland's Castaway Cove, opened 1993.

Zombie Xtreme, Seaside Heights Boardwalk, opening date not available.

Alice in Wonderland, Storybook Land, opened early 1970s.

Log Flumes

Log Flume, Casino Pier and Water Works, opened 1997.

Neptune's Revenge, Clementon Amusement Park and Splash World, opened 1983.

Pelican Splash, Funtown Pier, opened 2000.

Canyon River Rapids, Gillian's Wonderland Pier, opened 1992.

Pelican Splash, Keansburg Amusement Park, opened 1998.

Zoom Phloom, Morey's Piers–25th Avenue, opened 1985.

Seal Flume, Morey's Piers–Schellenger Avenue, opened 1999.

High Seas, Playland's Castaway Cove, opened 2000.

Pelican Splash, Playland's Castaway Cove, opened 1996.

Poland Spring Plunge, Six Flags Great Adventure, opened 1975.

Saw Mill Log Flume, Six Flags Great Adventure, opened 1974.

Log Flume, Steel Pier, opened 2002.

River Rapid Rides

Congo Rapids, Six Flags Great Adventure, opened 1981.

Splash-water Rides

Movietown Water Effect, Six Flags Great Adventure, opened 1987.

Giant Ferris Wheels

Casino Pier and Water Works, 66 feet tall, opened 1998.

Clementon Amusement Park and Splash World, 100 feet tall, opened 1995.

Fantasy Island, 66 feet tall, opened 1994.

Funtown Pier, 120 feet tall, opened 1989.

Gillian's Wonderland Pier, 148 feet tall, opened 2001.
Morey's Pier–Schellenger Avenue, 150 feet tall, opened 1985.
Playland's Castaway Cove, 90 feet tall, opened 1997.
Six Flags Great Adventure, 154 feet tall, opened 1974.
Steel Pier, 66 feet tall, opened 2003.

BIBLIOGRAPHY

Books

Adams, Judith A. *The American Amusement Park Industry: A History of Technology and Thrills.* Boston: Twayne Publishers, 1991.

Anderson, Norman. *Ferris Wheels: An Illustrated History.* Bowling Green, OH: Bowling Green State University Popular Press, 1992.

Bailey, Shirley R., and Jim Parkhurst. *Early South Jersey Amusement Parks.* Millville, NJ: South Jersey Publishing Co., 1979.

Bush, Leo, O., and Richard F. Hershey. *Conneaut Lake Park: The First 100 Years of Fun.* Fairview Park, OH: Amusement Park Books, 1992.

Cartmell, Robert. *The Incredible Scream Machine: A History of the Roller Coaster.* Fairview Park, OH: Amusement Park Books; Bowling Green, OH: Bowling Green State University Popular Press, 1987.

Francis, David W., Diane DeMali Francis, and Robert Scully. *Wildwood by the Sea.* Fairview Park, OH: Amusement Park Books, 1998.

Fried, Frederick. *A Pictorial History of the Carousel.* Vestal, NY: Vestal Press, 1964.

Gabrielan, Randall. *Images of America: Keansburg.* Dover, NH: Arcadia Publishing, 1997.

Gargiulo, Vince. *Palisades Amusement Park: A Century of Fond Memories.* New Brunswick, NJ: Rutgers University Press, 1995.

Griffin, Al. *Step Right Up Folks.* Chicago: Henry Regnery Company, 1974.

Kane, Martin, and Laura Kane. *Images of America: Greetings from Bertrand Island Amusement Park.* Dover, NH: Arcadia Publishing, 2000.

Kyrazi, Gary. *The Great American Amusement Parks.* Seacaucus, NJ: Citadel Press, 1976.

Levi, Vicki Gold, and Lee Eisenberg. *Atlantic City: 125 Years of Ocean Madness.* Berkeley, CA: Ten Speed Press, 1979.

Mangels, William F. *The Outdoor Amusement Industry.* New York: Vantage Press, 1952.

Manns, William. *Painted Ponies: American Carousel Art.* Millwood, NY: Zon International Publishing Co., 1986.

O'Brien, Tim. *The Amusement Park Guide.* Old Saybrook, CT: Globe Pequot Press, 2003.

Reed, James. *Amusement Park Guidebook.* New Holland, PA: Reed Publishing, 1987.

Siegel, Alan A. *Smile: A Picture History of Olympic Park, 1887 to 1965.* Irvington, NJ: American Graphic, 1983.

Magazines and Newspapers

Amusement Business. 1961 to present. Billboard Music Group, P.O. Box 24970, Nashville, TN 37203

Amusement Park Journal. 1979 to 1987. Amusement Park Journal, P.O. Box 478, Jefferson, OH 44047-0478

Carousel News and Trader. 1986 to present. Carousel News and Trader, 87 Park Ave. West, Suite 206, Mansfield, OH 44902-1657

Merry-Go-Roundup. 1975 to present. National Carousel Association, 128 Courtshire Lane, Penfield, NY 14526

NAPHA News. 1978 to present. National Amusement Park Historical Association, P.O. Box 83, Mount Prospect, IL 60056

Roller Coaster. 1978 to present. American Coaster Enthusiasts, 5800 Foxridge Dr., Suite 115, Mission, KS 66202-2333

Selections from 1908 *Street Railway Journal,* in *Traction Heritage* 9, no. 4 (July 1976), Indianapolis.

INDEX

Abrams, Sol, 34, 36
Action Park, 39, 41
Adventure Rivers, 194–95
Adventure Station, 208
Adventure Village, 33, 41
Aerial wave, 76
Aeroplane, 10
Airplane Swing, 68
Alcyon Park, 41
Alice in Wonderland, 35, 137
Allen, John, 15, 39, 158
Alpine slide, 39
American Carousel Society, 19
American Coaster Enthusiasts (ACE), 19
Amusement Center, 170
Applegate's Pier, 27, 28
Aqua Circus (Steel Pier), 56
Arnold's Park, 21
Arrow Development Corp., 17
Arrow Dynamics, 193
Arrow Manufacturing, 145
Asbury Park, 24–25, 36, 39
  Palace and Casino, 43–44, 46
Astroliner, 17, 82, 85, 171
Astroworld, 14
Atlantic City
  casinos, impact of, 40, 58
  Central Pier, 31, 32, 40, 41
  early development of, 25–29
  Million Dollar Pier, 29, 40, 42, 53
  Steel Pier, 28, 35, 40, 45, 47–61

Steeplechase Pier, 28, 40, 42
  Tivoli Pier, 42, 45
Auditorium (Keansburg Amusement
  Park), 64, 66
Auditorium Pier, 28

Baker, Abe, 82–83
Barnes, Joe, 34, 173
Bartlett, Norman, 9
Batman & Robin: The Chiller, 196
Batman the Ride, 195
Bayern Kurve, 36, 145
Bayonne Kiddieland, 41
Bayonne Pleasure Park, 41
Beastie roller coaster, 15
Beer gardens, 2
Belleville, 30
Bellewood Park, 30, 31, 41
Belmar Playland, 24, 41
Belmont Park, 21
Belvidere Beach, 31, 41
Bennett, Bob, 105, 108, 110
Bergen County Traction Co., 30
Bergen Point Park, 41
Bertrand Island, 32, 40, 41, 42
Bevelheimer, Ned, 207, 208
Big Chip, 200
Big Splash, 61
Bingham family, 112
Blackbeard's Cave, 207–10
Black Hole, 130

Blast Fun Park, 211
Boardwalks, early, 24
Bobsled roller coaster, 7
Bolliger & Mabilliard, 195, 198
Boo Fun House, 80
Borelli, M. D., 113, 142
Bowcraft Amusement Park, 118–23
Boyton, Paul, 4–5
Bradley, James, 24
Brigantine Castle & Amusement Pier, 41
Brown, Mike, 145
Bubble Bounce, 69
Bubbles, the Coaster, 139
Bumper boats, 104, 207
Bumper cars, 8
Burke, Kieran, 197
Burlington Island Park, 41
Busch Gardens, 15

Calypso, 36
Camden Children's Garden, 211
Cannon, Freddie "Boom Boom," 36
Cantalupo, Tony, 69
Captain Good Times, 41
Carmel, Charles, 96–97, 142
Carousels, 1
  at Casino Pier (Floyd Moreland), 35,
    96–97, 99, 107, 110
  at Clementon Amusement Park, 76,
    79, 83, 84
  early, 8, 24
  at Fantasy Island, 204
  at Freeman's Amusements, 141, 142
  at Gillian's Wonderland Pier, 35, 156,
    157–58
  at Jenkinson's Boardwalk, 91
  at Keansburg Amusement Park,
    64, 70
  list of wooden, 214
  at Playland's Castaway Cove, 113, 114
  selling of, 39
  at Six Flags Great Adventure, 35,
    183–84, 190
  at Steel Pier, 57
Carowinds, 15
Carver, Lorena, 51
Carver, W. F., 51
Casino Amusements, 32, 39, 41
Casino Arcade, 41, 44, 45
Casino building (Steel Pier), 47–48
Casino Pier and Water Works, 32
  description of, 96–111

Cassidy, Leon, 9, 67
Catanoso family, 59–60
Cedar Point, 16, 18
Central Pier, 31, 32, 40, 41
Chair Swing, 60, 100
Chance Rides, 204
Children's Storybook Farm, 41
Christmas Fantasy with Lights, 137–38
Christopher, John, 98
City Jet roller coaster, 57, 58, 159
City of Keansburg, 66–67
Clementon Amusement Park and Splash
  World, 39
  description of, 75–87
Clementon Lake Park, 30
Cobb, Bill, 191
Columbia Park, 31, 41
Coney Island (Cincinnati), 14
Coney Island (New York), 2–3, 7–8
  Dreamland, 6–7
  Luna Park, 5–6, 7
  Sea Lion Park, 5
  Steeplechase Park, 5, 7
Conneaut Lake Community Park, 21
Cortina Bob, 36
Cowboy City, 33, 41
Crazy Mouse, 60–61
Creative Engineering, 171
Crystal Maze, 24
Cyclone roller coaster (Coney
  Island), 8

Dark Ride and Fun House Enthusiasts,
  19
Dark Ride and Fun House Historical
  Society, 19
Dark rides, 9, 35, 36, 40
  at Casino Pier, 98, 102, 103–04, 108
  at Keansburg Amusement Park, 67
  list of, 214
  at Morey's Piers, 171
  at Playland's Castaway Cove, 113
  at the Steel Pier, 56
Days of Fun, 41
Dayton Fun House Co., 8–9
Den of Lost Thieves, 35
Dentzel, William, 81, 96, 141, 156
Dinosaur Beach Adventure Theme Park,
  41, 45–46
Dip-lo-do-cus, 37
Disco Star, 60
Disney, Walt, 12, 14

Disneyland, 12–13
  Tokyo, 18
Disney World, 14
Diving Bell (Steel Pier), 50, 54, 58
Diving Horse (Steel Pier), 51, 53, 54,
  58, 59–60
Dodgem Corp., 9
Doo Wop, 178–80
Dragon Coaster, 10
Dreamland (Coney Island), 6–7
Dreamland Park (Elizabeth), 32, 41
Droge, Nick, 64
Dundy, Elmer, 5
Dyrehavs Bakken, 1

Ed Brown's Playground, 41
Eldred, Mildred, 81
Electric Park, 30, 31, 41
Eli Bridge Co., 8, 156
Elysian Fields, 23–24
Encyclopedial Wheel, 26
Enterprises for the Preservation of
  Old Americana, 149
European Coaster Club, 19
Exhilarama, 41
Exposition parks, 5–6
Extension Kiddieland, 41

Fairyland, 30, 41
Fairy Tale Forest, 41
Family entertainment centers,
  20–21, 207
Fantasy Island, 200–06
Feltman, Charles, 3
Ferris wheels
  in Atlantic City, 26, 55, 60
  at Casino Pier, 102, 108
  early, 1, 4, 8, 24
  at Keansburg Amusement Park, 63
  list of, 215–16
  at Six Flags Great Adventure, 183
Fisher, Eddie, 34
FitzGerald, John, 98
Flip Flap, 5
Flitzer roller coasters, 114, 171
Florimont, Ed, 201–02, 206
Flyer roller coaster, 45
Flying Turns, 9
Freedomland, 13–14
Freeman, Frank, 141
Freeman's Amusements, 141–42, 144
Frey, Tom, 202

Fricanos family, 133–34, 136–37
Fun City, 41
Fun Fair, 41, 90, 91
Fun houses, 34
  at Clementon Amusement Park,
    79–80, 82
  at Jenkinson's Boardwalk, 35, 93–94
  list of, 215
  at the Steel Pier, 52, 55
Funland, 11
Fun Pier, 34, 41, 45, 163, 173–74
Funplex, 212
Funtime America, 211
Funtown Pier, 141–48
FunTown USA Association, 144–45

Galaxy roller coaster, 43
Garden of Marvels, 184, 194
Garden Pier, 29
Gardner, Al, 57
Gavioli band organ 64, 67
Geauga Lake, 16–17
Gelhaus, Hank, 70–71, 73
Gelhaus, Henry, 69, 70
Gelhaus, William, 62–63, 69
Gelhaus, William (brother), 71, 72, 73
Ghost Town, 13
Giant Dipper roller coaster, 21
Giant Wheel
  at Fantasy Island, 205
  at Morey's Piers, 172, 173
Gibbs, Edgar, 78–79
Gibbs, Theodore, 75–76, 78
Gibbs, Willard, 78–79
Gilbert, Linus, 96–98
Gillian, Bob, 154, 158
Gillian, David, 153–54, 160
Gillian, Jim, 160
Gillian, Roy, 154, 156–61
Gillian's Fun Deck, 32, 39, 41, 154,
  158–59, 160
Gillian's Island, 160
Gillian's Wonderland Pier, 35, 39
  description of, 153–61
Gingerbread Castle, 41
Go-carts, 59
Goldberg, Maxwell, 57
Golden City Park, 34
Gold Nugget Mine Ride, 34
Goliath roller coaster, 18
Grandal Enterprises, 69
Gravatt, Frank, 50, 51, 52, 53

Gravitron, 171
Great Adventure, 15, 183–84, 187–90
Great American Scream Machine, 193
Great Escape, 13
Great Nor'easter roller coaster, 175
Great Southwest Corp., 14
Great White roller coaster, 163, 176
Guenther, Henry, 37

Hamid, George, 51, 53, 54–55, 56
Hamid, George, Jr., 54, 56–57
Hardwicke Companies, 182, 188
Hartman's Amusement Park, 41, 200
Harvey Comics, 36
Haunted Castle (Six Flags Great
    Adventure), 40, 192
Haunted Castle (Steel Pier), 52
Haunted Swing, 27, 35
Heim, Jake, 25
Heinz, H. J., 28
Helicopter, Steel Pier, 35, 61
Herman's Amusements/Schiffel's, 41,
    91–92
Herschell, Allan, 91, 113, 138, 144
Hersheypark, 16
Hillside Pleasure Park, 30, 42
Himalaya ride, 100–01
Hitchcock Manor, 171
Hoffman's Playland, 11
Holiday Playland, 91
Holiday World, 13
Hot dog, invention of, 3
Houdini's Great Escape, 35, 197
Howard's Pier, 27
Hughes, Carl, 12–13
Hughes, Morgan, 34, 36, 38
Hummingbird roller coaster, 37
Hunt's Pier, 34, 42, 44, 45–46, 163, 179
Hunt, William, 34, 45
Hydroworks, 175

Illions, Marcus, 97, 113, 142
International Amusement Devices, 8
Iron Pier, 28
Iron Tower, 3

Jack Rabbit roller coaster
    at Clementon Amusement Park, 79,
    84–85
    at Keansburg Amusement Park, 66, 68
    at Nickels Midway Pier, 44
    at Playland, 32

J&J Railroad, 139
Jazzland, 18
Jeepers!, 211
Jenkinson, Charles, 87–88
Jenkinson, Orlo, 88
Jenkinson's Boardwalk, 35
    description of, 87–95
Jenkinson's South, 39, 91
Jet Star roller coaster
    at Casino Pier and Water Works, 103,
    104, 110
    at Funtown Pier, 146
    at Morey's Piers, 175, 179
    at Palisades Park, 36
Johnson, Taft, 59
Jolly Caterpillar, 69, 72–73
Jolly Trolley, 134, 136, 137
Jones Woods, 2
Jumbo Jet roller coaster, 168–69, 174,
    188–89
Jungleland, 34, 45

Katapult, 173, 174
Keansburg, 24, 37
Keansburg Amusement Park and
    Runaway Rapids, 36, 39, 40, 45
    description of, 62–74
Keansburg Steamboat Co., 63
Kennywood, 16, 21
Kiddie Karnival, 33, 42
Kiddieland, 11, 32–33
Kiddieland (Pennsauken), 42
Kiddieland (Saddle River Township), 42
Kiddie Park, 11
Kid's World, 42, 43
King Amusement Co., 157
King Kong ride, 164, 167, 171
Kings Dominion, 15
Kings Island, 14–15
Knott's Berry Farm, 13, 17

Lagoon, 17
Lake Compounce, 3
Lakemont Park, 21
Lakeside Park, 6
Land of Make Believe, 124–32
Leap the Dips roller coaster, 21
Legoland, 18
Lenape Park, 30, 39
LeRoy, Warner, 182–84, 187
Lightning Loops, 191
Lincoln Park, 42

Little Leaper, 60
Log flumes
    at Casino Pier, 108
    at Clementon Amusement Park, 83
    early, 4–5, 14
    at Funtown Pier, 145–46
    list of, 215
    at Six Flags Great Adventure,
        183, 188
Long Branch, 24
    Pier, 42–43
Looff, Charles, 96
Loop-O-Plane, 69, 157
Lost City dark ride, 57
Luna Park (Cleveland), 6
Luna Park, Coney Island (NY), 5–6, 7
Luna Park (Pittsburgh), 6
Lusse Brothers, 156
Luv Bugs, 104

Macdonald, Clinton C., 11
Mad-O-Rama, 43
Magic Carpet, 60
Magic Mountain (Denver), 13
Magic Mountain (Los Angeles), 14
Magnum XL 200 roller coaster, 18
Mahana, Fred, 167, 171
Maier, Christopher, 128, 129
Maier, Eddie, 100, 101
Maier, Hermann, 124–26
Major, Bill, 146
William F. Mangels Co., 8, 64, 113
Marine Ballroom (Steel Pier), 55–56
Marine Pier Amusements and Playland,
    32, 42, 44, 163, 169–71
Mariner's Landing, 163, 170–73, 178–79
Marke family, 120, 122
Matterhorn, 36
Mays Landing, 30
Medusa roller coaster, 197
Memphis Kiddie Park, 11
Merry-go-rounds. *See* Carousels
Midway, 4
Miler Coaster Co., 130, 139
Miler Manufacturing, Fred, 108,
    110, 114
Mill Chute ride, 40, 79
Millennium Force, 18
Miller, John, 9, 66
Miller, Ted, 118–20
Million Dollar Pier, 29, 40, 42, 53
Miniature golf course, 101

Miss America Pageant, 53
Moreland, Floyd, 35, 96–97, 99,
    107, 110
Morey family, 44, 163–81
Morey Organization, 45, 46, 176, 178
Morey's Piers, 35, 36, 45
    description of, 162–81
Mountain Creek Waterpark, 39, 211
Mount Olive, 38
Mystery Ride
    at Clementon Amusement Park, 81
    at Keansburg Amusement Park, 67
    at the Steel Pier, 56

Nagashima Spaland, Japan, 18
National Amusement Devices Co., 8
National Amusement Park Historical
    Association (NAPHA), 20
National Association of Amusement
    Parks, Pools and Beaches, 13
National Carousel Association, 20
NBGS (New Brunfels General
    Store), 130
Neptune's Revenge, 83
Neustadter, Milton, 57
Newman, Andrew, 75
New Point Comfort Beach Co., 62–63
Nickels Midway Pier, 44, 46
Nienauber, Justus, 149, 150
Nitro roller coaster, 197
Noah's Ark, 79–80, 81
Nolan's Point, 42
Norton, Gad, 3

Observation Roundabout, 26
Observation Tower, 24
Ocean City, 24, 32
Ocean Discovery (Steel Pier), 58
Ocean Grove, 24
Oceanic Amusements, 43
Ocean Pier, 33, 34, 42
Ocean World (Steel Pier), 56
Olwell, Edward, 59
Olympic Park, 30, 37, 42
Opryland, 14
Ott, Robert, 12, 13

Pacific Ocean Park, 13
Palace Amusements, 39, 42
Palisades Park, 30–31, 34, 36, 38, 42
Pan American Exposition, 5
Parachuter's Perch, 191

Parrot Club, 97, 103
Paul Bunyan Center, 13
Pavilion of Fun, 7
Philadelphia Aquarama, 56
Philadelphia Toboggan Co. (PTC), 8, 79, 156, 157, 158
Philips, Gary, 202
Picadilly Playland, 211
Piers
    See also under name of
    early use of, 25, 27–28
Pirate's Cove, 130
Pirate Ship Skua, 34, 45
Pittman, Robert, 195
Pixie Playland, 11
Planet of the Apes, 168
Playland (Rye, New York), 9–10, 21
Playland's Castaway Cove (Ocean City), 32, 39
    description of, 112–17
Playland (Wildwood), 32, 39, 42, 170
Pleasure gardens, 1
Pleasure Island, 13
Pleasure Railway, 24
Point Pleasant Beach, 24
Potsdam Railway, 9
Power Surge, 108
Prater, 1
Premier Parks, 190
Pretzel Amusement Co., 9, 67, 98
Pritzker family, 188
Python roller coaster, 114

Racer roller coaster (Kings Island), 15
Raging Waters, 173, 174
Ramagosa, Gil, 158, 167
Reid, Al, 69
Reisenrad Ferris wheel, 36
Rendezvous Park, 31–32, 42, 51
Resorts International, 40, 58, 59
Rex Plex, 211
Reynolds, Debbie, 34, 36
Ride reservation system, 189
Riverside, 17
Riverview Beach, 37–38, 42
Riverview Park, 9
Roaring Rapids, 191
Rocket Ship (Steel Pier), 54, 55, 61
Rock-O-Plane, 69
Rocky Point Park (Rhode Island), 3
Roller Coaster Club of Great Britain (RCCGB), 20

Roller coasters
    See also under name of
    in Atlantic City, 26
    early development, 1, 3, 5, 8, 9, 10
    list of steel track, 213–14
    list of wood, 213
    looping, 17, 28, 172
    in the 1980s, 18
    with spinning cars, 37, 60–61
Rolling Green Park, 157
Rolling Thunder roller coaster, 191
Roll-O-Plane
    at Casino Pier, 100
    at Clementon Amusement Park, 80
    at Keansburg Amusement Park, 69
Rosenthal, Irving, 34, 36, 38
Rosenthal, Jack, 34, 36
Rotor ride, first, 36
Runaway Mine Train roller coaster, 14
Runaway Rapids water park, 72, 73

Safari, at Great Adventure, 183
Santa Claus Land, 13
Santa's Workshop, 13
Savage, Frederick, 183–84, 190
Scenic Railway, 26, 64, 66
Schenck Brothers, 31
Scheutzen Park, 42
Schnitzler, Ernest, 24
Schwarzkopf, Anton, 57, 103, 168
Scooby Doo roller coaster, 15
Sea Lion Park, 5
Sea Serpent roller coasters, 172
Seaside communities/resorts, 24–25
Seaside Heights, 24
Seaside Park, 24
Sea View Excursion House, 26
Sea World, 14
Sea World Texas, 18
Sellner Manufacturing, 130
Shock Wave roller coaster, 18
Shockwave roller coaster, 194
Shoot the Chutes, 4–5
Sidewinder, 131
Silver Streak, 98
Simpson, David, 112, 114
Simpson, Scott, 114
Simulator rides, 17–18
Six Flags, Inc., 190
Six Flags Great Adventure, 35, 39, 40, 45
    description of, 182–99

Six Flags Great America, 18
Six Flags Magic Mountain, 18
Six Flags New England, 17
Six Flags New Orleans, 18
Six Flags Over Georgia, 14
Six Flags Over Mid-America, 14
Six Flags Over Texas, 14, 190
Six Flags Worlds of Adventure, 16–17
Skull Mountain, 196
Sky Flyer (Steel Pier), 60
Sky Ride
    at Casino Pier, 102, 106
    at Fun Pier, 34
    at Funtown Pier, 144–45, 146, 147
    at Morey's Piers-Spencer Avenue, 35
    at Six Flags Great Adventure, 183
Skyscraper, 110
Slingshot, 110
Somers, William, 26
Sousa, John Philip, 51
Spillman Engineering, 153
Spinning Top Gondola ride, 190
Splashwater Falls, 193
Splash World, 84–86
Splash Zone, 170, 212
Spook House, 36, 40, 67
Sportland Pier, 32, 39, 42, 44, 45, 167
Sportsland, 207
Sports World, 212
Stabile, Michael, 150–52
Stainton, Howard, 154, 156
Stainton's Playland, 32, 42, 154
Star Tours, 18
Steel Dragon roller coaster (Japan), 18
Steel Pier, 28, 40, 45
    description of, 47–61
    Diving Bell (Steel Pier), 50, 54, 58
    Diving Horse (Steel Pier), 51, 53, 54,
        58, 59–60
    fun houses, 52
    Grand Opera Co., 51
    helicopter rides, 35, 61
    people who performed at, 53,
        54–55, 58
    rides at, 57
Steel Pier, 52
Steeplechase Park, 5, 7
Steeplechase Pier, 28, 40, 42
Stevens, John, 23
Storino, Pasquale, 90–93, 110
Storybook Land, 33, 35
    description of, 133–40

Storybook parks, 33
Storyland Village, 33, 42
Storytown USA, 13
Superman roller coaster, 198
Surfside Pier, 162, 164
Swiss Toboggan, 91
Switchback Railroad, 3
Switchback Railway, 26

Taft Broadcasting, 14
Taj Mahal, 59
Tarvas, Fred, 112, 114
Themed roadside attractions, 33
Thompson, Frederick, 5
Thompson, LaMarcus, 3, 26
Thunderbolt roller coaster, 7
Thundering Surf Waterpark, 212
Tilt-A-Whirl, 9
Tilyou, George, 5, 7, 28
Tivoli Pier, 42, 45
Tomahawk Lake, 212
Tony Grant Stars of Tomorrow Show,
    54, 58
Top Thrill Dragster, 18
Tornado roller coaster, 7
Tower of Fear, 147
Tower of Jewels, 6
Townsend, Otis, 153
Trabant, 69, 102, 158
Trip to the Moon, 5
Trolley lines and parks, 4, 30
Trump, Donald, 59
Tsunami roller coaster, 85
Tumble Bug, 9
Tumbling Dam Park, 30, 42
Tumbling Run Park, 9
Tunney, J. Stanley, 141–42, 144
TW Sports, 42

Ultra Twister roller coaster, 192
Universal Design, 34
Utopia 2000, 103–04

Valleyfair, 15, 16
Vanderslice, Joseph, 141
Vertical Limit, 85
Viper roller coaster, 195–96
Visionland, 18

Warner Brothers Jungle Habitat,
    38–39, 42
Washington Park, 30, 31, 42

Water Chutes, 4–5
Water parks, rides, and slides
  at Casino Pier and Water Works,
    96–111
  at Clementon Amusement Park,
    83–86
  early, 4–5
  at Gillian's Island, 160
  at Gillian's Wonderland Pier, 158
  at Keansburg Amusement Park,
    71–73
  at Land of Make Believe, 129–32
  at Morey's Piers, 170, 173, 174, 175
  in the 1970s, 39–40, 170
  in the 1980s, 17
  at Six Flags Great Adventure, 191,
    193, 194–95, 197
  vertical loop, 39
Wet 'n Wild (Orlando), 17
Whip rides, 8
White City Amusement Park, 51
White City (Chicago), 6
White City (Trenton), 30, 42
Wildcat roller coaster
  at Bertrand Island, 40
  at Keansburg Amusement Park, 70
  at Palisades Park, 36
  at Riverview Beach, 37, 38
  at Steel Pier, 60

Wild Mouse roller coaster
  at Casino Pier, 100, 102, 103, 108
  at Funtown Pier, 144
  at Keansburg Amusement Park, 69
  at Playland's Castaway Cove, 114
Wild West City, 33, 149–52
Wild West parks, 33
Wild Wheels Raceway and Adventure
    Pier, 45, 163, 175
Wildwood, 25, 32, 33–34, 35, 44–46
Wipe Out (Morey's Piers), 36, 164
Wipeout (Steel Pier), 60
Wizard's Cavern, 104
Wonderland, 6
Wonder Wheel, 8
Woodbury, 30
Woodlynne Park, 30, 31, 42
World's Columbian Exposition, 4
Wuest Casino, 42
Wynne, Angus, 190
Wynne, Ken, 98, 100–03, 105,
    107, 108

Young, John, 27–28, 29
Young's Pier, 28, 31
Yum Yum Palace, 187

Zoom Phloom, 173
Zugspitz, 36, 159

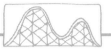

ABOUT THE AUTHOR

JIM FUTRELL BECAME FASCINATED WITH THE AMUSEMENT PARK INDUSTRY at a young age as he followed the development of the Great America theme park near his boyhood home of Northbrook, IL. Since then, he has visited 268 amusement parks around the world and ridden 336 different roller coasters. Through the years, Jim has worked as a consultant for several Pennsylvania amusement parks (Kennywood in West Mifflin, Idlewild in Ligonier, Conneaut Lake Park in Conneaut Lake Park, and Bushkill Park in Easton. He has authored numerous articles on the industry, is an avid collector of amusement park memorabilia, and serves as historian for the National Amusement Park Historical Association. His first book, *Amusement Parks of Pennsylvania,* was released in 2002. Jim lives with his wife Marlowe and three sons, Jimmy, Christopher, and Matthew, near Pittsburgh, where he works as a market research director for a regional economic development agency.